I DWELL IN POSSIBILITY

The Cross-Cultural Memoir Series introduces original, significant memoirs from women whose compelling histories map the sources of our differences: generations, national boundaries, race, ethnicity, class, ability, and sexual orientation. The series features stories of contemporary women's lives, providing a record of social transformation, growth in consciousness, and the passionate commitment of individuals who make far-reaching change possible.

I DWELL IN POSSIBILITY
A Memoir by Toni McNaron

Revised and Expanded Edition

With a New Foreword by Louise DeSalvo

The Feminist Press at the City University of New York
New York

Published by the Feminist Press at the City University of New York
The Graduate Center, Suite 5406, 365 Fifth Avenue, New York, NY 10016
www.feministpress.org

Library of Congress Cataloging-in-Publication Data

McNaron, Toni A. H.
   I dwell in possibility: a memoir / by Toni McNaron ; with a new foreword by Louise DeSalvo.
Rev. and expanded ed., 2nd ed.
         p. cm. – (The cross-cultural memoir series)
      ISBN 1-55861-280-7 (acid-free paper)
   1. McNaron, Toni A. H. 2. English teachers—United States—Biography. 3. University of Minnesota—
Faculty—Biography. 4. Alcoholics—United States—Biography. 5. Feminists—United States—Biography.
6. Lesbians —United States—Biography. 7. Alabama—Social Conditions. 8. Racism—Alabama. I. Title.
II. Series.

PE64.M38 A3 2001
976.1'781063'092—dc21
[B]   2001050127

This publication is made possible, in part, by public funds from the New York State Council on the Arts and the National Endowment for the Arts. The Feminist Press would also like to thank Janet E. Brown, Mariam K. Chamberlain, Johnnetta B. Cole, Florence Howe, Joanne Markell, and Genevieve Vaughan for their generous support.

NATIONAL
ENDOWMENT
FOR THE ARTS

State of the Arts
NYSCA

Text design by Paula Martinac
Text composition by Dayna Navaro

Printed on acid-free paper by McNaughton & Gunn.
Manufactured in the United States of America.

06 05 04 03 02 01   6 5 4 3 2 1

To Theresa Louise Hurley and Erskine Lamar McNaron

And to all the students who have enriched my life over so many years

I dwell in Possibility —
A fairer House than Prose —
More numerous of Windows —
Superior — for Doors —

Of Chambers as the Cedars —
Impregnable of Eye —
And for an Everlasting Roof
The Gambrels of the Sky —

Of Visitors — the fairest —
For Occupation — This —
The spreading wide my narrow Hands —
To gather Paradise —

Emily Dickinson

Contents

Foreword

Making the Possible, Probable:
A Long Overdue Thank-You to Toni McNaron

July 11, 2001

Dear Toni,

This is the letter I should have written years ago when I first encountered your miraculous *I Dwell in Possibility.* At the time, I was reading as many memoirs as I could to prepare for the writing of my first memoir, *Vertigo.* You had sent your book to me sometime during 1993 after I had come to speak at the University of Minnesota-Minneapolis, where you were teaching. You were too shy, you told me years later, to give it to me in person.

We had met as professors and critics, feminists reinterpreting Virginia Woolf's life and works in those heady years during the 1970s and 1980s. We attacked the literary critical establishment for what we believed to be gross misrepresentations of her work, and we tried to change old ways of thinking about Woolf as a dreamy, apolitical writer of incomprehensible novels. You changed how readers thought about Woolf's sexuality by writing about her lesbianism—Quentin Bell, her nephew and biographer, had proclaimed her sexually timid and frigid; he did not view her love of women and her physical relationships with them as sexual. I was writing about Woolf as an incest survivor and how this had profoundly affected her life and work—Bell had written that her adverse response to sexual abuse showed she was "neurotic." Our work provoked and enraged, but also persuaded; we believed our work was righteous.

We knew one another then as colleagues, and corresponded, and respected each other's scholarly work. Yet, when we met in person, we did not speak much about our personal histories although our anthem was that *the personal is political.* Many feminist critics and scholars used this as a major axiom in our scholarly work. But I had kept the personal strictly personal. I wanted my work to stand on its own; I also feared that if reviewers of my work knew that I, too, was an incest survivor, they would fault my work as biased.

So I didn't know until I read your memoir how very much we had in common, though you were raised in Fairfield, Alabama, and I was raised in Hoboken, New Jersey. I didn't know that our class backgrounds were similar, that our mothers were disappointed in us because we both rejected traditional "feminine" behavior models and developed rough, wrangling personalities to survive. That you, too, were a sexual rebel—you, with girls; I, with boys.

And no, I am not sorry that I learned about how much alike we were by reading your life. I *loved* that I got to know you as Virginia Woolf had initially come to know Vita Sackville-West—by reading her books. Fancy that: a woman like me, a second generation Italian American born into the working class, learning about the life of someone she knew through her work. It seemed a measure of how far I had come in the world, reading the book of a person *I actually knew.*

When your memoir first arrived, I read it immediately. I felt instinctively that I *needed* to read it and that it would have an important impact upon my understanding of the entire genre. I was planning to write my own memoir and also to teach Cross-Cultural Memoir at Hunter College in New York City. I believed that reading a book about your life in Jim Crow's South and the development of your lesbian identity would provoke important classroom discussion about racism and sexual identity. Many of my students came from the South; many were gay, and your book, I believed, would prompt reexaminations of my students' lives. I wanted to teach your book alongside Maya Angelou's *I Know Why the Caged Bird Sings,* Esmeralda Santiago's *When I Was Puerto Rican,* Mary Crow Dog's *Lakota Woman,* Richard Rodriguez's *Hunger of Memory,* Le Ly Hayslip's *When Heaven and Earth Changed Places,* and Meena Alexander's *Fault Lines*—all works that address the impact of culture upon the formation of personality.

As I read *I Dwell in Possibility,* I saw how important your book would be in helping my students better comprehend their own lives—how gender roles are taught, how it feels to be an outsider, how we deal with sexual desire, how our lives can be creative responses to our circumstances. I saw, too, that reading your memoir would help them understand the larger historical events that you witnessed in Birmingham, Alabama, during political actions by black citizens—nonviolent protests that had been violently disbanded by Eugene "Bull" Connor's enforcement of Jim Crow laws. Never before had I read about these incidents from the point of view of a white southern woman who had actually seen and lived through them, though I had read much history about nonviolent integration efforts in the South, as had many of my students.

I also began to realize that *I Dwell in Possibility* could be an important model for my own writing. Unlike so many memoirists, you situated your life in the context of the historical moment into which you were born. Reading your book gave me a new perspective on what growing up white and female in Jim Crow's Alabama had felt like; without flinching, you described what it was like to be a silent witness and reluctant heir to racism. You learned about describing moments of being—what living *feels* like to the person living the life—I know, from reading Virginia Woolf. You *showed* the reader what it was like (and, by extension, what it meant) to have as a child African American friends whose names you never knew; what it felt like not to conform to southern dictates of how a white girl should act; what it was to be locked into the often brutal reality of race relations in the United States.

Simply stated, *I Dwell in Possibility* made me rethink my life and reflect more deeply on the impact growing up during World War II in an Italian American working-class neighborhood had on me. You helped me to discard the notion that my life began and ended within the confines of my immediate family. I would have to excavate the *meaning* of being born an Italian American woman in the 1940s as you had excavated the meaning of being born a white woman in the late 1930s in Alabama. In writing about my family, I had to write about the *history* of my family. In following your example, I had to take the lessons of feminism and apply them to the study of my own life. This would become the most significant challenge of my writing life, changing forever the way I understood myself, my ethnicity, my parents, and my grandparents' history as Southern Italian peasants forced by poverty and repression to emigrate to the United States.

Writing narratives of growth and development as if they were played out solely within the confines of the nuclear family, without referring to the political world beyond the home, without taking into account what "family" means within a culture, misrepresents the lived life. The subtext of such memoirs—and I had read many—was clear: you become who you are because of your family. Period. But your work, and the other memoirs I read in preparation for my course, showed me that the development of all children is profoundly affected by their times, by the impact of being born into families that had lived through wartime, that had been born poor and despised, that had endured slavery, that had suffered attempts to exterminate their people—or that had borne anguished yet privileged witness to these events.

You showed your readers that the only way we can know ourselves fully is to understand the formation of our personalities in the context of political history, in the context of racism and classism, sexism and homophobia. Although, as critics, we wrote about our *subjects* in the context of their times, you were among the first of our generation to write openly about yourself, about your life in the context of Jim Crow's South—indeed, yours was the inaugural memoir in the highly influential Feminist Press Cross-Cultural Memoir Series. In so doing, you disturbed, too, essentialist stereotypes about white womankind in the South.

Feminism teaches that the deepest meaning of our lives lies in discovering the connections among the personal, the historical, and the political. This paradigm, when applied to the writing of one's own life, demands a different kind of courage; here, you were pioneer and model. As we both learned, courage comes *as you do the work*, not *before you do the work*. Writing our lives enables us to witness our survival. But writing our lives also forces us to face those painful and unpleasant truths that we learn about ourselves and about our families, caregivers, forebears, and natal communities: our capacity for cruelty and compliance; our inability to act heroically; our tolerance of injustice.

I knew from reading *I Dwell in Possibility* that I would have to write about some difficult, heretofore unspeakable issues in my family: my mother's depression, my sister's suicide, my father's violence, my sexual abuse by a caregiver. I also learned that I would have to write about my failings. Your work provided an example of enormous courage, for *you* wrote about difficult matters—your relationships with the black women who worked for your family as housekeepers, your awakening as a lesbian, your anguish at not acting to stop the racist violence that you witnessed—all told, your understanding of what it means to be born into the paradox of racial privilege and sexual repression.

Your work even suggested the form mine might take. I liked that you broke your work into chapters, that you used titles for each— "Out of the Nest," "First Lessons," "Child's Play"—that also functioned as metaphors. Somehow, thinking of a life as composed of chapters made the writing of my own life, the understanding of it, seem possible. And so, the chapter titles for my own work— "Combat Zones," "Vertigo," "Safe Houses"—slowly came into my consciousness. I began to scribble chapter headings as I read your memoir, long before I would write all that needed to follow.

In 1995, I am rereading *I Dwell in Possibility* for my course Cross-Cultural Issues in Memoir. As I reread your account of your alcoholism, I realize that I haven't yet described my own alcoholism as a teenager although I am very near the end of my writing.

Urged on by your account, I begin to pen mine. Alongside notes about your work, one of my diary entries from this time reads: *I also want to write about how much I drank.* And another: *I wrote the scene of me on the yellow line of the highway, passed out drunk. Susan [my best friend] standing above me, trying to take care of me.*

From there, I begin exploring the reasons for my own alcoholism, coming to understand that yours was, in part, a response to your experience as a passive witness to atrocity; that mine was, in part, a response to the sexual abuse by a caregiver I experienced as a child. Linking these events—between and within our lives— explained what had been, for me, the formerly inexplicable: my alcoholism, hypervigilance, chronic illness.

As Virginia Woolf wrote, no book is a single birth. Each is related to other books and must be so understood. And so it is with your book and my book.

It is the spring of 1995, and I am walking to Hunter College. I carry in my briefcase a copy of *I Dwell in Possibility*, which I will be teaching. This day, like each day I walk to Hunter, I am edgy and careful, not knowing what I will encounter upon my arrival. For several days during the semester, the college had been surrounded by police vans in anticipation of another student protest against budget cuts and tuition hikes. Throughout the early spring, there have been sit-ins and teach-ins; recently there was a march and a peaceful protest of students and faculty in front of City Hall. During the demonstration, protesters were corralled closer and closer together by mounted police. The periphery is sealed. No one can leave. *I thought they wanted us to stampede so they could fire upon us,* a colleague later tells me. *We were all shouting, "Stay calm, stay calm," but we felt like we were suffocating. I thought that many of us would die.*

I turn the corner and see a phalanx of police in full riot gear with bandoleers of bullets across their chest. They are ranged across Lexington Avenue, the street that fronts our college, and they are holding automatic weapons.

The policemen are there not because there is a student demonstration, but because there might be one. Rudolph Giuliani is mayor, and his administration is dedicated to maintaining law and order. My students and I are experiencing, firsthand, what this means. Many of us feel like we are living in a police state where one false move, even during peaceful protest, can result in carnage.

The students' favorite protest strategy is to form a human barricade across Lexington Avenue, the downtown traffic artery that fronts the main entrance to Hunter College. It is a very clever and very successful strategy because stopping traffic on just this one block snarls traffic all along Manhattan's East Side.

Even when traffic isn't stopped, student leaders set up portable microphones and give speeches, explaining how the proud tradition of free tuition at the City University (of which Hunter is a part) has been abandoned. The student leaders remind us that investing in the education of the city's poor makes good economic sense long-term. They excoriate the city's leadership for its hostility toward the City University, which can only be explained by racism and classism.

I am proud of my activist students. I have some of them in my classes, for I always teach literature courses that discuss issues of race, class, and gender, and student activists gravitate to these courses. This is an important time in the City University's history, when the ability of poor students—my students—to afford a quality education is being severely threatened. I know that if tuition hikes go through, many of my students will have to postpone their education or curtail it completely.

That I am teaching *I Dwell in Possibility* during this historical moment in my life, in my students' lives, enables us to understand your work more deeply and to understand our own historical moment. Through your work we come to feel what it is like to live through and bear witness to violence as you did. Many of us are nervous; many of us are having nightmares. My body has broken out in enormous hives. Many students come to me during office hours to discuss whether they will take part in protests; many come telling me they feel they are in danger.

At the beginning of the semester, before we read your work, we talk about the kind of people who might write memoir. The students tell me that only important people—leaders who participate in history and important events—write memoirs. Ordinary people like themselves, who live their lives largely on the periphery of events, have nothing important to tell the world. Even my most activist students do not believe they have important narratives to record.

One reason I teach memoir is to obliterate this false notion. To show my students that each life has a story. That each life is lived in history. That each life merits recording—insights so intrinsic to *I Dwell in Possibility.*

In my diary I wrote: *The students loved Toni McNaron's memoir. They were upset by her description of what happened to black families during the civil rights movement in Birmingham. We discussed how President Clinton spoke about how hate groups and hate speech fuel violence. And what a scary country this is and always has been, some of my students said. Founded on racism and exploitation. One student, whose family was from the South, said she was glad to read this history from this point of view; that she liked seeing such a frank examination of racism from a white person's perspective. We applied the insights from McNaron's book to what is happening at Hunter now.*

During that semester, my students wrote you letters of appreciation. They told you that reading your work allowed them to think about their lives in a new way—that they, like you, lived in a historical moment; and that being a "silent witness" to history means that you have participated in it, too—a paradox you unlocked for them.

All this they learned when they read that unforgettable moment you wrote about. It was on a Sunday in the summer of 1956: a group of black families brought their lunches to the park near the Birmingham Public Library for an event planned by the NAACP to integrate the city's open spaces. You witnessed "a crowd of rowdy whites" heckling and cursing the families, you saw them becoming increasingly more abusive, and then the police cars arrived, and you had hope that the picnicking families would be protected; but this was Jim Crow's South, and so, instead, the police unleashed their dogs and they corralled the people and terrorized them, the children too, for half an hour, and you saw a dog bite a woman's buttocks, and the black people carted off to jail.

I stood, mute and paralyzed, you wrote.

And then, again, later in that summer, another group of black families came to the park, and this time the police hooked up power hoses to fire hydrants and turned them on the crowd. You saw grown men and women, children, blasted along the ground, their skin scraping, their bodies hurtling; you saw them choked and blinded by the water; you saw mothers crazed with terror at the sight of their little ones being hurt. And, as you wrote,

No white person had made a single move to stop this atrocity, including me.

Those moments in your life, and your memory of them, and your reflection upon them, forced you into thinking about *what it means* to be a silent witness to atrocity. And, importantly, all this forced you to think about your place in history, your responsibility, and your silence. Now, many years later, I am beginning a fourth memoir, about my Southern Italian grandparents, and returning to *I Dwell in Possibility.* I can only imagine where my third reading will take me.

When you like a book, Henry Miller said, write a letter to the writer, to the publisher, and to a friend: reading a book begins a conversation. And reading important writing that has had an impact upon your life puts you in the author's debt, and you have an ethical obligation to repay it.

As significant as your book was to me and though I incurred a great debt in reading it, life intervened—parents became ill, a grandbaby was born, teaching duties became overwhelming, writing deadlines loomed, illness descended—and I never did then what Henry Miller said we all must do. I never wrote you that letter of appreciation and thanks.

Now, finally, I have been given a chance to repay the debt I have owed you these many years.

Thank you, Toni, for writing *I Dwell in Possibility.*

With love, and enormous appreciation,
Louise DeSalvo
Teaneck, New Jersey

Preface

In 1940, when I was about three, my mother planted a small magnolia tree in our backyard. It had come from a friend whose family lived in the heart of agricultural Alabama. This friend believed having the sapling would remind my mother of her childhood days in Selma.

In all my young years of driving around the South, I never saw a magnolia tree growing in a black family's yard or a black section of town. I concluded that even the trees, like the picture show, water fountains, restrooms, and library, were for "Whites Only." In 1987, after I had been living in the North for over twenty years, I attended a National Women's Studies Association conference held at Spelman College in Atlanta, Georgia. Founded in 1880, this black women's college boasts stately buildings, open grounds, and a solid row of magnolias along its outer fence. As I walked onto campus the first evening, I remembered my earlier impressions of where they could grow.

I caught my breath at their majesty: the trees rising conically, reaching for the sky, their waxy leaves so green as to appear almost black, their branches clotted all the way up with great white blooms. As a child, I believed some giant had placed the blooms among the leaves as a whimsical gesture.

On the ground beneath one tree, I found several brilliant red seed cores from fallen flower heads, full of prickly whiskers that had once held graceful petals in place. In my hand, they were pulpy, and the whiskers sprang back softly when I pushed them against the center.

Also on the ground were several petals from fallen blooms. Picking up one, now a deep ochre, I felt its succulent thickness and realized for the first time what helps keep the blooms intact for so long. These artful petals are actually useful, sucking in each afternoon's rain, holding moisture against the next day's relentless heat.

The South and its signs are more complicated than I could know growing up in their midst. My growing up itself was more complicated than I sometimes constructed it. Perhaps, I thought, by studying myself as carefully as I had these magnolias, I could unearth my own mysteries.

It all began when Sara Evans, a feminist colleague in history at the University of Minnesota, taped my memories of the civil rights movement in Birmingham. She enjoined me to write my story since I had been present at events of great historical moment. The project quickly broadened to include early memories of playing with black children, only later to be taught to feel superior to them. Once I had opened that door to my childhood, other powerful scenes crowded into my consciousness. Eventually I shifted from the original focus on race to a more open-ended exploration into the formation of the self I now consider "me." As I explored my earliest memories of family and my gradual sense that we were different from the black families who lived so near us geographically, I soon found myself enmeshed in other central questions of my growing up: Why did my father call me "Son"? Why did my mother "protect" me from other children? Why did I never tell her the most important things about myself? I saw that the self that I was shaping differed significantly from the one my parents had imagined. I remembered a woman who felt confused and isolated, who was an alcoholic. Yet I also began to connect my developing creativity with a sense of myself as a sexual person, my emergence as a lesbian, and my passion for literature and teaching.

The first edition of this memoir was more than six years in the making, while Part IV took more than ten months to create. That's an incredibly long time for someone who prefers breaking through plaster walls to sweeping up the debris, washing or hanging out clothes to folding and putting them away, hatching a grand idea to tracing down footnotes or laboring on a third or fourth revision. Often I experienced great frustration, among other things, during this second writing process, thinking: People who liked the initial version will not want to buy or read this new expanded volume, so why am I working all summer to make it clearer? From all that transpired, however, it became clear that much of my story remained to be told, even parts already "covered" in the original edition. Now my part in the process is over, a fact that fills me with excitement and satisfaction. My lingering discomfort with the work's being read by strangers, however, comes from my sure knowledge that others in this account would tell different stories from the ones that I record. My fantasies are wild: "Someone will sue me," even though everyone in my family, except my sister Betty, is long dead; "Betty will never speak to me again, deny me my mother's antiques, turn me from her door when I visit," though she has adjusted to my telling her that I am a lesbian, an alcoholic, an autobiographer, and someone who found growing up in our family painful as well as wonderful.

None of these things will happen. Instead, I will live with my periodic concern that I have been unfair, lopsided, cruel, vindictive. The act of putting my life onto paper has allowed me to see it more distinctly, both in its worst and best lights. I accept that it is populated by individuals who were who they had to be rather than who I might have wanted them to be. By facing their ghosts, I stand strangely less encumbered by their ideas of me. I think of Virginia Woolf and Maxine Hong Kingston, and keep coming out of the shadows.

Toni McNaron

Acknowledgments

*B*ecause this work has been fostered by so many, I feel compelled to acknowledge some of the most important of them: the Graduate School of the University of Minnesota for a summer research grant that allowed me to make much more rapid progress than normally possible; my brother-in-law, Leon, who helped me purchase a home computer without which the numerous revisions, full of "block moves," would have proved daunting; Anita Kunin for providing me with photocopies of the early manuscript, thereby facilitating my finding my publisher; my women's writing group for reading and responding to early portions of the first two sections; Chris Gordon, Judy Remington, and Ellie Siegel for reading manuscript drafts and giving me essential editorial suggestions; and my tireless editors—Kathy Casto, who lent clarity and good humor to my work on the original memoir; and Jocelyn Burrell, whose close and demanding reading of the expanded manuscript led me to produce a more trenchant and honest version.

Florence Howe's expert editorial skills, together with her extraordinary generosity, have challenged and touched me all along the way. I am indebted to my dear friends and colleagues, Shirley Garner and Mimi Sprengnether, not only for their quick and sharp responses to specific sections but more importantly for their unflinching belief in me and in the value of this project.

Finally, I acknowledge my family members—Blue and Slate, our dog and cat, who kept me company many a late night or early morning as I struggled to articulate what memory was offering me; Minna and Sophie, our current and magical cats who sit and chew draft pages to encourage me to keep at it; and Susan Cygnet, my partner, who has helped me learn that intimacy is worth the effort and risk involved, spurring me to voice my ideas and feelings even, or most especially, when I feel reluctant to do so.

I Dwell in Possibility

Part I

Top: birthday party, 1941; *bottom:* the author's mother at Christmas, 1963. Courtesy of Toni McNaron.

Out of the Nest

I grew up in a one-story white frame house, with living room, dining room, and kitchen on one side of a long hall, three bedrooms and a bath on the other. The house was in Fairfield, Alabama, home of Tennessee Coal and Iron (TCI), a subsidiary of United States Steel. Called the Pittsburgh of the South, TCI boasted a model steel workers' town, with low-cost housing and schools located near the plant. Nothing was said about the grit that appeared on window sills and furniture within hours of dusting. Because the worst of the manual labor in the hellish blast furnaces was done by blacks, they outnumbered whites. Everyone in Birmingham, the city to which Fairfield was attached, worked directly for "the company" or for one of its necessary feeder industries and services. It was the late thirties, and the South had only just begun to pull out of the Great Depression.

My father progressed from working in the wire mill as junior bookkeeper to being chief accountant for TCI, and we lived where we did for his convenience. He liked to come home for lunch, and the mill was only about ten minutes from our house. Though an unpretentious house in a working-class neighborhood, my home was full of antiques. A few of them, including a delicate drop-leaf, three-drawer sewing table, came down the Mississippi on a flatboat with my maternal great-grandmother. With her French Huguenot family, she had fled one of many persecutions and landed in Canada. Some of the other fine pieces were gifts to my mother, primarily from my sister but occasionally from my father. I remember a fishing trip from which he returned with a four-branch gas chandelier and no fish. He had spied it in the barn of a farm where he had stopped to get fresh eggs. Painted red, it was being used by the local chickens, attested to by wisps of straw still falling from the lamp bases. My father bought it for a couple of dollars, and we all watched as it became a gorgeous brass light that hung from then on in our living room.

Most of the antique furniture was acquired by my mother in her many jaunts to shops filled with old chests and tables, china, silver, and other bric-a-brac. In the forties, Alabama shopkeepers were not always aware of the value of their holdings, but my mother knew wood grains, silver markings, porcelain symbols. Often I accompanied her to serve as decoy. We would arrive at a shop and browse until the proprietor asked if he could help us. Somehow, Mamie (the name my sister had used as a baby that became what most people called my mother) turned the conversation to me, and I launched into one of my distracting recitals. Since I knew names of rivers, oceans, continents, and other phyla, I could charm adults fairly easily. While I spouted off something years ahead of my comprehension, my mother slipped into remoter rooms of unfinished furniture. Using the pearl-handled penknife always in her purse, she quickly chipped through some colored paint on a washstand or end table. When she found cherry or mahoghany, or, on rare occasions, rosewood, she returned to me smiling. At the next lull in whatever conversation the owner and I were having, she would say in all innocence, "Oh, I happened to notice the little painted piece in back—how much is that if I just take it with me now and not bother you with refinishing it?" If the price was right, a bargain was struck, and the piece piled into the back of our old black Plymouth. Once home, and the newest treasure in the basement, she and I stripped off the bad color, restoring the wood to its original beauty.

Perhaps had my mother lived in another age or been able to tell herself a different story, she might have opened an elegant little shop. Then she could have bought up old painted pieces, restored them, and sold them to people wanting the pleasure of owning them. Instead, we accumulated pieces of antique furniture as my schoolmates' parents might collect matchboxes or miniature china horses. Inside my house, I often felt overwhelmed by objects I had been told were priceless and feared I might accidently knock to the floor at any moment.

My mother seldom did anything on a small scale. Though she was only four feet eleven inches tall, her imagination and energy formed a force field that lent her at least an additional foot. This commanding presence left me often feeling eclipsed, effaced, though Mamie clearly adored me. I still remember going into our house on Holly Court some five months after she had died and being met instantly by the smell of her perfume. It was as if she had just stepped out and would return at any moment.

When I first knew her, she was already forty, so I have very little sense of her as a girl or young woman. Old photos show her in typical twenties styles—tight-fitting black dresses with lace, low-slung wide belts, large ornamental pins on her equally large bodice, funny hats with feathers. One story from her youth that I heard repeatedly was about a dance in Montgomery to which she went, along with Zelda Sayre of whom my mother was an acknowledged look alike. She and Zelda reputedly decided to play a joke on Scott Fitzgerald, in town on furlough from the army. My mother was to "play" Zelda for a time to see if Scott could tell the difference. I listened as Mamie spun her tale about dancing with the dashing soldier who would become one of America's great writers. The joke seems to have worked, at least in her reminiscence.

But the person I knew in childhood had changed in some major ways from that storybook character. No longer svelte, my mother was always either on a diet or about to go on one. Given her frame, at 160 or so, she was twenty to thirty pounds overweight. Rising in the morning full of resolution, she ate her two squares of zwieback and drank a cup of tea while pointing out her virtue to us egg and toast munchers. By lunch, resolve had weakened to allow a taste of whatever dessert she had made for the rest of us; by dinner, caution had flown into the southern air. Mamie was a fine and proud cook, preferring French dishes with rich sauces and elaborate sweets of all sorts. Her cream puffs were legendary, shared with many townspeople when she had to make her contracted monies for the church coffers. Birthdays brought out all her creative talents, not only in the cake of one's choice but in the side dishes: sweet potatoes mashed and put into scooped-out orange halves complete with handles; fried chicken wings or pork chops dressed in paper "shoes" to keep fingers greaseless; tiny Parker House rolls shaped like miniature English pasties.

Her weight in no way obscured her elegance. Most weekdays, Mamie wore a house dress and a smock during the morning as she cleaned or cooked. In mid-afternoon, she took a leisurely bath and "dressed"—nice clothes over massive foundation garments, careful make-up to give her a certain old world beauty. Her hair was brownish with auburn tints, often worn wrapped around a thick rat that lent a halo effect not unlike Greer Garson. The wreath, which softened her face, also cast her backward in time.

Throughout my childhood, my mother wore tiny pince-nez glasses. Whenever she took them off, two bright red ellipses appeared on either side of her patrician nose. I called these "holes" and worried because they took so long to fade. When she finally succumbed to tortoise-shell glasses with regulation ear pieces, she lost some of her exoticism.

Early in the twentieth century, when she was nearing twenty, Mamie had won a scholarship to study piano outside the South. But before she could leave Selma, Alabama, she met, fell in love with, and married Mac, as she called my father. They carried on a brief courtship when he was on shore leave from Newport News, Virginia, and were married over Thanksgiving of 1917, because Daddy could get away at holiday time. Most of the photographs in their early years are of them in bathing suits or other casual wear at some beach with lots of relatives. A little later they appear with my sister, Betty, born about a year after they were wed.

My father was handsome in a craggy sort of way. About five feet six or seven, he had steel blue eyes that stare out of photographs much as they did in real life. He seems almost always to have worn his hair in a close crew cut. It was totally gray when I was born, the story being that it turned overnight after his father died. When I knew him, he too was overweight, though he never seemed to be doing anything to change that. My mother tried to get him to wear belts, but he insisted they cut him and so he preferred suspenders. They allowed him to buy trousers that were loose, that let him breathe. As a child I often watched in excited horror on those occasions when his trousers inched down over his stomach, lower and lower, until, suddenly recalling them, he hitched them back to his waist. He was the perfect antidote to Mamie, in her half-body girdles and massive brassieres.

But his laxity in the matter of fitted clothes was delusive. I was constantly surprised by the particular forms of his fastidiousness. One that seemed especially romantic to me as a child involved his donning a smoking jacket some weekday evenings after supper and on weekends for most of the afternoon. I thought him dashing and relaxed, especially in the silk one I gave him when I was twelve. The other manifestation felt much more oppressive. It involved forcing me to be letter and number perfect in school subjects. Nights often found me sitting on the cedar chest across from his favorite easy chair. We were there to go over my history or geography lesson, and Daddy defined that activity as follows: he would announce a topic heading; I would recite, word for word, the material underneath. If I missed even a preposition or con-junction, I had to do it over. Similarly, when I brought home tests graded 97 or 98, his only response was, "Well, why didn't you get 100?"

Of course I adored him, as my first memory of him shows: It is early Christmas morning, and I am nine months old. Warm in my flannel sack, I come out of sleep to see my father leaning over my baby bed. His face smiles, his eyes twinkle; his prematurely gray hair is cut unusually crew for the holiday. He calls to me: "Wake up, Jay Bird Blue, it's Christmas."

Daddy had another special name for me—Son—that he used in private for the first six years of my life. In the South, a saying went, "If you can kiss your elbow, you'll turn into a boy." One summer when I wanted desperately to be Daddy's son and was old enough to realize that I was only a daughter, I would sit in my back yard, alone, in my seersucker playsuit, contorting my arms, trying to get a lip over to an elbow. Once I even asked a girl friend to bend my arm further than I could. That night I lay awake in my canopied bed aching from my trial.

Failing the elbow trick, I tried other devices to pass. I asked for and got boys' toys: a jungle gym, chemistry sets, Lincoln logs, tinker toys, baseballs and gloves and bats, and all manner of guns during World War II. I wore cowboy shirts with my school skirts; I learned to run fast, to play hard ball, to shoot marbles, and to throw a pocketknife so that it landed blade in ground.

When Daddy stopped calling me Son, my attempts to be one merely became more subtle. To avoid being a "dizzy blond," I learned all I could as fast as I could. Because Daddy once showed me pictures of the Axis army's territories and chuckled when I tried to say the French or German names, I studied history with a passion. Because I heard him humming the tune to "Ghost Riders in the Sky," I read cowboy books until I could spout the lingo like a native. Because my father once said he admired Alan Ladd in *Whispering Smith,* I wore two six-shooters and leather chaps even in the hottest summer weather. When I saw neighbor boys working in the yard or on the family car so their dads could read the Sunday funnies, I pretended to like mowing the grass and washing our old Plymouth. When I began menstruating, I denied my pain so I wouldn't be like "those silly girls" who stayed home from school the first day, lying under heating pads or hot water bottles. I carried books for boys I had crushes on in junior and senior high school, not even aware of how confused I was about my gender identity. Embarrassed in adolescence not to be able to shave my face, I took a razor to my underarms every morning, causing rashes that stung most of the day.

As I was growing up, I longed to hear my father call me Jay Bird Blue or some other term of endearment. But he stopped calling me pet names or any names as he and I got older. Something about me was causing my idol to fade from sight. Rare moments, to which I have attached tremendous importance, stand out. When I was four or so, he occasionally let me crawl up into his lap after supper and listen while he read me the daily funnies: "Major Hoople's Boarding House," "Gasoline Alley," "Hazel," "Dagwood and Blondie"—domestic strips in which well-meaning men were henpecked by imposing women.

In about 1943, I decided that my father bore some physical resemblance to Adolf Hitler—he too wore a small mustache in the center of his upper lip and had dark eyebrows. I would beg him to let me wet comb his crew cut over to the right. With his hair plastered down, the image was remarkably like the Führer's. When he indulged me in this fantasy, I imagined him powerful and assertive, full of words and passion.

Wanting desperately to spend time with him away from home, I asked to go fishing from the time I was about seven. Though he often promised—"The very next trip, you can go, but not just now"—I never got to go on one of these magical adventures. He preferred the company of his friend Mr. Kelton, a huge beefy man over six feet tall, whom my mother disliked intensely. On lucky Saturday afternoons, Daddy offered to take me for a treat, when he was not off fishing. What we actually did was go over to Mr. Kelton's house, and he and Daddy talked, while I played relatively unsupervised in a back yard, fenced in for Mr. Kelton's hound dog.

Once when I was ten, Daddy took me to a professional baseball game at night under huge flood lights that attracted thousands of southern summer bugs. Birmingham had two baseball teams—the Barons and the Black Barons. The Barons were a farm team for the Boston Red Sox, while the Black Barons trained the earliest blacks who broke into major league baseball. Spectators for each team were absolutely segregated. Sitting in the bleachers with my father, I felt excited to be there. I ate a hot dog and drank Coca-Cola in a paper cup with Walt Dropo's picture on it. Walt was my hero since he, like I, was a left-handed first baseman. Near the end of play, Daddy bought me an ice cream sandwich. But he was annoyed by my questions: "Why do they fall onto the ground near home plate?" "Can we move down into those seats where nobody's sitting and we could see more?" "Why is that man with the red face yelling at the umpire?" "Wasn't that a strike, not a ball?" "Why can't I have a Popsicle?" He never took me to another ball game.

With his sudden death in 1954 when I was almost seventeen, my father became even more a mystery to me than his shadowy presence had caused him to seem. From that time until I entered therapy twenty-five years later, I made up stories about him and what he would think about his daughter/"Son" as I matured.

Early memories of my mother are much more troubled. I see her face, moon-round, smiling but often slightly strained, coming closer than was comfortable for me. "Don't cross the street, honey, you'll get hurt." Hearing her say this, I feel instantly defiant and angry. Within half an hour, I've gone outside, toddled over to the curbing, looked across the road at nothing of interest, and crossed that street. No hurt comes to me, so I feel tricked.

Mamie seemed full of "don'ts," sentences telling me what not to do in order to avoid danger: "Don't go barefoot outside, you'll get impetigo." "Don't go swimming in public, you'll get polio." "Don't run and play, you'll get overexertion exhaustion." "Don't get your nice starched white pinafore wrinkled." "Don't go out of your yard, the stray dogs will get you." "Don't lie in the dirt, you'll get eaten by ants." "Don't play pitch, you'll hurt your fingers for piano practice." "Don't perspire, it's not nice." "Don't spit out your watermelon seeds, it's common." "Don't ever eat ice cream and watermelon on the same day or you'll die like Mrs. Munson did last Fourth of July." I explored all these warnings and found only one true—when I played pitch frantically with a hard ball, I did sprain fingers, making piano playing virtually impossible.

My mother was acting out of her best sense of what was necessary for me to become only a slightly modernized version of the southern belle she had been. Two images of me clearly illustrate her hopes: All through childhood, I wore my golden blond hair waist long. Wanting me to look like someone in *Gone with the Wind*, my mother rolled hunks of my thick hair on worn-out boys' socks that she scavenged from neighbors with growing sons. Trying to sleep on eight or ten wads of hair was an ordeal, and I felt only relief when my locks were finally shorn as I entered junior high. All through childhood, I also wore a starched white pinafore each morning over my dotted swiss or polka dot piqué dresses. Mamie would get me ready for a morning presumably of play, put her hands lovingly on my shoulders, look me hard in the eyes, and say: "Now, go outside and have a good time, honey, but remember not to get your little pinafore wrinkled or dirty, in case we have company this afternoon."

My way of coping with so many don'ts was to lie, not merely to avoid trouble but as a way of life. Most of the time I wasn't found out, but fear haunted me. When I was caught, it was shameful and full of pain for us both. One summer between college terms, I insisted, when Mamie asked if I was bored with spending so much time with her, that I liked playing two-handed solitaire every afternoon and sitting in front of the TV trying to think of something other than the programs or her occasional contented snoring. I wrote my true feelings to my roommate and buried her answering letter in my underwear drawer. My mother periodically inspected my drawers, insuring that my clothes were neatly stacked. The day she met me at the front door, tears in her eyes and Jean's letter in her hands, I lied extra hard to calm her and to cover my rage. "There's only a month left till we can go back to Tuscaloosa and freedom" meant that Jean was unhappy with her home life, not that I had said anything about mine. "Your mom is like mine—they want their little girls close, just in case" was really saying how much we appreciated the loving watchfulness from our mothers as we got older. "Just put on a smiling face and count the days": I couldn't construct any other meaning for that one.

If I managed to get away with most of my lies, my disobedient acts were more flagrant and perceptible. Mamie's mode of dealing with me was effective. As an active child, I ran and played as many hours as possible. Feeling trapped inside my house, I stayed outside except for lunch and occasional bathroom breaks, though I even preferred to squat in our back yard behind a hydrangea bush so as not to interrupt my play. Knowing all this, Mamie devised "Punishment." Never spanked, I was forced to sit perfectly still in a rocking chair in my parents' bedroom every time I disobeyed. There was a direct correlation between degree of defiance and number of minutes in that chair. The range was from five to thirty: five minutes can be a long time for puppies and little girls; thirty an eternity. I couldn't take anything of mine into the room—no crayons, paper, books, games. They would distract me from contemplating what a "bad girl" I had just been. My mother never understood that I was trying to be a bad girl, since that was the closest I could get to being a boy.

What I did, shut in that room without a clock to let me see how my confinement was progressing, was fantasize. Within a few months, I was able to become sufficiently involved so that sometimes, out of sheer spite, I refused to leave. Mamie would come to the still-closed door when the last minutes were passing and say, "Time's up, honey, you can go out and play now." Mostly I just sat out my fantasy, prolonging the last scenes while she waited for my appearance. Rarely, I said, "Just a minute, I'm busy." She'd stand it as long as she could and then burst into her own room and urge me out into family space. Once or twice she cried from sheer frustration, saying over and over, "I just don't know why you hurt me this way."

After one of my refusals to leave the room on her schedule, Mamie smarted around the house for the rest of that day overlooking smaller disobediences. I comprehended that I had won something; I felt smug and mean and lonely.

Most of my schoolmates lived in situations where at least the bathroom was private. I did not. The excuse went something like: "Oh, honey, excuse me, but we only have one bathroom and I just have to. . . ." There was a turn bolt on that door and my sister used it. When I tried, I was sharply reprimanded for inconveniencing Mamie who, after all, was responsible for dinner or lunch or whatever was currently important. More than I resented those intrusions, I disliked being called in while she bathed and dressed for the day. We talked there, or I was asked to help her into one of her several armoring garments—brassiere, massive girdle, tight-fitting slip. The intimacy and role reversals that surrounded these meetings several times a week for years seem even at this great distance to be troublesome.

I always sat on a little wicker clothes hamper, my eight-year-old feet barely touching the cool tile floor. I stayed very still, hoping my mother would forget I was there. Mouse quiet, I gazed at her, drying from her morning bath. She stood before me, huge and strong and all soft, rounded folds—layers of folds—face, breasts, stomach, thighs, ass, or as she insisted on calling it, "derrière."

Once dry, she would start all over, this time with a powder puff bigger than my whole hand. The powder made me want to sneeze, but I would hold fingers like a clothespin on my nose so she would go on, forgetting me. With short quick motions, she dusted under her melon bosoms, slowly so they poised between rise and flop. Then she moved down to her satin stomach with its big open space she called a navel— to me a cave. Then her puff-hidden hand moved down, but I have blocked that scene. At this point I would jump off the hamper and ask "why" about some silly thing. I wanted to make her dress; I could not watch her any more.

My question broke into her lazy ritual, and she started to pile on ladies' armor that crushed her lovely folds. First, a vest, soft but hiding. Then a brassiere one size too small so that her floppy breasts looked like iron ones. Was she really a lady knight in disguise? Then came the girdle I helped her close; I snapped the snaps—one … two … three … four— from waist to … Then came hooks and eyes over what I eventually learned was pubic hair. Then soft panties over that and a clingy slip over everything. At the very last, she smeared on Mum, a white cream for marble-shaved underarms, rouged her cheeks, and lined her full lips with a hard red stick.

Then she would loom over me—a statue in a mask—ready to fight her own dragons, I thought. I could not see any skin and had no hope for a soft hug; I would hurt myself on some new-made edge.

The other person living in our house was my sister, Betty. Sixteen and a half when I was born, she had been an only child until then. My first knowledge of her stems from a story Mamie told: when Betty found out that I was on the way, she is supposed to have replied, "If I can't name the brat, I won't speak to it." My mother recounted this to relatives, neighbors, friends. She found it humorous, but I did not like being called "brat" or "it." Betty was allowed to name me, and she chose Toni. Had I been a boy, I would have been called Tony. Many people do not understand the fine point of this gender-based spelling, so that all my life I have gotten mail addressed to Mr. McNaron. Once when I was going to church camp, I was mistakenly put into the boys' cabin, only to be moved immediately upon arrival.

My sister is essentially verbal. From the beginning, she taught me words that I at first had no idea about, which I remembered by sound or later by spelling: "postprandial divertissement" was one of my earliest phrases, along with "marsupials are indigenous to Australia" and "the prolixity of *lapins* is horrific." I see her sitting beside me rattling off these words, being amused and proud when I could repeat them to her latest swain.

In order to get finer instruction in Greek and French, Betty went to New Orleans to Sophie Newcomb College, then the women's arm of Tulane University, but returned after one semester with a case of severe homesickness. The family doctor advised bringing her back home in

November, but Daddy insisted she stay in New Orleans the whole semester; otherwise, he could not get a partial tuition refund. The story I always heard was that for the rest of that fall, Betty would call Mamie and cry into the long distance telephone.

Born a year after my parents were married, Betty was reared largely by her maternal grandparents. The Hurleys lived in Selma, Alabama, the seat of southern culture and agriculture. Adoring Betty, they lavished upon her clothes ordered from Bergdorf Goodman in New York, toys from Switzerland, and unconditional love. Since my mother's father worked for a railroad, Mamie had unlimited passes to travel the eighty miles south from Birmingham. Mamie spent the last month or so of her pregnancy back home, and my father commuted on weekends. Once Betty was born, Mamie remained with her mother for several more months.

Grandparental showering at such an early age convinced Betty that her family was without fault or flaw and that she would always be taken care of. When I was growing up under strict rules about keeping my room pristine at all times, my closet neat, and all my clothes properly hung or drawered, I chafed under tales of Betty's youth. It seems that she often let her nightgown slip from her body onto the floor, only to have the faithful old family servant, Annie Belle Royal, come along to pick it up and put it away. I could not make sense out of two antithetical codes for children with the same mother.

Though the South of Betty's youth and courting age was different from my mother's, both women fulfilled the requirements of "belle." My sister was what the forties termed glamorous. I remember one photo in particular; lightly tinted, it shows Betty in a soft hat with a huge brim that dips over her face just like Garbo's or Rita Hayworth's always did. Her smile is subtle, even alluring, and her soft hazel eyes glance upward from slightly shaded lids.

My sister had her own food story, as did everyone in our family. Determined to be thin at any cost but adoring sweets, she established a bizarre regimen. Breakfast was usually one piece of cheese toast and a mammoth cup of hot tea; lunch, a Hershey bar and Coca-Cola; dinner, tiny servings of food topped by a large dessert. If her morning ritual on the scale found the indicator pointing beyond her top weight (110 pounds), she ate virtually nothing that day except the Hershey bar and Coca-Cola. Next day, when things were back to acceptable, the earlier plan resumed. To this day, Betty has retained what can only be called a girlish figure, feeding others sumptuous meals while nibbling at

Lilliputian helpings herself. Recently her doctor warned her that her blood sugar level was dangerously high, that sweets were off her diet. Realizing the genuine crisis this constituted, I quickly searched my co-op shelves for substitute snacks. But sesame sticks and trail mix hardly replace Lundt's latest delight, a giant Hershey, or bulk chocolate triangles by the pound.

Her looks and charm made her quite popular with boys, who somehow did not hold it against her that she was also extremely smart. Since I was a flop at "boys" because they resented my success at my studies, I held my sister in some degree of awe. Betty was unwilling to sit home and pine, however, so she hid her all-A report cards, telling chums that she "did all right" at the end of each grading period. When I was preschool age, she had endless beaux wishing to marry her, all of whom she carefully kept at bay. Several of them paid court to Mamie, sensing that the way to Betty's heart was through her mother. Others chose to focus on me in their struggle for supremacy: I was carried off to bed many nights on the shoulders of a sweet hulk of a man named "Box" Willingham, who threw me into the air to my delight and let me blow his army sergeant's whistle. These World War II veterans played with me the way other children's dads did, and I loved them fiercely.

Every now and then, Betty would prefer me out of the living room so she and her current visitor could be "alone." In addition to the proverbial nickel for an ice cream cone, I was bought off in clever ways. The most original was the time Betty finagled me into turning the crank of her old blue Victrola while she and Tookie Teague waltzed. I was intrigued by the magical machine that made sounds if you cranked and by the graceful swirls my sister made. She negotiated the furniture and ornaments so much better than I.

During the war when men were off fighting Germans, Betty worked as a public school teacher. I picture her, frantic in our living room, watching a high school senior doing calisthenics that she herself would have to lead her class in the next day; or helping Mamie cut out endless patterns of leaves for borders in her third-grade room; or standing in tears in the middle of the floor having vainly tried to locate middle C on a pitch pipe, readying herself to teach music class. Finally, she got to be the librarian for a year until the regular guardian returned from her stint in the navy.

Books suited my sister better than basketballs or chalk pointers, so after being replaced in the schools, she found her way to the Birmingham Public Library. Beginning in the circulation department, checking out books, she quickly rose to be head of the popular literature wing. In those days, libraries tried to maintain quiet. Betty loved jewelry, especially gold charm bracelets. I can still hear her clinking delicately around shelves, urging three more novels on one patron, four more books on camping on another. Circulation doubled during her first year in the job, since her customers, especially the men, simply could not refuse her recommendations. Who knows whether they read every word, but they certainly exposed themselves to much more culture and information than they had intended. Though she complained about the hours, my sister probably liked her job—not exactly a salon, her section of the library was definitely her domain.

Betty left the library in the early sixties, returning to teaching, this time in a private school across town from where we lived. But in 1963, in December, our mother died suddenly, and Betty was permanently changed. One sign was her decision never to return to work. She asked a friend to bring any personal belongings from her desk when he came to pay his respects. Her last check was mailed to her at home.

We had what is now thought of as a closed nuclear family. When I was born in 1937, three of my grandparents were dead and the fourth died when I was three. My parents were old enough to be my grandparents, and my sister could have been a youngish mother. Though one of my mother's brothers and one of my father's sisters lived in Birmingham, I spent very little time in their homes or getting to know them. They visited us at Christmas, and occasionally we went to their houses for some special event. They called on my parents when they needed help, or when one of their sons (they all had only boys) got into some kind of trouble. I resented their arriving on our doorstep with their newest crisis, expecting Mamie or Daddy to solve it. I resented even more Mamie's and Daddy's persistent willingness to do just that, even when it meant hardship or strain for them.

My family's insularity meant I was shut out of my history as well as on-going holiday clan gatherings. Neither parent liked to talk about the past: my mother said it was too painful; my father simply never mentioned his. I have been told that the annual July 4th celebrations in Selma took place on my mother's parents' lawn and that Mamie's father worked for the railroad. Mostly, he dressed himself in starched white shirts and immaculate suits, summer or winter. Daddy was born and reared on Sand Mountain, at the tail of the Appalachians. His family was supposedly dirt poor and uncultured. My father's father walked out on him, his mother, and two sisters when Daddy was in his teens, forcing him to end his youth and go to work to help support the family.

I know these shadowy ancestors from faded pictures, shown me under duress and at my insistence. I held back questions and responses so as not to upset whoever was showing them. Daddy's father looks like a slightly ill kempt, overgrown kid, usually with some old hound dog at his feet, holding a bottle or glass in one hand, a string of dead fish in the other. His eyes are not quite focused, and he looks as if he could run at any moment. The first time I saw a snapshot of him after I had gone through treatment for years of alcoholic drinking, I felt I was meeting a kinsman. My father's refusal to touch liquor at home suddenly made more sense.

Daddy's mother came to live with him and my mother and sister when Betty was a child. Mamie told a story about sterilizing dishes and glasses in order to protect her child, only to have Mrs. McNaron, who suffered from tuberculosis, go into fits of hurt or affronted self-pity over the special treatment. Whenever my mother and father were in deep wrangles, Mamie would drag out her recital of these scenes, guaranteeing a yelled out, "I don't want to hear that story one more time, Old Lady" (my father's affectionate name for his wife). In the single snapshot of her that I have seen, my paternal grandmother stares out of eyes filled with betrayal, holds herself like a ramrod, seems afraid to smile. She is as thin and sparse and held in as her husband is fat, messy, and without boundaries. I would describe her as handsome rather than beautiful, him as childish and irresponsible.

I have many more photographs of Mamie's side of the family, especially of her father. He is dressed to the hilt: rounded high collars centered by tasteful ties always adorned with a stick pin, never lacking a suit coat, framed in oval, arty tintypes taken by a professional photographer in downtown Selma. "Doc," as Mamie's father was called, smiles from his neat borders and reminds me of the Mona Lisa—reputedly enigmatic if not downright profound but vapid to me. In the full-standing photos, this saintly creature always has a pocket watch, visible from the gold chain and jeweled fob that show just below the center of his buttoned vest. Betty remembers him as "the sweetest man that ever lived." All I remember about him is a walk down Holly Court hill when I was a baby of about two and a half. I needed to hold his hand to steady myself. Because it would have been less than gentlemanly to walk any way other than upright, I had to strain my short arm because he was too tall to walk upright and still reach down to my level.

Mamie's mother looks like a matriarch from the United Daughters of the Confederacy, though we never belonged to that group: buxom and tightly corseted; tall and big boned; eyes looking straight ahead, unflinching and steely; hair pulled back from her face severely, only to roll into a soft circle around her head. When Betty showed me this picture a few years ago, my unvoiced but immediate response was, "I wouldn't want to have her mad at me 'cause she could hold on to it forever."

My mother's mother died quite suddenly one summer in Foley, Alabama, in a movie house. Every year, my family vacationed there, staying in the cabin owned by Mamie's parents. Foley boasted a picture show among its more modern attractions and Mamie's mother took Betty and a boy cousin to afternoon matinees as often as the feature changed. There, in the darkened theater, my grandmother had a heart attack, and while my sister held her head her cousin ran for a doctor. My grandmother died, and my mother fell into a depression that lasted three years before my father intervened. At his insistence, they visited Dr. John, the family doctor. When my father asked what they might do to "cure Old Lady," Dr. John recommended having another child. Though my parents were almost forty, I was conceived. Whenever Mamie told the story of Dr. John's suggesting that she and Mac have a baby to "cheer Theresa up," I felt like running. I grew up in the shadow of that expectation, always trying to please, so often sensing that what I did was not quite enough.

I felt too important to the adults in my house. They kept close watch over me, encouraging me to be what they were not or could not be, reluctant to let me be myself. As a result, my childhood was full of instances in which I very much wanted their attention, but when it came in quantities, I would feel compelled to pull away. For instance, my junior high school teachers seemed intent on having us create "projects," assignments that caused me considerable consternation. Visual effects were to accompany our written reports, and we all knew that decorations determined whether our work received a B for competence or an A for "creativity." Part of me welcomed the help readily forthcoming from Mamie, with Betty as her assistant, since I was not particularly artistic. They would cheerfully volunteer to make my covers, correct my spelling, encourage me to do yet more reading and writing to insure the coveted A. Somewhere in the middle of this process, my gratitude would turn sour, and I would feel taken over, unable to own my work but equally unable to snatch it from them.

My family taught me to see myself as superior to virtually everyone and to isolate myself in the name of precocity or independence or some other large, empty word. One result was that I developed an extraordinarily active imagination, another was few companions my own age. Angry and confused, I took my feelings outside where I ran and played, day after day, to the point of exhaustion.

First Lessons

*O*ne house, a hedge, and an unpaved alley from where I grew up was the "colored section" of town, popularly known as the "quarters" or "nigger town." The former term recalled the plantation days of slavery, while the latter reflected more contemporary race hatred. The world across that alley fascinated me. When I was three and four, I would sit by my bedroom window and look over at unpainted wooden houses where people lived who were supposed to be different from me. Occasionally, cruising policemen yelled at them, "Get your ass inside, nigger"; after a judicious time lapse, the figures returned to their porches and resumed their activities.

There were three houses up the slant alley. The one nearest the top had once been whitewashed, and traces of peeling green trim persisted. All were built of weathered boards with spaces between, offering no protection against heat, rain, cold, or dust. The family in the first house had a beat-up jalopy that mostly did not run. When they wanted to use it, they would push it into the alley, then try to start it. If the engine failed to turn over, they quickly pushed the car back into their packed dirt yard before the garbage truck filled with white people's trash came or before some white teenaged boy decided to gun his motor all the way up that alley, raising so much dust that it drifted across the vacant lot to my window sills.

Behind "my" three houses (I thought of them as somehow special to me) lay miles of equally poor dwellings in which many hundred blacks eked out whatever existence they could. The neighborhood stretched up a gradual hill so that from my watch-window I could just barely make out houses and an occasional church tower way off in the distance. Within its boundaries, that part of town contained several classes of blacks. The absolute poorest lived nearest us—an odd phenomenon—while middle-class people had better houses further within the tangle of short streets that made up the center of the section. These houses had brick foundations with clapboard siding from about half way up. Window boxes graced virtually every house, as did old rusty gliders painted fresh every other spring. In every yard grew brilliant flowers—waist-high zinnias in reds, oranges, and yellows; fertile roses that looked like they should be wearing blue ribbons; the tallest black-eyed susans I had ever seen. I learned about these distinctions as I rode with my father to take Hettie, our housekeeper, and her successor, Josephine, home when they worked past dark.

When I was ready for junior high school, I had to get to the other side of Fairfield. To walk there the proper way, through white neighborhoods and shopping areas, took about half an hour. But there was a shorter route: once on the street below our house, I could cut ten minutes by going down a little side street that took me over the imaginary line from between white and black Fairfield. I would walk right through the black section, past a tiny store where I could stop for a few jawbreakers or Tootsie Roll Pops on the way home. I was usually the only white child in the place, and the man behind the counter always grinned as he asked, "How you today, Miss?" Along the counter behind which he stood were big jars filled with all kinds of hard candies, "penny" candies that cost two or three cents in white stores. Once I asked my parents why the A & P lied about its candy and the black man's store told the truth. I got no answer but was scolded yet again for refusing to take the "long" (read white) route to school. One of the things I liked about this route was the absence of other white schoolchildren, since in their presence I felt awkward and isolated. In the black neighborhood, I felt more at ease partly because black women on their porches often spoke to me as I went along, ignorant of the pressure I created for them and their children.

The entire South of my childhood was unreconstructed. Blacks were not allowed into white neighborhoods except to get to the houses where they might work. Though Fairfield had a larger population of Negroes (as we called blacks then if we were being polite) than whites, this numerical majority did not matter at all, since every remotely powerful office was held by white men. There were no hotels in Birmingham where blacks could stay except for Gaston Motor Court, owned by one of the few black attorneys in Birmingham but still located miles out of town. Though blacks were allowed to spend money in downtown stores, I never saw them except in department stores my mother said were "common," visited by us only when we needed some specific item unavailable anywhere else. The only exception was Loveman, Joseph, and Loeb, a major department store where blacks did shop regularly.

Once when I was small, my mother and I were in Loveman's looking for some cotton mesh gloves. I never liked these trips downtown, and, on this occasion, I manufactured a major thirst that meant I needed to leave my mother at the counter to find a drinking fountain. I found two fountains, one lower than the other. Since I still could barely reach the regular ones, I used the one nearer my level. As I drank, I felt myself yanked away with a force that almost cost me my footing. Mamie dragged me to one side, whispering loudly, "Can't you read that this one is for coloreds?" I had not seen the clearly painted black letters on the cream wall above the porcelain basin, COLORED. Beside it, above the fountain that was too high for me, I saw an equally clear sign reading WHITE.

"Is the water different in the fountains?" I innocently asked. "Of course not," my mother whispered in a tone that made me think I might be demented. "Then why can't I use the one that's easier for me to get water from?" We had never talked about race relations in our home and so whatever was going on eluded my childishly literal mind. "Just do as I ask, please, honey. Now come on back and try on these nice beige gloves I've found for you."

In the next weeks, I noticed other things: when Daddy took Hettie home, she rode in the back seat, leaving him alone in the front. If children from across the alley ran carelessly into the paved street, their mothers called in voices that sounded like Mamie's when she was afraid I had fallen and hurt myself badly. We kept the dishes and glasses used by Hettie and the yard man, Charlie, in different places from our own. I felt hurt and angry about the car and dishes, since I adored Hettie and Charlie and couldn't comprehend why they were being treated differently. Occasionally at Loveman's I sneaked a quick drink from the forbidden fountains, but my motive was to disobey my mother.

Even though we lived close to Fairfield's black section, no one ever talked about "them," and I was told by my family not to pay any attention to the things I might see or hear from "across the alley." But I needed time away from all the beautiful objects waiting to be knocked to the floor, and I needed very early to disobey. So I began to travel the short physical distance past the last white house, slip through the hedge, and arrive at alien ground—the alley. Though I spent play time in that unpaved area between what I knew were entirely different worlds, I seldom went into the yard of a black person's house. Once or twice I ventured into a field near the three ramshackle houses to play softball with a group of blacks and a few whites who did not live on my block.

I played in the alley often. Two or three other white children not yet in school who lived on my block also played there, along with nine or ten black boys and girls. A black boy, older than the rest, taught me to play marbles, and I was good. We dug out little cup holes in the clay and drew boundaries with a stick; then everyone put the same number of marbles inside the circle as ante. Then one by one we used our special shooter to try and knock marbles into holes. Every marble we got to go into a hole was a keeper. If we lost all our players and only had a shooter, it was legal to put it inside the circle, matched by five to ten regular marbles of anyone who wanted to risk that big a loss. I always risked, winning some stunning shooters called rollerpackers. The risk answered some deep impulse that was being systematically repressed in the rest of my life.

To be a proper southern girl, I needed to learn prudence at all costs, since one false move might reveal some unacceptable tendency. At my first birthday party, for instance, we played the games popular among white children of the time: drop the clothespin in the milk bottle, pin the tail on the donkey, drop the handkerchief, blindman's buff, and how-many-little-words-can-you-make-from-this-big-word. Mamie had bought wonderful prizes to be given the winners— brightly colored tops, packages of metal jacks, wooden paddles with tiny red rubber balls attached by long rubber strings, bags of cat's eye marbles complete with a shooter. I won all the games, but my mother made me give the prizes to my guests, saying, "You wouldn't want your little friends to think you're selfish or greedy, would you?" What I wanted was fairness, but I saw that being polite might well exclude that possibility.

By the fifth grade of my all-white school, I comprehended that life among my so-called white peers was far more hazardous and cruel than it had been in the alley. None of us who played there minded whether we lost or won on a given day; it was exciting just to make holes, draw circles, and risk. Consequently, when I saw white boys playing marbles using pretty much the same strategy I had learned, I asked to play with them. They let me but giggled behind their hands at some private joke. When I won, consistently and heavily, their giggles turned into ugly snarls. They talked about me in ways that caused girls to avoid me, especially in the restroom. The back of my neck stung and turned red in spite of my willpower, but I went ahead and used the toilet when what I wanted most was to run out of the bathroom, out of the school, out of my world. But I refused to play marbles less well than I knew how, so the process of exclusion and derision continued.

As it did, I gradually formed distinctly negative attitudes toward white boys. I did not like how mean and nasty they could be to the black children across the alley from me. They routinely dropped terrified cats and kittens off high back porches, laughing uproariously when they landed with thuds I could hear from two houses away. And I very much hated them when they rubbed my nose in pink buttercup flowers until I sneezed and coughed my way into my house. Without knowing it, I was coming to associate white boys with bullies who went after white girls and all blacks.

Given these strained relations with my white classmates, I still puzzle over why that black boy taught me to play marbles so well and over why he and other black boys did not seem to mind when I won their marbles. Surely it is facile to say they won mine too and so it evened out. Did they already feel like such total losers in the world around them that a few marbles more or less couldn't matter? Did the black boy have a fantasy that I would do just what I did and so teach me well in order to cause me pain? Did he do it to get back at the white boys who routinely shot BB guns into his front yard, scaring him and his sisters back into their house? Did he, like I, sense without words some connection between us deeper than color and gender? Or were we just having fun, was it just a game?

I refer to my alley associates as "that black boy" or "a black girl" because we never told names, white or black, though we played together for several years. In fact we hardly used words at all, which was another blessing about the alley. Inside my house, language was everything, and everyone knew lots more of it than I did, no matter how hard I tried to catch up. I now believe that we maintained that amazing anonymity and silence as protection. My mother often asked me who I was with "out there in all that red clay dust." Because I knew nobody's name, I could answer truthfully, "I don't know, they're just some kids—we have fun and I like them." Perhaps their mothers asked similar questions. But somebody could have gotten into lots of trouble if the grownups had traced our gang. Our silence had its painful edge, since it acknowledged the impossibility of any of our becoming friends.

When I was about to enter the first grade, my mother took me aside and tried to tell me something about race relations in the South. Her success was only slightly greater than when she tried years later to tell me about menstruation by saying, to calm my fears at blood coming out of me, "Oh, honey, be glad, now you can have babies." All I heard that afternoon when I was seven was that I was forbidden to play in the alley. That was on a Sunday, the usual day for long talkings-to by my mother. On Monday, I started school and hated it instantly.

On the first day of first grade, everyone's mother brought her reluctant child inside a hot, stuffy old brick building, into a strange room full of small desks and large blackboards. Presiding over it all was a woman I would come to see as kindly enough, but my initial encounter with Miss Leslie left me angry and confused. It seems that part of our "lessons" was to be the acquisition of manners—of which I already had more than enough as far as I was concerned. But Miss Leslie felt it her social duty to show her little girls and boys how to set a table properly and how to sit by a *papier maché* fireplace and engage in chat, that essential southern practice.

In an attempt to involve us in setting up these ersatz spaces, she asked the class to bring various items from home: cushions for the little straight chairs we were to chat in; paper place mats for the little table where we were to have tea; vases for flowers or other decorations. Then she looked at the fireplace area, turned to us with a deep smile, and said: "Now the last thing we need may be hard to find, since not everyone will have one in their home. But we lack a little hearth broom." I was confused about what she wanted, since she pronounced hearth "herth." Guessing what she meant, since we did have a red straw broom by our fireplace that I used regularly to sweep up ashes or stray coal pieces, I raised my hand eagerly. "I can bring a hearth broom from home—we have one." I pronounced the word as it should be.

"Well, thank you, my dear, I'm sure you can, but first you must learn to pronounce it correctly—"herth," not "harth"—come along now, I'm sure you can say that."

Proper pronunciation was sacred in our household. I knew that h-e-a-r-t-h did not rhyme with e-a-r-t-h, even though they might look alike if you took away the "h." My confidence in the correctness of my way of saying it urged me on to what was probably stupid bravery. I looked Miss Leslie in the eye and said, "Oh, no ma'am, it's "harth," not "herth."

My mother whispered in my unbelieving ear, "Honey, just say what the teacher asks you to here and keep saying it right at home. And say you're sorry, like a good girl. Go on, now." This from the same person who drilled correctness into me, even refusing to let me use street slang in order to blend in with the other children on my block. My anger flared as I turned on my mother and spat out, "You tell her *you're* sorry if you are—I'm not sorry—I'm right and I don't understand why you want me to lie."

Deciding not to push the issue further just then, Miss Leslie went ahead with her plans for next day, saying only, "Why don't you bring along your little broom and we'll put it by this nice fireplace and you can show us all how you sweep the ashes." When the long half-day finally ended, my mother went up to the teacher's desk and spoke in hushed tones. I have no idea what she said, but I was disappointed in her for seeming to collude with someone who could not even pronounce a simple word correctly.

We got out at noon, and by two o'clock I was back in my play clothes, sitting in the alley with my black playmates. After a few days, I noticed that the handful of other white children who occasionally played there were gone. Other parents may have conducted similar awkward, muddled conversations about no longer playing in the clay strip between worlds. No matter how muddled the message, the others obeyed. I was slow to grasp that my entry into that dull and hypocritical space where first grade happened was my formal exposure to southern racial and sexual politics. In that schoolroom, no such Never Never land as my alley could exist. There, everything was black or white, and I was definitely white.

As a child, I came into contact with two black women, both of whom worked for my family as domestic servants: Hettie Holmes and Josephine Zeak. Mamie took an interest in Hettie's welfare, giving her old clothes and food to take home to Mr. Holmes. As a child who loved to choose for myself, I wondered if Hettie might not prefer money to go downtown and buy something new.

On several occasions, Mamie sent Daddy to the local jail on

Sunday mornings to bail Hettie out. Hettie, my mother told me, drank whiskey on the weekend and fought with her husband, who drank whiskey all week. Their weapons were knives, and Hettie came to work more than once with new cut marks on her neck and upper arms, though never on her powerful and beautiful face. I imagined Mr. Holmes agreed with me about her face. Once, when I raged against him for hurting her, she said laughingly: "Oh, sugar, you should see him, he looks a whole lot worse." They stayed married all the time I knew her.

Hettie was short, dark skinned, and pudgy, wore faded house-dresses, and cleaned our house in bare feet. But to me at three and five, she seemed mysterious, warm, and free spirited. She dipped Red Devil snuff from little flat aluminum cans. Wanting to do everything she did, one morning I asked her to let me have some snuff. "No, child, this'll make you some sick." I insisted, putting Hettie into an ancient black–white tug in which a child of five can order a grown woman to do her bidding. I won, of course, and took a small pinch of the rich brown smelly stuff. Sticking it carefully between my gum and lower lip, I tried hard to copy my model. In about three minutes, I felt lightheaded, then nauseated for the rest of the morning. After that I was content to watch my hero fill her own lower lip until it stuck out bravely.

Hettie Holmes cooked things my mother did not know how to fix. Her corn bread—crisp and delicate all at once—tasted so good I ate it without butter or jelly. Her version of pork chops and onions had a succulence and pungency that spoiled me for all future offerings of that popular southern dish. Hettie could serve peas and beans that still tasted of peas and beans, unlike my mother's, which had no particular taste because they were disguised in a thick French sauce.

My mother prepared *haute cuisine* when I wanted greasy vege-tables from a frying pan. The frying pan urge obsessed me for months. Hettie made our lunch and served it in the dining room where we always ate. Then she had her own food at a table in the kitchen, carefully placed so Mamie could see and talk with her. Mamie enjoyed Hettie's company but could not conceive in 1943 of their eating in the same physical space. Hettie took the cast-iron pan from which our food had just been served, set it on a dish towel on her table, and ate directly from it. When she had eaten all she could with a fork, she took a piece of bread and sopped up remaining traces of gravy or "pot licker." I was punished severely for using my bread that way.

Whenever Mamie went to town to shop or attend her many clubs (garden, book, church auxiliary, forensic, library), I lunched out of that frying pan, sitting proudly at the kitchen table. Hettie, on the other hand, watched and listened nervously for Mamie's possible untimely return. At least once, we were almost caught. I was in the middle of pork chops and onions, peas, and corn bread, when Mamie rang the door bell at the front screen door. While Hettie kept my mother at bay with some story about her hands being in dishwater, I dumped my food onto a china plate and ran for the dining room. When I first saw Lillian Smith's title, *Strange Fruit,* I recalled those stolen childhood lunches at which I could relax about whether I was using the correct implement or putting my glass back at the right angle in relation to my knife and plate.

In Alabama, torrential downpours can drop inches of rain in a very short time. We lived on the plateau of a high hillside that had been terraced for housing. Houses across the street had many cement steps going from the street up to their front porches, while our front entrance was on the street level. When it rained hard, the water surged down those stone steps into our yard before it ran down the hill toward our back alley. I was scared of those sheets of water. If a storm began on an afternoon when Hettie was keeping me, she stopped whatever she was doing to stand beside me at the living room window. I was fixed in amazement at the deluge of clay-colored water washing down, making creases in all the lawns, noisy even through our closed windows, bringing small objects with it. Standing behind me, her hand resting reassuringly on my back, Hettie would talk in her low, husky voice: "God's making soup out of rain for his people and what you see washing down the steps is his pots boiling over, like mine do in the kitchen if I go off and forget them." She told me the trees were not going to blow over but were yawning to wake up and feel the wind blow through them. She told me lightning was a message from the Lord telling us to work harder and look especially to our house-keeping. She told me thunder was Jesus in his private bowling alley, knocking over ten golden pins, having fun for a change.

Hettie Holmes stopped working for us when I was about nine, and I never heard of her again. When I asked why she was not coming to work, I received no answer. I was angry and hurt to have so central a person removed from my daily life without a word of explanation. Maybe she became more alcoholic and could not work a steady job; maybe Daddy stopped being willing to bail her out of jail; maybe she cooked up one mess too many of greasy magic peas and corn bread for Mamie's ego. Maybe she got tired of being grateful to Mamie for handouts. Or maybe she secretly resented being bailed out of jail by my father. I made up lots of maybes. But none of them took away my ache or filled the void I felt when Hettie vanished. She is surely long dead but I think of her sometimes when it storms or when I eat black-eyed peas that never quite taste right.

Shortly after Hettie Holmes stopped working for us, we heard about a young black woman reputed to be good at cleaning and ironing. She arrived one day in 1947 and stayed until we sold the house in 1964 after Mamie died. Josephine Zeak was her name, and I liked her right away. I had never known a person whose name began with "z." Josephine was tall and thin with cocoa brown skin and shiny straightened black hair. Her nose was Western, her cheek bones were statuesque African. She wore stockings and spoke softly. Her dresses had belts. She used a napkin when she ate her lunch and read magazines while her food digested. It was a major source of irritation to my mother and sister that Josephine would not hop up from lunch to scrub the kitchen floor or at least wash the lunch dishes. She insisted on half an hour between her last mouthful and any resumption of work, so that her food could digest properly. I remember Mamie getting up from her lunch, returning to her knees to finish polishing a part of the floor between the living and dining rooms that got waxed once a week and was hazardous to walk on. While she did that, Josephine waited for her hamburger patty to settle, reading to my mother from *Life* magazine about some movie actor they both liked. She refused to wash curtains, wax floors, or iron with starch, leaving those odious tasks for my mother.

When Josephine arrived, I thought myself old enough to take some responsibility in training her. Dusting and vacuuming were my specialities, so I "taught" her to do those things. She was canny enough to mask her feelings, never letting on that she already knew how to do such chores all too well. In her early thirties when I met her, she had been cleaning houses since she was a teenager. Whereas Hettie Holmes had come every day unless she was too hung over or in jail, Josephine stipulated which three days a week she could come and what her hours would be. Because Mamie had never dealt with a black person who was not completely deferential, she was speechless. All she could do was complain to Betty about Josephine's "insolence" and how that was probably tied to her being light skinned. Neither of them considered firing or confronting her.

Sometimes Josephine and I cleaned the bedrooms together so she would have time to iron in the afternoons. Those were good times for me because I went into the basement where the ironing board stayed and talked to Josephine. I learned about her two daughters and soon met Joann, who was only three or four months older than I. Our talks about school subjects and dating seemed stiff to me. Joann was dating and I was not, so I felt inferior when that topic came up. But when we talked about anything else, she hung back, trying to show what her mother undoubtedly would have taught her was appropriate deference. We graduated from high school the same year, and that next fall she married a soldier named Sport and moved to Georgia, while I went to the white state university. One rainy afternoon in the basement Josephine shared a dream with me: she was determined to help her girls advance themselves, so they would not have to clean houses.

Sometimes I read to Josephine while she ironed, and then we discussed what I had read. As I grew older, I realized how unfair it was for anyone so intelligent to have to clean white ladies' houses in order to make money. Many years after she came to work for us, I asked her about all this, and she said, "I once thought of being something, but then I married and had the babies and it did not seem very practical to try. It was easy to get work cleaning houses. White ladies liked me to do that but didn't particularly want me to do other things."

Since my exodus from the South in 1961, my contact with Josephine has been mostly through our monthly letters. Hers are full of the weather, her health, her children, grandchildren, great-grandchildren, the white ladies she has worked for, her hopes that I am well and happy. When I went to Wisconsin to graduate school and her older daughter went to Alaska with her army husband, Josephine said she felt lonely and less useful. But on one occasion, she was more helpful to me than either of us understood at the time. I was in the process of writing my Ph.D. dissertation. My mother and sister had just spent the summer with me in Madison, Wisconsin, and I could see that Mamie was not well and that Betty was discontented. That fall, just months before my mother died of a heart attack, Josephine called me long distance (a huge cost to her) to say she was worried about "Miss Mamie." Under strenuous questioning, she revealed that Betty was pushing harder than usual to leave Holly Court. My sister had wanted to move across town to a better neighborhood for years. My mother flatly refused—perhaps that was the only time she refused my sister.

She owned her house; it was her only security; she liked having Betty and her husband live with her. To reverse that arrangement would mean a loss of power. As Josephine talked with me, she cried, saying, "Oh, Toni, I'm scared for Miss Mamie." I sat right down and wrote my mother immediately, supporting her wish to stay where she felt more secure. Josephine had taken a great risk to speak so directly to me.

Though I have never told Josephine in so many words that I am a lesbian, she has known about several women with whom I have lived. She has accepted this part of me as easily as she did my telling her at ten how to vacuum. She sends greetings to my present lover, remembers her name, is happy that I am not living alone. Each time I have moved, she has written to say, "Wish I could come help clean so your space will be fit to live in." Statements like this one are followed by, "Smile," written in parentheses. Her sense of humor continues to touch me as does her determination to grow old gracefully. A few years ago she moved away from her husband, Mr. Zeak (she never called him anything else in front of me). She wrote me that things had not been so good between them, and she had decided to live more peacefully in her old age. Now she rents an apartment in the same building as her sister. Her income gets smaller every year since housecleaning has become too strenuous. Though she worked hard for over fifty years, she has no pension and virtually no Social Security. Her daughters help her out financially, and my sister and I send her money occasionally, which she calls a "token." When I see the word, I feel that no amount we ever send can make up for the years of cheap labor she gave us. Her meaning for the word is that my sister or I have sent her another sign of how much we value and care for her.

On a trip south in 1974, I looked forward most of all to seeing Josephine. She invited me to her house for lunch, and I accepted gladly. The psychosomatic laryngitis I had developed shortly after my uncle had greeted me with, "God made them niggers black, you know," magically vanished as I crossed Josephine's threshold. Her space was safe space, a place where I could speak without fear of offending. The decorations in her house were a strange blend of simple furniture and linoleum on the floors and exquisite ornaments from our house on Holly Court, given to her first by Mamie and then by Betty after Mamie's death.

We were to have lunch in the kitchen so I stood and talked with her while she fixed things. She had remembered my favorite lunch: Campbell's tomato soup and a hamburger made of ground round steak on bread with mayonnaise and catsup. I cried while Josephine stirred my soup; no one else that trip seemed to focus on me at all, preferring to make me into who or what they expected. Maybe that was part of why I always loved the women who worked for us so fiercely and was so devastated when they vanished: they gave me sympathy, kindness, and affectionate acceptance without being able to demand anything in return.

When I noticed that Josephine was cooking only one hamburger patty, I asked why. "Oh, I ate my lunch before you came, so I could listen better to all you have to say." Then I noticed only one place setting at the table. "Oh, I'll just stand here by the stove, in case you want something more; then when you finish, we can go into the living room and have a nice talk." I felt wounded for both of us and insisted that she sit with me while I ate.

I decided to ask her about being black in Fairfield, Alabama, and she decided to tell me. She spoke with tears in her eyes about Dr. King and his vision. She spoke with fear in her eyes about young blacks, especially men, out of jobs, restless, eager to act violently toward anyone in their way. She admitted that it had made her angry to be treated badly by white ladies and hurt her not to be able to give her children more of what she wished for them. I told her I was in favor of total integration. She replied, "Oh, child, I'm too old and grew up a long time ago; if we go that far, it's just more hurt and blood for us here." Her worst terror was that, as some blacks rebelled, all would be punished. So she preferred moderation, a slower pace. From my position of white safety, I told her the pace was killingly slow now and that I wanted change within my lifetime.

After a couple of hours, Josephine began noticeably to fidget. When I asked, she admitted, "I'm a little worried about how long you've been here. My neighbors are sure to have seen the car when it drove up; they'll know it held a white lady." I had stayed longer than any errand could have possibly taken and so must not be an employer. Recently a "nice colored lady" from her church had been slapped around by young black boys because she had been seen being too friendly with some white person at a grocery store on Fairfield's main street. Josephine was frightened and yet sad to have to wish me gone. I asked her to come outside and let me take a picture of her, which she did. I could get her to do this, against her better judgment, because the basic power imbalance between us was still present. Having hugged in her kitchen, I was careful not to appear too close or to touch her. It felt entirely too familiar to me, holding in spontaneous affection for a woman I love.

For many years, Josephine sent me a homemade pound cake at Christmas. That meant laying in eggs, sugar, flour, butter, vanilla, ingredients alone at a cost of about eight dollars. Josephine made five dollars a day, cleaning houses. To make my cake, she took a day off, losing her much-needed money, in order to sift, mash, and beat by hand. Then she went to elaborate lengths to wrap my cake so it would hold its freshness through the U.S. mail. It came in a cardboard box, mailed first class, marked fragile, handle with care—expensive. Inside the big box was a bakery box secured into the heavier one by layers of grocery store brown bags. These would have cost her as well, since stores gave free extra bags only to whites. Inside the boxes lay the cake, made in a doughnut hole pan, even more delicate than if it were solid. The cake was wrapped first in waxed paper, then aluminum foil, then paper toweling. Each material was folded with utmost attention to closing out any air that could dry the texture. Wads of paper towels were gently stuffed into the center, so the form arrived intact. Tissue paper wrapped the bakery box, holding it firmly yet softly in its container. Every year when it came, I cried: all that time and love and sacrifice for me. I was possessive about my cake, unwilling to share it even with lovers. Several years ago, I gave up sugar but could not bring myself to tell Josephine for a long time afterward. I liked feeling that taken care of. I still miss my package.

Hettie and Josephine filled that peculiarly southern role of black mothers to a white child, mothers marked by the cruel inequities of a racist culture. I took advantage of them even while I adored them and would fight to defend them if neighbor children called them "nigger." My mother had severely punished me the day I came in from playing with friends on the block and asked if our yard man was a "shiftless old nigger." "Never let me hear you call any of the colored people who work here by that common, white-trash word, do you hear me?" I heard her and never did it again, since my mother had gone on to say, once her fury had abated, that it would hurt their feelings badly to hear me say that word. Though I often took spiteful pleasure in disobeying my mother, about this subject I lived up to her demand. I did that because I loved Hettie and Josephine more than almost anybody in my life and because they loved me back through the dense barriers of race. But their love had to filter through an ingrained and justified fear and hatred of my whiteness. They surely made distinctions between me and the faceless white boys who shot up their front yards with BB guns. For all I know, they defended me against names used within their own world for the racist bigots who lounged on the street corners of town. But the trap of racism held us, so I have to live with knowing that my love for them was mixed with my liking having power over someone in my world, and their love for me was interlaced with ambiguity and maintained at perhaps too high a price to their own sense of selfhood.

A black man named Charlie Teague mowed our lawn once a week and helped my mother in her large garden. He was very big and dark and full of an infectious laugh that hid his worries from whites. While he cut the grass or weeded, he sang or talked to himself. His monologues were hard to follow, since the whole left side of his face was full of Brown Mule chewing tobacco. After my disaster with snuff, I stood in awe of him: how did Charlie stay upright with all that raw tobacco lodged in his mouth? Every five minutes of so, he shot out a long, straight stream of juice that arced perfectly through the hot air to land with a mighty splat on the sidewalk or in the gutter or the dust.

I felt proud when Charlie deigned to talk to me instead of himself. He would stop work, wipe sweat off his face, and listen to my latest story. During the 1940s, like most children, I had a helmet and machine gun. I also carried an old World War I medal my father had given me, and a lot of hostility that emerged when I played soldier. Charlie indulged my fantasies by calling me Sergeant, or, when he felt especially playful, Sarge. He would pretend to take orders from me about mowing or weeding, answering me with a mock salute and a "Yessir, Sarge, whatever you say."

One July day, Charlie was working in our side yard, overgrown with high weeds because my mother had recently been in the hospital to see if a lump in her breast was malignant. He was using a big sickle that had once been fire engine red and was almost as tall as I. Deciding that I wanted to swing that sickle, I asked Charlie for it. When he demurred, pleading that it was too heavy for me, I commanded him as a white army sergeant to let me use that tool. He obeyed as a black hired man.

Feeling cocky, I swung the big blade out to the right. That part went fine, but then the sickle fell back toward me, grazing my right big toe. A large slice of me went with it, stuck to the grassy blade, and my toe began to bleed. Afraid it would not stop, I held my toe under the yard hose, since cold water had often stopped my nicks and cuts from bleeding. This had no effect except to make little pools of reddish water in the dust. Charlie was scared speechless and did not even bother to say "I told you so." What difference would that make to my hysterical mother when she found out that he let me swing the blade?

After a long time, my blood slowed enough for me to walk a few steps in my sandals before having to mop my toe. I sneaked into the house and ran for my room to put on socks to hide the wound. Lunch was ready, and Mamie expected me to take Charlie's tray out to him as I usually did. He ate what we did, even if he had special dishes that stayed in the basement. His tea was served in an old Blue Plate mayonnaise quart jar full of ice cubes and a lemon slice. Once I asked why Charlie's dishes were kept in our basement when Hettie Holmes's special plates were just stacked on a separate shelf in the kitchen. Whatever Mamie said, the message was that since Charlie was a man, he did dirtier things than Hettie when he was at home or on the streets.

Eager not to arouse any suspicion by my delay, I hurriedly pulled on the darkest blue and red socks I owned, strapped on my sandals and walked to the kitchen to get the tray. By now my toe was throbbing, but I refused to limp or show any signs of pain. When I took the tray out to Charlie, he was still wearing a look of terror, but I smiled innocently and told him just to call if he wanted more corn or iced tea. Back inside, my socks soaked up the blood, and I got through lunch. When I took them off, later, blood had clotted so thickly that the right one had to be gently peeled away. I never told on Charlie, and Charlie never told on me. Occasionally one of us would make a veiled reference to "the blade" or "that big toe" and fall into gales of laughter.

Every fall I saved enough of my allowance to let me buy Charlie a Christmas present: several plugs of Brown Mule and a quart of Mogen David red wine, his favorite thing to drink. Mamie gave him old shirts and pants of my father's plus some food she made. Charlie always showed delight over his presents, laughing more than usual, breaking off an extra big chew of tobacco since he felt flush with his supply from me, talking loudly about "what wonderful white folks ya'll are."

Like other black people in my life, at some point Charlie simply vanished. By that time, I had stopped asking where they went or why they no longer came to our house, but I never learned to stop missing them.

In 1950, while American soldiers were killing Asians in Korea, I entered a high school full of white boys who rode through the black section of town at night and on weekends, shooting it up or throwing glass bottles into streets, onto lawns, against sides of houses. All that seemed very far away to me as I struggled vainly to keep my starched Peter Pan collars straight, my bobby socks rolled to just the right length, and my lipstick on past second period math. I had trouble making friends my own age and often felt lonely. I have almost no clear memories of those years.

But I do remember sitting on my bed for hours, looking out my burglar-barred windows at the alley, the three houses down its slope, and further off, the expanse of dwellings that made up the black neighborhood. In my yearning for something I could not have named, I romanticized the people who lived there even as I continued to benefit from my automatically privileged position. We were all caught in the web of southern racism and sexism. Those blacks who lived in solid brick houses on paved streets in the center of their community near churches and food markets were imprisoned by their color. Once out of their neat yards filled with tall red–orange callas and prize-quality roses, they were as vulnerable as their poorest fellows living in wooden shanties along dirt roads full of potholes. Similarly, though hardly with the same possibilities of permanence, when I ventured away from my house and yard into the larger world of white teenage activities, I felt like an exposed failure, no matter how many A's or honors I accumulated.

One night during this time stands vividly in my memory. I awoke to an eerie glow, sat up in bed, and raised my shade. Columns of flame deep inside the black section frightened me enough to cause me to wake my parents. We heard faint sounds of one or two fire engines though the flames ranged over blocks, burning out of control. (Blacks depended on the city of Fairfield for public services, so I suspect one or two engines was all they ever got.) I sat on the edge of my bed crying until almost daylight, long after Mamie and Daddy had gone back to bed and encouraged me to do the same. The flames finally subsided, replaced by ominous clouds of black and then ugly grey smoke. To me, it seemed as though that smoke came from the people, not the fire. Years later when I saw pictures of columns of smoke from the ovens of the Holocaust, I would flash back to that night in Alabama.

Though I searched the white newspaper for several days, I found no word about the big fire. There was lots of news about the local domino club's victory over a neighboring team, majorettes from Fairfield High who attended a conference of other majorettes, the latest discount on chicken at the Piggly Wiggly—nothing about what must have been the worst fire in my town's history. I wanted to go see where it had been, but my parents refused to take me near the place. When Josephine came to work the next day, I asked her about it, but she brushed me off, saying, "Some folks say white boys from the high school lit a Coke bottle filled with gasoline-coated rags and threw it into some lady's yard, but I'm sure it was just old newspapers stacked in a building." I remembered the stories about boys at school who routinely invaded the black world, looking for idle amusement, and I knew who started the fire. Breaking my silence about that fire now, forty years later, I feel a ferocity coupled with that sense of helplessness that was to wash over me more often the older I got.

Child's Play

"Toni's so talented—she can amuse herself for hours." My mother said this often to our family and friends as proof of my creativity and resourcefulness. Hearing it, I always see myself sitting alone in a room, coloring or reading or building some new fantasy world.

The story began in my baby bed with its several rows of colored wooden beads strung on thin metal rods like an abacus. From the time I could stand, I moved the beads in endless mutations to produce colors and spaces. At three, I was given a little slate with a real abacus for its top. When my mother handed me my slate and piece of chalk, she said: "Here, honey, now draw a cat or print your ABC's." As long as she watched, I demonstrated what I gather were my precocious motor and mental skills. But as soon as she went into some other room, I put down the chalk and began to count and arrange the beads. I loved the click of one against another and the gliding sound as I moved a whole row from left to right, fast. Their bright reds, blues, greens, and yellows cheered me up, reminding me of my baby bed and of how much I liked standing up in it, staring at the big colored spheres.

At about four, I began to catch my feces in my hands before they fell into the toilet bowl, take them into my bedroom and hide them in an old shoebox my sister gave me. That box stayed under my bed, near the windows. When the grownups were busy elsewhere, I would steal into my room, crawl down between my bed and the wall, haul out my box and make wonderful creations. At its height my collection included ten figures and four or five cars. One day as I was busily executing my new idea for a giraffe, my mother discovered me. Deeply shocked, she gave me a severe lecture about "niceness," then punished me by having me sit quietly in a chair for some five minutes. A few days later, she presented me with a box of colored modelling clay, but I refused to use it, saying, "Clay is for babies."

I learned during this earliest phase of my artistic development that what I made could not last long, and that lesson was reinforced throughout my childhood. As payroll master for his company, my father brought home bags of bills and change every Thursday, only to take them away on Fridays to hand out in small brown envelopes to the workers. But while they were in our house, I could dump out and play with their contents. Each unbleached muslin bag from the First National Bank of Fairfield could hold several hundred copper pennies. I loved to hear them tumble onto my bedroom floor, then watch them scatter under my bed, into corners, out into the hall. Because Daddy worried that a coin or two might get lost under some piece of furniture, he urged me to play on the living room rug. The public nature of this space frustrated me, since people tracked back and forth on their way out the door. In the middle of an elaborate design, a large foot could invade my work area, disrupting my pennies, causing me to cry quietly as I tried to restore them.

The pennies served as borders for buildings, people, objects. But almost as soon as I had finished a town or barnyard or sentence, Mamie came and scooped them up because she needed the room for something, or Daddy rebagged them so he could get to bed in time to feel rested at 4:00 A.M., his wake-up hour.

The effect of these interruptions on my creativity was marked. Unlike some I know, I never kept a diary or journal, and I have no signs of childhood art, though I engaged almost daily in the act of making. I remember feeling quiet and steadied by such activities, safer than when talking. From a very early age, I was able to lose myself in such creative play, going far from 5130 Holly Court, Fairfield, Alabama. But writing any of it down seemed dangerous to me; someone could easily take my stories or plans away if they existed on paper. So I lived out my mother's proud boast—I did indeed amuse myself for hours, leaving no record for anyone to find, not even me.

I was a skinny child with a head full of long blond hair that I wore in curls like Scarlett O'Hara. This hair was mostly a bother as I ran wildly outside. Summers, Mamie plaited it into two stubbly braids held with rubber bands that pulled and were covered with grosgrain ribbons of various colors. Try as she did, my mother seemed incapable of making tight, neat braids like I saw on girls at school, but at least my neck was partly cleared so sweat could roll down easier. Every late afternoon, my hair had to be brushed, since my rambunctious playing tangled it horribly. Tender headed, I cried through most of this ritual. But all adults seemed convinced that my hair was my "crowning glory," so there was no getting away from the torture. To this day, I have to force myself to brush the recommended fifty strokes and prefer simply to wash my hair and run my hands through it as it dries.

The reason I was skinny is my food story. At a rather early age I learned that if I did not eat my lunch or dinner, my mother would stay at the table coaxing me. Wanting her undivided attention sometimes fiercely, I began what must have been a tedious ritual. I picked and poked at my food until my father and sister were long gone from the table. Then Mamie and I were left to battle out the carrots or spinach or even mashed potatoes and gravy. "Eat, honey," was the refrain to which I turned deaf ears, knowing I could outsit her and keep her talking.

The hard part of my regimen was that food got cold and inedible, so that finally no one would have wanted to have it. To handle this unforeseen development, I figured out how to toss bits of congealed vegetables or cold meat down the big furnace duct that came up to the dining room floor and was covered with a metal grating that I polished monthly to keep its brass coating shiny. While Mamie was in the kitchen getting another glass of iced tea, I would deftly get rid of some of the odious food. When she returned, I would brag about my cooperative behavior, "See all I've eaten while you were gone; aren't I a good and brave girl now?" My poor mother praised me for what she took to be eating but what in reality was lying and having sure wrist action that later helped me throw a baseball to first base with amazing accuracy.

One day when I was about eleven and had been tossing unwanted food down the grate for years, I was shocked to learn that we were going to have the furnace cleaned out. On the appointed day, I made myself scarce the moment the burly white workman arrived at about nine in the morning. Ironically, we were all having lunch when he knocked on the basement door, came into our dining room, and unwrapped a small bundle. "I can't tell how this stuff ever got into your furnace, ma'am, but I took it out. Do you want me to throw it away or what?" To my horror, the bundle contained parched chicken bones, unrecognizably shrunken things that must once have been carrots or beans or squash, dust-coated blobs of years-old potatoes.

My mother graciously scooped it all up, saying over her shoulder as she fled into the kitchen, "Oh, never mind, I can just put it here in the trash, probably a cat or mouse did it." Lame by any measure, and we both knew it.

When Mamie returned from the back porch, she sat down resignedly and looked right at me. "Toni, honey, how could you have told me such stories all these years. I thought you were trying to eat, and you were doing something no nice person could imagine. Wherever did you get such an idea in the first place?" I answered not at all but glumly chewed the vegetable before me. I never really answered Mamie, and she never required it. From then on, I had to invent new schemes to cover my not eating. Stashing small amounts in a pocket or trying to attract the cat's attention without also alerting my mother were far less effective than the furnace trick had been.

Though I resisted real food, for years I played something called "store" and a variation I named "drugstore." Mamie saved Rice Krispies and Grapenuts Flakes containers, Quaker Oats tins, RC Cola bottles, Oxydol boxes. Being resourceful, I also badgered our next door neighbor lady for such rareties as Black Jack shoe polish cans, Sauer's almond extract bottles, and Blue Bonnet margarine holders. On makeshift shelves or tall cardboard crates, I set up my wares, each marked with a tiny price tag, and sat patiently waiting for other children to come "buy" something. We never actually paid money for such empties but gave each other rocks or shards of pretty colored glass that had been given designated values.

"Drugstore" was beautiful. I saved old medicine bottles, of which we seemed to have a great abundance, what with the vague illnesses that kept me home from school and my mother's various potions. Into each clear bottle went first tap water, then a few drops of food dye. The result was a rainbow of bottles, each having a label on which I wrote the virtues of the exotic contents. "Sure cure for toenails hanging part way off." "Take one spoonful daily and never again have circles under your eyes." "Drink regularly for itchy heads or rashes between your toes." Each evening, I stored all the pretty liquids in the basement, only to set up the entire show next day even though almost no one ever came to see or buy my magic elixirs. The colors fascinated me, just as the beads on my baby bed had years before and just as organic chemistry and stained-glass windows would years later.

My artistic flair was inhibited by all the rules of public school.

Teachers wanted me to sit still for hours, coloring within the lines, making trees green and cows brown and people light pink. Once in second grade I argued for the trueness of a picture. I had drawn a brown person and a pink cow because I had seen brown people out in country fields with scrawny pinkish-red cows. My teacher, driven by racism as much as a narrow view of art, threw my piece of construction paper into the waste basket, saying, "If you insist that there are brown people and pink cows, I'll report you to the principal who will talk to your mother about your disrespectful attitude." I got a C in conduct that semester.

As a very little girl, I loved to make musical sounds—song snatches, whistles, simple noises that felt good. My mother sang and encouraged me to hum along with her at home and church. In grammar school, I learned there was someone called "the music teacher" who would come to our classes one hour a week. I was elated, since it meant I would learn real tunes and words. I even fancied being able to teach Mamie a song. The teacher was a tall, thin woman with fading auburn hair and big feet and hands. She would stride into our classroom, go straight to the old spinet that was wildly out of tune, and begin playing some song whose lyrics were much too advanced for us. I learned "On the Road to Mandalay" without having any idea where or what Mandalay was. But I was quite drawn to "flying fishes"; they reminded me of brown people and pink cows, and I wished I lived "in China across the bay" since maybe there they would let me color as I saw things and not worry about the lines.

The music teacher did not like my voice because it was too low. She forced me to sing soprano notes. I squeaked and cracked and sounded awful. Everyone laughed at me for singing off key, and my record began to say I was "unmusical." To help me retain self-respect and some interest in singing, my mother assured me, "Just keep singing out as loudly as you want at church, honey, and if it isn't quite right, no one will mind." She also told me that singing an octave lower than other girls was perfectly all right, that if I ever joined a choir, I would be placed with people called altos because their voices were "mellow." That word became a lifeline to counter "unmusical" as I fought to hang on to my love of making sounds. No wonder I came to prefer cellos and French horns, contraltos and basses, the left hand on the piano, fog horns at sea.

Too many of the people who taught me spent most of their time trying to help marginally literate students. Consequently the few teachers who did excite me remain in my mind like crystal. Much of my free time was spent in their rooms, where I helped them arrange borders above the blackboard or clean their space. I often lost potential friends because I chose to answer the questions teachers asked in class. Although it was painful not to be accepted, I did not regret my choices even when I was making them. Those women were generous to me, in class and out. They told me extra things about geography or math or sentence diagramming; they let me take heavy books or satchels full of our homework to their cars; occasionally they even asked me to read spelling quizzes or other students' test papers when the answers just involved numbers or letters.

The first time this happened was in second grade. My teacher was Miss Virginia Lindsay, a slight honey-blond woman in her late thirties. She was known for her long hikes even in damp Alabama winters and for her summer travels to exotic places not in America. After about three months as her pupil, I was allowed to help grade spelling papers on Wednesdays after lunch. I would bolt my food and race back to Miss Lindsay's room where we sat together at her big desk. She gave me a red pencil like hers to put check marks beside misspelled words. Being left-handed, I made check marks that looked backwards, so I learned to reverse them. I would not give away our secret. Miss Lindsay always patted me on the arm when we were done and said, "You'll make a fine teacher someday."

In fifth-grade, a tall, fleshy, not-so-smart woman named Bernice Brown taught us things I already knew, but she was warm and affectionate and liked me. One afternoon she took me aside, and put her arm around me: "Now, Toni, you know, don't you, that you're a special little girl who will keep going to school for a long time? And when you've gotten big degrees and I'm old, I'll feel so proud that you were in my fifth-grade room. And if you aren't popular, just wait till you're older." The elliptical nature of her last remark haunted me even as the rest of her speech made me feel special and proud.

And I remember Miss Gray, a wiry woman probably only two or three years from retirement, who taught sixth-grade math with an iron fist. On rainy days after she had drilled us in fractions or simple equations or long word problems, she showed us a softer side. She would recite long poems, my favorite being one that began, "Now, William, come here sir." Miss Gray never prepared us for her shift from math to poetry but suddenly would turn her small head capped by thinning frizzly hair and bellow out this or some other first line. I always jumped at first but then settled in for the treat that her recitation was. The lasting thing Miss Gray taught me was that math and poetry do not need to be disconnected. She primed me for my later fascination with Jacob Bronowski and Buckminster Fuller, who urged adults to stop talking about the gulf between science and the humanities.

But most of the time I was just bored by what went on in that stuffy brick building where too many students did not know how to read or write. I began being absent often, having one form or another of a cold-flu-sore-throat ailment just bad enough to keep me home but not so bad as to keep me from reading or playing games by myself. My report cards tell it all: for the first eight years of school, I consistently ran up higher numbers in the "times absent" column than in the "times present" one, though I collected zeroes in the "times tardy" slot. One school year they went: first semester—absent 64 days, present 26; second semester—absent 57 days, present 33. In the space for accompanying remarks appears: "Toni seems quite bright, but could you encourage her to come to school more often?"

When I did not attend school, I had to stay in bed quietly during the mornings, since I was "sick." However, if by lunch time I had no fever, I could play quietly in the side yard during the afternoon. I quickly found ways to insure a reading of 98.5 degrees. As soon as Mamie placed the cool tube under my tongue, I maneuvered it on top. The only drawback to this practice was that sometimes the result was so low as to raise suspicion. But when it worked, I could get up as long as I promised not to run around.

Most days I played the same solitary game. Outside our bathroom window stood a massive oak tree. Forgetting mosquitos, gnats, and other southern bugs that attack anyone who stays outside for more than a few minutes, I spent hours hunkered down on the ground.

First I would scoop out dirt from around roots, then mold wet clay tunnels that leaned against them, and finally turn twigs and carefully sculpted leaves into road signs that meant "Right Turn Only" or "Do Not Enter" or "Danger High Voltage." They only meant that to me, but then if I were not there, things merely looked scuffed up, as if a squirrel had scratched around for stray acorns. Once my highway was complete, I carefully smuggled tiny metal cars and trucks outside. Though for some reason unknown to me my parents bought me such toys never intended for little girls, they were to stay in the house so as not to get dirty or broken. For hours I intently moved cars and trucks along my dirt roads, twisting and turning through the system of tunnels and overpasses. Sometimes several cars stopped at once so the riders could get out to share inside information about road conditions or talk about where to go next. Occasionally a truck turned over going too fast around a sharp curve. Upset, I rushed vehicles to the scene to rescue the unlucky driver and his family who were with him on an outing. If asked the name of my game, I would have said without blinking an eye, "Running Away." I imagined going first into town, then to places nearby whose names I knew—Bessemer, Tarrant City, Dolomite, Powderly, Ensley. If I needed to go farther away, I picked Mobile or Florida or Mandalay.

Though I could play alone for an unusually long time without becoming distracted, this ability became a way to handle my increasing sense of difference from other children my age and the resulting isolation. Occasionally an exception emerged, some child in our neighborhood or at school with whom I formed a tight bond at least for a brief period. I have photographs of two of these friends. One is a tiny snapshot of Sue Brooks and me at my third birthday party. Binky (Sue's nickname) and I are perched on a little stepstool placed on the sidewalk as part of some game. We are each holding a balloon chosen from the great cache Mamie had suspended from the dining room chandelier. We are looking innocently and intently into one another's faces, seemingly with no heed of the camera, the photographer, or the other children. The outside world had vanished for that frozen moment.

The other photo dates from high school days. I am at Sarah Jones's house after school, palling around with her and Sue Hood, another schoolmate. The three of us were fast friends for a year until Sarah and Sue began having predictable dates with boys, and I sunk further into my inability to secure any such prize. On this afternoon, we are posing suggestively: Sarah lounges on her front step while I stand near her in a pose I'd seen Hedy Lamarr strike in movies. We look content and connected, something I was not to feel often outside the confines of my home.

When I was eight, I made my first and only penny peep show and experienced a devastating blow to my efforts to share my creative self outside my family. My mother carefully taught me how to construct such a spectacle. First you must find a sloping hillside (we had a huge one in our vacant lot filled with flower beds). Then you take a trowel—

or better yet your hands—and burrow into the slope. When the space is the right size, you line it with cardboard to keep out falling dirt and curious bugs. With the frame complete, the real work begins. A penny peep show is made up of tiny bits of paper or material, formed into recognizable objects, all placed in that hollowed-out space and covered with a piece of window glass. The glass in turn is covered with a cloth or strip of cardboard, thus hiding your "show" from view. People are then invited to take a peep at the cost of a penny. These projects were popular in my childhood, and I paid lots of pennies to see other children's shows.

When I came to make my own, I decided to be more elaborate in my choice of objects to put in the boxed-in space. I made tables and chairs of match sticks, painstakingly gluing each slim stick to its fellows. I constructed people from wads of cotton, dressing them in scraps of cloth from my mother's hooked rug work basket. Finally, I wrapped live flowers in tiny waxed-paper containers that would hold water longer than newspaper. After almost a week of preparations, I invited neighbor children and even a few select adults to "peep" by writing crude invitations that I dropped into mailboxes. On the appointed day, I stationed myself beside my wonder half an hour before showtime, just in case someone tried to get a free sneak preview. As viewers began to arrive and give me their pennies, my heart pounded with what I would only later understand to be artist's nerves before an unveiling.

After about ten people had come, I took advantage of a lull to run inside to the bathroom. Less than five minutes later, I returned to find the glass smashed in, the flowers crushed, and the little matchstick furniture in shambles. I burst into angry tears and screams that lasted over an hour. I was inconsolable, filled with fury for whoever had destroyed some inner part of me that I had lovingly presented to be "peeped" at. My mother never convinced me to build another show, though she often would sit on the ground with me and begin putting things together from the dirt around us. I would watch her for a few moments and then break into sobs until she had to take me inside and comfort me with candy or some other sweet.

The next Easter Mamie gave me a gorgeous spun sugar egg: a peep show with an isinglass window that opened onto a resplendent garden filled with every imaginable flower and a bunny for good measure. The next year, she began giving me special decorated eggs made of thin milk glass. Each bore my name, the date, and some lovely design: tiny blue forget-me-nots; a bouquet of purple violets; a wreath of yellow jonquils. I have moved this collection around with me over the past thirty-five years.

I do not remember making anything for a long time after my peep show was wrecked. Determined to protect myself, I retreated into my head, where images and creations seemed safer than when set out for public display. I crammed in story after story of little girls who saved friends from disaster and then gradually focused on horses or cats or more exotic animals once I had read Kipling. In the animal stories, I was always the undying champion who rescued them from capture and caging in zoos, or from natural predators.

One of my favorites, which I told myself from the ages of eight to eleven, with minor variations, focused on the same subject as my game with trucks among the oak roots—running away:

A little girl packs a wicker picnic basket with all the leftover fried chicken and biscuits from her mother's refrigerator, leaving room for her floppy-eared harlequin rabbit and a story book. Then she tiptoes out of her house while her mother fixes lunch. She runs as fast as she can, as long as she can, and winds up on the edge of town where the road begins to open onto lush meadows filled with butterflies and brown-skinned hopping rabbits.

She runs into the very center of this grass sea, plops down with her cache of chicken and biscuits, and begins unwrapping little packets of food. She can never eat just the one she's made for that afternoon but keeps at it until all the food is gone. Her stomach full, she lies down in the field, reads a little, quickly falls into a sleep filled with magical dreams. Usually she is awakened by a beautiful yellow and blue butterfly lighting on her nose or by a furry rabbit sniffing loudly around her hair and face. These interruptions never frighten her, because she never wakes to find it dark.

Once the little girl sits up, she realizes that she is hungry. It is dusk and the sun is going down. She begins to feel cold and lonely, hugs her rabbit to her chest, and sings herself back to sleep. She is protected during the night by fairies or brownies and rises to a glorious sunrise and a little dish of Cream of Wheat.

After eating, she sets out for far places that she always reaches safely. These journeys lead the little girl to cities and countries whose names her big sister has taught her, places like Borneo and Atlanta and Walla Walla, Washington, her favorite place in the world to say out loud.

My stories never had endings. I just stopped telling them or let them trail off into shadowy scenes while I went into the kitchen to help my mother do the dishes. As I retrace their outline, I realize that what is missing is another human being. Though I was able to surround my heroine with benign and affectionate nature, I could not conceive a companion of her own kind.

The closest I ever came to such a person was my make-believe baby sister. Between the ages of seven and ten, disliking dolls, I fabricated Sarah Sue, much my junior. I bossed her around unmercifully but defended her from the ornaments that were likely to slip off their marble-top tables at any moment and from the adults who could interrupt her at their whim. She was an admiring audience for my roly poly bug collections, my June bug captures, my skating up and down the sidewalk that marked our property boundaries. She consoled me about having to eat at least one or two of the carrots on my plate or about having to sit quietly after lunch in the summer. When my mother took me downtown while she shopped at all her favorite department stores, Sarah Sue listened to my endless complaining and shared my dislike of such activities. I do not remember why I stopped creating her, but I suspect it had something to do with her getting too big to handle and having a will of her own. In any event, I eventually gave her up rather than continuing to drag her around as a flimsy sign of my imaginary power.

Just about the time I lost Sarah Sue, I entered into one of the most purely creative if bizarre stages of my young life. I felt increasing pressure to become more lady-like, as Mamie talked about brassieres and lipstick and ruffled dresses. I decided to withdraw from the irksome business of growing up, since I knew that I did not want to become a southern lady, learning how to faint without hurting myself or letting my skirt rise above my knees, or how to lower my eyes, hold them down, and then raise them slowly and alluringly. While my mother indoctrinated me into the culture she believed I was destined for, something inside me resisted fiercely. Sensing that Toni, the defiant ten year old, would lose, I cleverly chose to become a horse. I had already read many cowboy stories as well as technical studies of horses that described breeds, named body parts, and defined various gaits and habits.

Borrowing from one of my favorite radio programs, "Tennessee Jed and His Great Horse Smokey," I became Smokey. Weekday afternoons an hour before the "Lone Ranger," the show was a southern version of the classic masked Samaritan. Having no gender, Smokey was a means for me to escape the confining behaviors appropriate for adolescent girls. I whinnied at the table when I wanted something, and my parents acknowledged but did not disrupt my fantasy. Years later, when I took psychology courses and learned that children are hospitalized for far less severe antisocial or withdrawal symptoms, I felt grateful to my family. Instead of mincing like a preadolescent girl, for two years I cantered, galloped, trotted, and occasionally even pranced.

During this period, my sister visited Boston. Her gift to me upon her return was a treasured black leather bridle, complete with steel bit. With that bit between my teeth, and her (or my mother) holding the reins, I ran around our front yard, neighing.

In the middle of my dilemma over how to express my creative energy without its being ridiculed, interrupted, or destroyed, my mother asked if I would like to take piano lessons. At first, I recoiled from the suggestion, since it would mean sitting inside for long periods and I preferred to run. But Mamie felt strongly that one of her daughters should play the piano, given her own talent and love for music.

After weeks of discussion, I agreed. My first teacher, Mrs. Bowen, lived near us and taught in her home. After about a year with her, I transferred to the Birmingham Conservatory of Music and half-hour lessons from Miss Edith Plosser. I was excited to have a music teacher with such an unusual name, though she seemed cold and stern. Her repeated complaint was that I did not practice seriously or long enough. Since we did not own a piano, practice meant calling our across-the-street neighbor, Nell Hill, to find out when it was convenient for me to come over to her house where there was an out-of-tune upright. At the same time that she complained about my sketchy practicing, Miss Plosser thought me potentially talented, so she set me to such masters as Bach, Scarlatti, and Clementi. They had no tunes and were terribly demanding technically. I began to cut practice times shorter than usual.

Once I was safely ensconced at the conservatory, Mamie convinced my father that I had to have a piano. Somehow, one was procured—a Betsy Ross spinet, made in America of partly seasoned wood because of the Second World War. Since our house was already liberally furnished, my piano was placed in the hallway outside my bedroom door. My sister's bedroom was at the end of that hall, so when I practiced, she was trapped in or barred from her room. Any time she interrupted, I welcomed the break, though the situation must have irritated Betty.

My third teacher, Mr. Parker, was over six feet tall with jet black hair and deep-set, searching eyes. His hands were enormous, reaching an octave plus two with ease. His span and temperament inclined him toward Franz Liszt, so I studied most of Liszt's corpus. My hands are also fairly large and by sheer determination, I can play an octave plus two. I gave that measure of determination because I was amazed at the raw emotion within the music. A part of me otherwise unknown and unencouraged was awakened, and putting my passion into the ivory keyboard had less risk than my previously chosen media. My interpretations pleased Mr. Parker, so he set me to such equally romantic giants as Rachmaninoff, Katchaturian, and the mature Chopin. I suddenly turned from a phlegmatic pupil into someone who went eagerly to her turquoise velvet piano stool and stayed there, hoping my sister would not need to get into or out of her bedroom, pounding away at the forte passages, rendering soft parts with maximum tragic sadness.

At first I exulted in the forte passages, hitting the keys with such ferocity that I sometimes made the crystal vase that sat atop the piano vibrate. After seeing Rubenstein at our local auditorium, I began to raise myself off the piano stool as I banged some percussive chord of a Chopin étude or Rachmaninoff concerto. Gradually, as I came to trust both the piano and myself more, I let myself pour years of accumulated melancholy and aloneness into the pianissimo phrases, knowing without language that the keyboard was a safer repository for such emotions than writing or speech. After all, the moment I struck the key, the act was over. Musical tears could always be explained away as deriving from Chopin's romanticism or Brahms's sweetness. Not having to "own" the emotions that sounded from my fingers emboldened me to express myself more deeply and fully than in any other circumstance or medium.

Playing the piano gave me even more satisfaction than playing pitch with a hard ball. Like my hero, Walt Dropo, I was left-handed and preferred to play first base, since it was one of the few instances in which being left-handed counted for rather than against me. I had a beautiful leather hardball glove with Walt's signature on the claw, and the clean "splop" of a ball landing solidly in the pocket of that mitt brought me small but distinct rushes through my mid-twenties when I finally abandoned playing pitch.

My two outlets became counterproductive, since the ferocity with which I played pitch endangered my hands for executing delicate piano runs. Mamie, of course, wanted me to give up pitch, but I refused. Once I went so far as to limit baseball to two hours a day during the month immediately preceding a major recital. I remember occasionally going to lessons (in the musty house where Mr. Parker and his ailing mother lived) with a sprained finger. My thumb took the worst beating: if I reached to catch a side ball incorrectly, my thumb bent back on itself from the force of the throw. When that happened, swelling set in, lasting at least three days. Often I could not play a note intended for the right thumb because mine was too big for the space between keys.

The worst scene in this battle of wits with my mother and between the selves warring within me occurred the month before my senior recital. After several solo pieces, I was to end by playing a Katchaturian duo with my teacher. By this point in my career, I knew I was good, at least at broadly romantic music. Maybe I panicked at the prospect of a career as a pianist. In any event, I entered into my pitch activity with renewed concentration, extending my allotment by however many minutes it took Mamie to realize my time was up.

A week before the big event at the concert grand, as I was catching a particularly hard throw by my playmate, Kenny, I felt searing pain. As my thumb folded back, I knew I had sprained it badly. I began immediately soaking my swollen finger religiously. After two days, my thumb barely fit into the key area. Lying about my pain, I practiced with a strange enthusiasm, leaving off my baseball fetish entirely. The night of my performance, pains shot from my thumb up into my right arm. No one knew I had taken six aspirin just before leaving home. I executed my solo pieces with clarity and passion, and in the final duo, Mr. Parker and I played superbly. The audience applauded enthusiastically, but I took that recital as further proof of something I was coming increasingly to believe and practice: people seemed satisfied, even pleased, with performances at which not quite all of me was present or in which not quite all of me was engaged.

My Mother, My Muse

Part of my coming to consciousness as a feminist has been a growing understanding that my mother was indeed an artist, whose media included church work, flower gardening, and decorating her home. In the South of her youth, girls seldom resisted the cultural pressures to marry and become mothers. My mother seems genuinely to have enjoyed her home and family. But the person talented enough to win a music scholarship surely must also have needed creative outlets. The intensity with which she carried out her Altar Guild duties, planted new bulbs, arranged flowers throughout the house, or created beauty in our living room impressed me even as a young child. As I struggled not to fear or suppress my own creativity, I believe I watched Mamie more closely, looking for clues to becoming a woman with deep longings for aesthetic and spiritual fulfillment.

I frankly have no idea what would have been done about my spiritual training without my mother's influence. Whatever Daddy may have believed about Christianity or any other religious system, he felt no need to attend church or to discuss religion with me as I was growing up. Once he did tell me that the part of the Bible he liked best was Psalm 1, so I read it repeatedly, trying to discover some clue about him or me or God. The psalm speaks angrily about the ways of the wicked being like "chaff which the wind driveth away," and of the wicked themselves perishing. One's only hope seems to be not to walk "in the counsel of the wicked" or sit "in the seat of the scorners," which to my father may have meant doing tax forms free for people whom the world deemed unworthy. To my young mind, however, these images called up harshness and punishment; they advocated strictness to the letter of the law if a person wanted to escape terrible con-

51

sequences. I did not find the God behind this psalm appealing and was not surprised that my father preferred to stay home on Sundays and read the paper.

But Christ was important to my mother, and she talked to me about him often. Her stories centered around a nice man who helped everyone, judged people not by their actions but rather by their inner wishes, and worked breathtaking miracles without a wand or vial or any of the aids that characters in my fairy tales needed. My mother also made sure I attended services with her regularly and that I found a serious personal belief system.

My experience with Christianity was aesthetic more than it was either theological or doctrinal. I loved the smells, sights, sounds, and, after confirmation, tastes that surrounded my hour in church. Being an Episcopalian was largely a sensory matter. Kneeling and rising at moments of joy and thanksgiving excited me. As I grew more ardent in my practice, I stayed on my knees throughout the Communion service. Some people knelt until it was their pew's turn to go up to the altar; the few who became my models resumed this distinctly less comfortable posture after they returned to their seats, witnessing more directly to the rigorous nature of the event.

Almost every Saturday afternoon, my mother went to church to perform some volunteer service. She waxed the floors twice a year, polished the pews every two months, washed and ironed altar linens once a month, and served altar duty at least that often. I asked to go with her because I liked being in church when no one was there. Cool even in summer, the atmosphere made me feel eerie—not scared exactly but more like someone in a fairy tale, stepping back in time. While Mamie did her chores, I walked or crawled around under pews, smelling the stale candle wax and lingering scent from the past Sunday's flowers. As I got older, I sometimes sat praying hard at the innermost rail reserved for the rector or bishop when he visited yearly for confirmation. My prayers were selfish, full of requests for more friends and less work around the house, for longer vacations and fewer days in school. I felt holy and important, very much an actor. I still remember standing outside myself, watching me on my knees, thinking, "God will surely hear me this time and show me a sign." My Bible story pictures showed blind men suddenly seeing, lame old women throwing down crutches, and lots of people eating from the same few fish and loaves of bread. Our Sunday school teacher told us these scenes were miracles proving Christ's power as God and confirming the faith of some believers. I thought I was a believer and wanted something dramatic to happen. Since questioning came to me quite young, I needed a sign to show that I could keep believing. If Mamie came upon me kneeling so devoutly, she smiled and gently encouraged me to move back to a regular pew, saying, "Now, honey, I'm glad you're praying but not here where Bishop Carpenter does. You come back here to our family pew and pray all you want."

My mother insisted that going to church in the wrong frame of mind lessened the experience. Rather than forcing me to say prayers or make lists of my wrongs, she suggested we leave time to read together from the Bible before going to service. Once we had eaten a light breakfast and dressed, including putting on our hats but not our gloves, we sat on my bed to prepare. Until I was about ten she read to me—always psalms—but from then on, I was expected to take my turn. We read our favorite psalm: the twenty-fourth for me; the ninety-first for her. Mine spoke of "clean hands and a pure heart," of not lifting up one's "soul unto vanity" or swearing deceitfully; I felt exhilarated just thinking about the "everlasting doors" through which the "King of Glory" would enter (heaven I assumed), and hopeful that I might "ascend the hill of the Lord" someday. Mamie's was all about protection in the face of one's direst enemies—"the pestilence that walkest in darkness," and "the destruction that wasteth at noonday." The "thou" of this psalm survives while ten thousand fall at his right hand and a thousand at his side. I caught my breath to think of the angels who could keep "thee" from dashing a foot against a stone or from falling at all. And I simply thrilled to hear, "Thou shalt tread on the lion and the adder, the young lion and the serpent shalt thou trample under foot."

Fired and comforted by our readings, we donned our gloves and set off for Christ Episcopal Church, some ten or twelve blocks from home. At the Communion rail I left my troubles (Why did my school-mates shun me? Would I ever have a teacher who interested me? Why couldn't I have an Erector Set when lots of boys I knew were getting them?), nagging guilt (I should have taken the garbage out before Mamie had to ask me three times; I ought to have memorized every word of my history lesson so Daddy would be really proud of me for getting a perfect score; I must start keeping my fingernails cleaner so Mamie won't have to worry so about my unladylikeness), even surface shame (Why had I lied to my teacher when she asked if I had helped Billy Mayo with his math? Would I really be punished for wishing my mother would stop badgering me to pick up my clothes before I left my room to go take a bath? Was I mean not to care that my playmate from across the street had gotten a rope burn when I lassoed him?). I was certain as I melted the awkward wafer and swallowed watered-down wine that I ingested calm and a powerful shield of protection. At no time did I seriously believe that these were even symbolic of Jesus's body and blood; they were a way to unify my ragged parts, to heal my raw places.

By the time I was ten, I was helping Mamie set up the altar for early Communion. I handled the objects that made church possible: beaten silver pitchers; a smooth silver plate that held little flat wafers that I eventually learned had no taste and often stuck to the roof of my mouth; linen napkins each with a beautifully embroidered cross and meticulously stitched border; the wine cup with its silver outside and gold inside, decorated with cross and dove; the choir cross on its polished wooden pole. As I carried that cross from its locked closet, where it was stored during the week, into the dimly lit nave and buckled it into its leather halter at the head of the choir stalls, I imagined myself a monk attending his Lord on some solemn occasion. All the objects seemed mysterious and came to inhabit my fantasies about escape and rescue, this time of a kind man named Jesus whom all the officials wanted dead. I imagined myself running to warn Jesus about the mean Pharisees who were coming for him, or beating up Sadducees who tried to trick him, or (most exciting fantasy of all) scaling the cross in time to cut Christ down before he died so the world could benefit longer from his good ideas.

When I was twelve, I learned names for all these holy toys—cruet, paten, chalice—and became fascinated by the changing seasons of the church year. Every time we went from one to the next, all the altar fittings changed color—from lime green to royal purple, white on holy days, black for Good Friday, scarlet for saints' days. Green and purple lasted the longest, causing me to conclude that there was a relationship between peace and growth, majesty and sacrifice. The symbolism for each color was woven into my daily thinking by the time I was in high school. Watching Mamie handling altar cloths or ironing little chalice napkins with more attention than she gave to Daddy's shirts impressed upon me that the house of God deserved my utmost care, that its ornaments were even more precious than the ones at home.

All through high school and college, as my Protestant friends drifted away or actively revolted against their religions, I increased my piety. My love for language and poetry kept me religiously active even when I knew that the theology no longer moved me. *The Book of Common Prayer* is after all a work of major literary merit, written in the sixteenth century by Thomas Cranmer, slightly before the King James Bible group completed its monumental task. At eighteen, I had invested Cranmer with mammoth physical and spiritual dimensions and felt personally attached to a man who could write such powerful prose. My favorite parts were the Collects—short readings intended for specific occasions such as sickness, travel, times of the day, the seasons. Some were also for people in certain circumstances or professions: prisoners, teachers, men at sea, the poor and dying. The imagery, the simplicity of diction, the uncanny understanding of the human condition and the human heart touched me. Phrases still float to the surface when I am extremely happy, sad, or tired: "O Lord, support us all the day long, until the shadows lengthen and the evening comes, and the busy world is hushed, and the fever of life is over," "Bless all who teach and all who learn," "Deliver us, we beseech thee, in our several callings, from the service of mammon," "Relieve the distressed, protect the innocent, awaken the guilty."

By attending chapel several times a week as a college student, I discovered a service—evening prayer—I had never attended at home, full of such sheer poetry as, "Let the floods clap their hands, and let the hills be joyful," or "He hath showed strength with his arm; he hath scattered the proud in the imagination of their hearts." Only Shakespeare and Keats evoked comparable shivers or yielded comparable rewards to my mind and spirit. During my senior year in college, partly to render service to the Episcopal Student Center and partly to satisfy my curiosity, I formally analyzed the Communion service only to discover that its structure was not unlike any well-made drama. Beginning slowly and quietly, the service builds gradually through recitations, prayers, and confessions spoken by the entire congregation. At the climax, when host and wine were elevated, my excitement rose with them. As I eagerly awaited my turn to walk the length of the aisle, I felt as if I were on my way to see a close friend. The fact that he was permanently out of town was softened by the mystical connection I could achieve by "receiving the sacrament."

The Episcopal church seldom mentions heaven and never deals in hell; the confessions indicate that through our daily actions, we make our own here on earth. The best mode of living is to recognize how we "have erred and strayed from Thy ways like lost sheep." Our best plan for salvation is to stop doing "those things we ought not to have done," and initiate "those things which we ought to have done." To succeed in this essentially ethical rather than theological program promises "health in us." In the midst of one of my several emotional crises during college, I looked up "salvation" in the dictionary and found that its root had to do with health of the spirit. As adulthood crept nearer and seemed more frightening, I needed such health badly. I spent increasing time in meditation and religious study, reading about Joan of Arc and the desert fathers, wondering how they escaped having to date and marry.

This vast store of magic and comfort might not have been mine without Mamie's need to exert herself in devotion to her church and her equally clear need to have me accompany her. I can only conjecture to what extent her seemingly domestic labors in church were in fact powerfully aesthetic for her. But I know that the church buoyed my mother. After a childhood and youth lived in the heart of a privileged South, she chose to make her life with a man who moved her to a dusty, industrial, working-class area. Her tastes were elegant and expensive, yet my father never made more than an adequate salary. Finally, Mamie's health was problematic for the last fifteen years of her life. On the one hand, her stamina was amazing to watch and hard to match, as I learned when we spent a month on vacation together. She outwalked me and was undaunted by attending nine plays in seven days in New York City. But her neuritis and arthritis clouded many of her days and pained her nights, and her shortness of breath scared her. Evenings when her body must have seemed strangely at odds with her spirit, Mamie would ask me to sit on the side of her bed and read that familiar Ninety-first Psalm to her slowly, sometimes twice for good measure. After my father's death, she told me repeatedly that without the church and her faith she could not have gone on. Yet that faith manifested itself in dailiness, never becoming theoretical or doctrinal.

She showed me how crucial a woman's view of Christian theology can be, and when I read Barbara Meyerhoff's moving account of a community of elderly Jews (*Number Our Days*), I understood perfectly what one of the women meant by "domestic religion"—a string of daily rituals over which the women in a family preside, that "makes the adrenaline flow" and "changes your entire view on things." Underscoring the femaleness of this phenomenon, a speaker insists,

"These things were injected into you in childhood and chained together with that beautiful grandmother, so ever since infancy you can't know life without it. . . . [I]n this domestic religion, you could never get rid of it. You could not just put it aside when you don't agree anymore. When it goes in this way, I describe, Jewish comes up in you from the roots and it stays with you all your life."

I no longer attend church services or adhere to the formal belief system of my past, but when I enter cool, dimly lit churches, tears come unbidden but familiar. I remember my mother, specifically and tenderly, going about her housewifely duties at church, infusing her and my very breath with something deeply spiritual and unforgettable, something that rises above creeds and denominational hypocrisies, something I cannot "put aside because [I] don't agree anymore."

My mother's yard and garden were legendary in our community. The actual gardening, which went on almost all year, began six months before I was born. Moving from their former house because the new arrival necessitated their having more room, my parents had also bought the vacant lot next door. During her last months of pregnancy, Mamie planted hundreds of iris and jonquil bulbs, sitting on a pillow and sliding down the inclining slope of our yard. That space became a magnificent display of flowers and shrubs.

At its very center stood a terra cotta birdbath. From that core fanned out a series of ever-widening circles bordered by rocks that were always kept in place and free from choking weeds. Within the first circle, surrounding the birdbath, old-fashioned pinks covered the entire ground area. The next somewhat wider circle contained special varieties of jonquils with multicolored centers; Mamie spaced these further apart to allow the best growing conditions for the bulbs and the best viewing for us. Concentric to this middle bed, the largest circle completed the central bedding expanse and housed gorgeous rose bushes in varying shades of red, yellow, and orange.

A second bordering system, made up of long, rectangular beds in which annuals were grown from seed, ran parallel to the lot line. Mamie had a major objection to the idea of using bedding plants. Perhaps it was an attempt to save money somewhere in her life, but I suspect that her motives stemmed from a desire first to watch seeds sending up shoots and then to separate the seedlings with her own hands.

These long edges of the garden area were especially showy at the height of summer: tough zinnias with their scratchy stems; brilliant marigolds, cosmos, dahlias, daisies of many varieties; sweet william and alyssum, baby's breath, ageratum, dwarf marigolds, tiny zinnias, blue phlox, fever few.

At the end of a bed that edged the property line grew the strangest and most wonderful of all Mamie's flowers—spider lilies. Their blossoms, at the tops of very tall single stalks, were deep fuchsia with slender tendrils. At their centers were tiny stamen with fuzzy black ends. They had no leaves and were airy and royal. When I moved to the midwest, I searched unsuccessfully for such a lily.

In our backyard there was a magnolia tree that had been planted in 1940 when I was only three. As I waited impatiently for it to grow, Mamie told me gothic stories of mammoth magnolias in Selma, where she had grown up in the first decades of the twentieth century. Our tiny tree had been given to us by a family friend whose father was a judge in the small town of Camden, in the heart of agricultural Alabama. Our friend fancied that having the sapling in her yard would help my mother survive in industrial Fairfield, reminding her of a gracious era vanished with her childhood.

By the time I was in high school, that magnolia was still only about three or four feet tall and was not giving my mother what she wanted most—sumptuous white blossoms, shade from the flaring heat of the sun, and that unmistakably sweet aroma. Then, one day, we were out driving in the country just outside Fairfield when we spied a magnolia tree in full growth and bloom. Nearby stood an old farmhouse to which my father walked to ask the woman of the house if he might buy a bloom or two for his wife. She agreed, and from that day onward, when Mamie was having a special celebration during late spring or summer, Daddy drove out to "our" magnolia, as we thought of it, and brought back a precious blossom or two. My mother lovingly washed off ants or other small bugs that had taken up residence in the spacious hollows and floated the massive flowers in a sterling silver bowl in the center of our dining room table.

Though the magnolia stayed small, we boasted a gigantic oak nearby. Around the base of this great tree, Mamie planted snowdrop bulbs. She said they hardly ever did well for her, but a few survived the damp winters and numerous squirrels who loved the taste of their leaves. They bloomed in February as the true harbinger of spring. All through January, from the time I was eight or nine until well into my teens, I watched them closely, going out back and turning over a few of the leaves my mother so scrupulously placed over them to hide them from the squirrels and to keep them warm. Finally a day would come when the first yellow-green showed above the mulch and dank earth. On that day, Mamie would let me remove the leaves and pour the first water lovingly from a kitchen pitcher. When the snow drops bloomed, I would sit beside them, drawn to the perfectly marked spot of green in the center of each scallop of each bloom. They were special because they were the only flower we grew that was green and because when I looked at the blossoms hanging their heads, I felt less alone in my shyness.

As soon as I knew about saving money, I began to reserve portions of my allowance each year for a special present. Two months before Mamie's September birthday, I looked through fancy iris catalogues, chose one specimen variety and proudly sent off my seven or eight dollars. She had never grown specimen iris. The hundreds that bloomed down our hillside were plain white, deep purple, sky blue, or lemon yellow fringed in brown. My mother loved those gifts from me because they allowed her to have one of a kind. Greeted with total enthusiasm, each year's iris was planted immediately in a bed made specially for the collection I had promised in a card accompanying the first bulb, which was called Black Orpheus.

Though my mother's talents for interior decoration were always in evidence, at Christmas time she outdid herself. A small touch that nonetheless delighted every child who came into our house was her wishbone tree. Mamie would buy the tiniest tree she could find at the YMCA lot, place it on a tier-top table in the living room, and hang on its delicate branches scores of gilded wishbones, saved from Sunday chickens and from the big hens she boiled up periodically for salad. All around this display were little boxes wrapped and bowed, each containing some bright trinket from the ten-cent store. Each child was allowed to select a wishbone from the tree and pull it with Mamie. The child who got the lucky piece took away a prize in one of the boxes. Those who got the unlucky piece received a handful of hard candies. Since Mamie seemed to enjoy the event as much as the children, everyone won.

Aside from this small ornament to cheer up children, everything about our decorations was a major production. Our front door project involved hours of hard scratchy work. I was allowed to help, so I know what it entailed. Around the facing, Mamie hung a swag of long-needled pine cuttings, intertwined with lights. She made her own swags because none she saw was thick enough for her taste. During my high school and college years, she and I would sit on the kitchen floor for hours, securing small clumps of pine to fat rope by wrapping picture wire around the sprig and then tying that to the rope. These clumps were overlapped like roofing shingles, the end result being a thick mass of pine with no hint of a rope beneath. Once we had tacked the swag to the wooden frame of the door, it remained to lace strings of multicolored lights through that mat of greens. I soon grasped that the swags sold at tree lots or florists were sparser in order to make it easier to attach lights. But my mother knew that expediency did not always coincide with beauty, and she chose beauty every time.

Once the swag was finished, Mamie began on our holiday wreath. She bought a basic green wreath with the tightest weave she could find. Then for days she gilded fresh fruit, sprinkling each piece while still wet with gold and silver sparkles purchased at a costume shop. These had to be nursed while they dried, since if they fell over they might lose sparkles. Once the fruit was dry, Mamie stuffed each piece into a length of old stocking saved from the rag bag, thereby making it possible to secure fruit to wreath. She loved della Robbia art, having seen pictures of the brothers' work, so her meticulous labor was an imitation of their ceramic designs.

The masterpiece of Christmas decorations was the living room mirror above the fireplace mantel. A huge pier mirror, it reached from the edge of the mantel to the ceiling. Mamie decided that something hanging from the top would be pretty reflected in the glass. She found a branch fallen from one of our trees, which became the base of her creation. After painting it white, she spent hours atop our rickety step ladder, with one knee on the top step, figuring how to get that branch to stay in the space between the top of the mirror and the ceiling. Finally she managed to get a tack or two into the ceiling and a curtain hook screwed into the mirror top. Achieving this sweet victory only spurred her on. She spent the next few days shopping for exactly the right balls and wire on which to string them. She wanted invisible wire that would create an illusion of floating magic in the mirror. Satisfied, she began attaching thin wire onto eight silver balls varying in size from huge to miniature.

Climbing back up on the ladder, she worked with this infinitesimal wire, trying to get the balls tied to the delicate, now-brittle branch twigs without breaking the branch or dropping the balls. Once a small twig did snap off, and one very large ball smashed to bits on the tile hearth. My mother glued the twig back onto its stem and marked it so she would never try to hang a ball from it in the future. Having replaced the big ball, she went back to work nimbly attaching wires to twigs. The result was a happy Mamie and a stunning mobile that not only was reflected in the mirror but moved gently whenever we had a fire. The motion and the shimmering images mesmerized me.

Few people commented on my mother's artwork. If she minded, it did not keep her from reassembling her mobile every year. The hardest part of the operation was storing the branch, since she was convinced she would never find a better one. We wrapped it in Kleenex, then in paper toweling, then newspapers, and finally stored it on a shelf in the basement far away from everything else. Ten years later, it was still intact and only needed a yearly coat of white enamel to resume its original splendor.

The photograph of Mamie that means the most to me shows her standing in front of the fireplace with her mobile above her head. It was taken two days after my father had died suddenly of a heart attack. She is as carefully dressed as ever and her hair and make-up are in place. But her face reveals a woman in deep grief. I remember thinking when it was taken that we probably would not have the tree branch up on the ceiling again. I was wrong, and that is why the photograph stands out in my memory. The next Christmas, my mother climbed back up the rickety ladder and turned her living room once again into a palace of art.

Many things changed when her husband died. But two things stayed the same—her garden and her decorating. She obviously had discovered that some creative acts are worth the pain they involve because life without them would be too bleak and empty to bear.

Part II

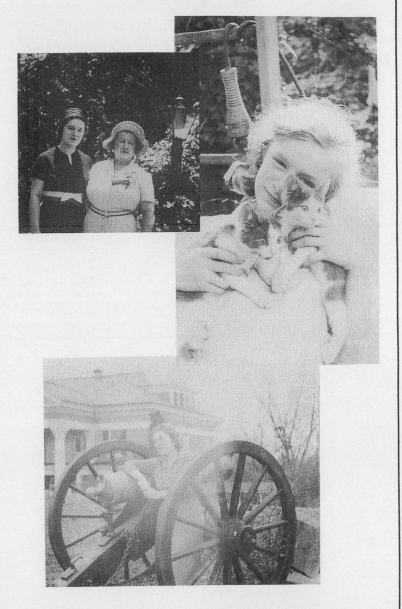

Top left: the author and her mother, 1957; *right:* the author, 1948; *bottom:* the author in Mississippi, 1959. Courtesy of Toni McNaron.

Men Come and Go

When I was thirteen, our family circle changed. It was 1950, and my sister married a man named Leon. I think I fell in love with him the way girls that age often do with older men. The first time I met him, he rode home with us from the Birmingham Public Library where he had been visiting Betty during her evening shift. Recently mustered out of the navy and beginning college on the GI bill, he was wearing a pea coat and dark blue high shoes of some sort. I thought him very dashing, and when he drove up to our house a few weeks later in a red and black Model A Ford, complete with rumble seat, I was his. It never dented my vision of him that the car seldom started once it arrived, and many's the time I was thrilled to pump the gas peddle vigorously while Leon turned the hand crank that stuck out of the radiator. I even liked it when the jalopy stalled on the streets of Fairfield, and we had to hop out and push it to an incline so the battery could reengage on the way down. That Model A had a horn with a rasp that irritated adults and pleased me. When Leon and Betty drove out into the country for Sunday afternoon courting, I was often asked to come along and ride in the rumble seat. The seat had no padding and my bottom was sore by the time we got home, but nothing would have kept me away. Little did I realize that I was serving as chaperone for my sister and perhaps for Leon too.

Openly jealous of Betty, I complained loudly to Leon who told me that he was coming to see Betty as an excuse to play with me. When I heard that they were to be married, I went to him in tears of rage and hurt, only to hear the same line—by marrying Betty, he would see more of me, and we could play more often and more easily.

When he asked my sister where she wanted to live, she replied

with surprise, "I want to live at home, of course." Leon moved into
Betty's bedroom. He did not seem to mind, since he inherited the use
of a big basement in which he played at welding, photographic
developing, and building fancy wooden things on his lathe. He let me
watch and even showed me how to use power tools and big machines.
I especially loved to pull down the handle of his free-standing power
drill and watch it quickly eat through the thickest piece of wood I
could find. And I was hypnotized by the vats of photographic fluids
into which he slid blank sheets of paper and out of which he drew
images of people or places. The moment the image began to emerge
was magical and persistent. Leon taught me how to mix and lay
cement, how to turn a staircase banister or a lamp base on a lathe, how
not to be afraid of electricity. I learned to use nail sets and screw
sinkers, so that all my finished surfaces came out smooth, nails and
screws invisible.

For the years Leon lived in our house while Daddy was alive, they
had arguments. My father did not particularly like his new son-in-
law—maybe because Leon played with me in ways Daddy did not;
maybe because he was very handy around the house and began
winning Mamie's praise by fixing electric outlets, small appliances,
sash cords, or by painting the outside of the house and making her
helpful objects like a cast-iron rack to hold fireplace wood. Saturdays
and Sundays were the most intense, with all five of us home much of
each day, getting into each other's way no matter how separate we
tried to be. The conflict over my father's chair and parceling out the
Sunday fried chicken are cases in point. Though we owned numerous
chairs from various historic periods, Daddy's was the lone stuffed
armchair, placed near a good reading lamp. I learned never to sit in it
when he was home, but Leon somehow missed this message. He
occasionally just wandered into the living room and sat down in the
Chair to read the paper for a while before dinner. Should Daddy come
out of his bedroom and find Leon there, he'd frown and return, not to
appear until Mamie announced dinner. At dinner we were sure to
have a scene—never over the chair, since my father was too silent or
lazy to confront the issue. The set-to would come over some topic of
conversation on which Leon ventured an opinion. Daddy would fume
and curse for a minute or two, then retreat into his usual silence.

For many years, when the four of us had eaten chicken, all had
been well, since everyone got the pieces asked for, even down to
giblets. I liked the heart best, Betty the gizzard, Daddy the liver, and

Mamie the neck. After my father's death, it came out that my mother had lied about her preferences. She had always sworn that her favorite pieces were the back and wings, pieces with virtually no meat. Once Daddy was dead, she began eating breasts, pulley bones,* even a leg or thigh occasionally.

When Leon began eating Sunday dinner with us, our delicate balance was tipped irreparably. He liked only white meat; my father liked only white meat. Betty took small pieces of white meat and a thigh while I liked only dark meat. We were all thrown. Either because Leon and Daddy were men or to keep the peace (unless these reasons are synonymous), we let them have their preferences. Neither Betty nor I was satisfied, forced into silent competition over a chicken thigh.

When I graduated from high school, Leon convinced me to declare myself a physics major at the University of Alabama. Russia had just launched Sputnik, and he was fiercely anti-Red. He berated fields of study like literature and jobs like teaching (things I thought fit me), saying "any girl" could do them. My math talents became his constant focus, while he played down the fact that I had caused a minor explosion in the chemistry lab twice in one semester. Wanting him to continue to think I was special, I listened. Still adoring him, I agreed. When at the end of my sophomore year, I had accumulated ten credits of C's and D's in physics and was miserable doing problems and never talking theory, I phoned my family to tell them I was becoming an English major. Mamie was a little disappointed; Betty supported my doing something verbal; Leon barely spoke to me for the next year. Even though I kept my math minor, I had failed him, preferring to do what any girl could to becoming the famous scientist he fantasized I might be.

Since sexuality never was discussed in our household I grew up ignorant and wary. When junior high boys began making references to the lengths and shapes of their penises, I was one of the last girls to understand. For a long time, I thought the cry in assembly of "six inches" as some boy touched his lower body meant that the boys were having some bizarre bathroom contest involving the measuring of turds. When I overheard girls in the lunch line say, "Nobody could have one eight inches long, 'cause it'd stick out of his pants in front,"

---

* A wishbone.

I realized my mistake and instantly felt profoundly out of step.

The summer I was fourteen, I got an older boy from across the street to let me lie on his squeaky glider while he lay on me, moved his hips from side to side, and breathed heavily. I had heard the glider from my own porch where I played with roly-poly bugs, watching them roll into tight balls whenever I poked them with finger or stick. I had also heard girls giggle ecstatically and felt compelled to see what caused both sounds. The experience was singularly boring. All I really felt was out of breath from the weight of Bobby's big body as it stayed flattened against mine. I pretended to like it, though, because somewhere I understood that was expected by him and by a code to which I was trying blindly to conform. But there was no fun in it. I preferred to crawl on my own belly in our basement across the red clay that smelled moist and rank all summer and was cool and smooth against my bare skin.

When I heard about "making out," I decided sex was uniformly unappealing, noisy, and dull. Part of my response came from early conditioning. From the time I was about three, I had slept in a canopied bed. On top of each of the four posters little pine cones were fitted down into the post, holding a lightweight frame in place. Over that skeletal form was draped a canopy, always white, always frilly like gauze or mosquito netting. When I was eleven and twelve, I fantasized often about becoming an orchestra conductor. Having been given my first record player—a square black box for playing 45 RPM records— and my first red plastic RCA records, I sat in my bed at night with my door partially closed, listening to Tchaikovsky or Rachmaninoff or Brahms. As the scores became more exciting, I began to conduct, swaying to the music, picturing myself complete with tuxedo and baton, doing what Eugene Ormandy and Toscanini did. Invariably, just at the climax of the score, the pine cones jarred loose and the frame slipped, bringing the canopy down dangerously close to my face. Of course, I could not finish my conducting, since I had to rescue the frilly netting from my passionate engagement with the music.

My mother would hear the frame slip and rush in to remind me that if I were that active, my bed would never last me into my own home. When I imagined my schoolmates thrashing around in a back seat of a car or on their family's temporarily abandoned sofa, I felt depressed. Any such vigorous movements in the name of sexual pleasure would surely bring down the canopy. So I internalized my culture's wish for me not to be too active in my own sexual enjoyment—to leave that to the males or, if one really wanted to be nice, to leave it out altogether. Sedate sex became the only kind I could fancy occurring in that bed that was to accompany me into my married life.

Since in high school dating seemed the only socially acceptable behavior, I tried, albeit unsuccessfully, to attract boys. I remember having a major crush on Harold Smith. Complete with thick, moist Victor Mature lips, Harold seemed mostly not to see me. To change his mind, I embarked on a vigorous campaign, carrying his books from class to locker, biking past his house each afternoon after school hoping he would be outside mowing or raking leaves or playing with his baby brother whose hair was even redder than his. My crush lasted well over a year without the slightest encouragement from my idol.

As time passed, my frenzy grew. Once I had a driver's license, I began driving past his house. If I was doing errands and spotted his car (I had of course memorized the license plate number), I would follow him to the grocery store or magazine stand or movie house. Though I constructed many fantasies about what would happen if I went into any of these places and just happened to run into Harold, I never had the courage to do it.

Because I was so fixated on my own crush, I missed a rather significant detail about Harold Smith: he did not date other girls either. He spent time at school horsing around with the boys; otherwise he was at home. The story was that his father did not live with them and that he took care of his mother.

On the few miraculous occasions when I had a date, it was usually with some skinny young man who avoided all unnecessary physical contact. Each time I managed to bring one of these strays home, the same event took place in our living room, which we called the sitting room. My mother would have on her usual afternoon attire: a muted linen dress if it were spring or fall; a dark blue or brown dress in winter; white linen with eyelet-embroidered neckline or cotton splashed with flower patterns in summer. For jewelry, she wore a bracelet, earrings, several rings, and an antique pin. Shod in heels and hose, carefully made-up and coiffed, my mother presented herself as lovely, gracious, and more formal than not.

Once the boy and I were inside, he was ushered onto the settee, while I sat in the gentleman's chair. Mamie sat utterly erect in the lady's chair and began her interview:

"Where do you live?" was her standard opening.

Whatever address came back was not right. Too far away, too close to downtown, a lower-class neighborhood, too near the mill, a section of town with apartment houses. No one ever came from the south side, which was the area Mamie wanted me to marry into.

"What does your father do?" she asked needlessly, since she had already decided against the boy from his first reply.

I usually felt like running out of the room as each boy told of his father's unacceptable job. The only person who saw through her was Joe Wheatley, whom I met my first year in college and who became my best friend for the next ten years. Joe was canny and read Mamie's rejection from her slight sneer and her change of position in the chair. His family was Irish, and Joe felt fierce pride in his heritage. When asked what his father did, he smiled thinly, even meanly, saying: "He runs the only Irish restaurant in Alabama." My mother was speechless for several seconds.

Once these excruciating interviews were over and the boy had gone permanently, Mamie would try to impress upon me yet again the importance of family and address.

One of the things my mother regretted was her inability to "bring out" her daughters into society. In Birmingham, Alabama, as in all major southern cities during my youth, spring meant more than jonquils and azaleas. Spring was debutante season. Between early April and mid-May the local newspaper was filled with long descriptions of afternoon teas held on spacious lawns under green and white striped canvas tents, of weekend brunches in solaria decked with orchids grown in adjacent greenhouses, of early evening buffets at which short white suit coats were acceptable if shirts met tuxedo standards—frilled fronts and cuffs with thin black edging that stood out when militantly starched. Concessions were made to the wealthiest families; their daughters were displayed at seated dinners of no less than five courses, followed by midnight-to-dawn dancing parties at the most expensive and exclusive of the city's country clubs. I knew what the deb wore, what her mother and father wore, what flowers and music provided the backdrop, which others from the season's crop of debs were invited, what refreshments were served, and the society editor's personal sense of the ambience. It became clear that some debutante parties and balls were more successful than others, and that this ranking was conveyed by the most subtle details and nuances of reporting. I recall one unfortunate girl who had served only sparkling burgundy at her cocktail tea for three hundred rather than the requisite champagne.

Whenever Mamie bewailed her failure to give me such a "coming out," I honestly reassured her that I would have wanted no part of such a thing. Just to read a newspaper account gave me a severe stomach-ache:

> Miss Camilla Carstairs was presented last evening under a starry canopy in the arbor of the BCC (Birmingham Country Club). Her mother, Agatha, and her father, Reginald, crowned her in a jeweled tiara interlaced with white orchids. Champagne flowed freely all evening and canapes supplied by Ross's Catering Service adorned several banquet-length tables covered in lime green linen with centerpieces of ice blue daisies requested by the deb as a sign of simplicity and wholeness. Miss Carstairs, or Cam as her close friends call her, was radiant with a glow that combined health and delight. Her party of complementary debs was composed of ten other lovelies, all coming out this season. Each of the girls presented Camilla with a bouquet of roses in varying shades of yellow or orange. Dance music was provided by a live band from Mobile, the Musical Mobilians. The festivities lasted until the wee hours, topped off by a bird breakfast lavishly donated by the proud father. Mrs. Carstairs was seen discreetly dabbing her eyes at several moments during the evening.

Putting myself in such a situation, I knew that I would have been all thumbs and feet, that my repartee would have been too serious and direct, my choice of flowers and music old-fashioned, and that my guest list would have included absolutely no one that anyone else knew as part of the current circle. In a word, I understood that I was not a debutante by any stretch of my mother's imagination and felt relief that our circumstances cut off all possibility of a debut.

Only one young man ever met my mother's standards—Don Reed, whom I also got to know during my first year in college. In response to her query about his address, he simply responded "Hartselle," which was a tiny town near Huntsville on the northern border of Alabama. Because it was a small, quiet hamlet about which she knew nothing, Mamie could romanticize the geography. When asked what his father did, Don could say, "He's dead," cutting off any further remarks, since any mention of death of a parent catapulted my mother into her own grief for hers. Because he was mannered, deferential, and an English major with verbal facility, he kept his head above water in our living room. In fact, he did that well enough to be asked into the dining room on several occasions to share one of Mamie's elegant meals.

My mother would have liked me to marry Don, and his family seemed equally interested in the match. What everyone probably knew, but no one acknowledged, of course, was that he was not the least interested in marrying me or any female. But we spent lots of time together out of genuine affection for one another and let our families think whatever was convenient. Their fantasies about our engagement meant fewer lectures about going out with someone.

My mother treated girls much as she did boys, saying about virtually any who spent time with me, "She's so frivolous; how can you stand to waste your time with anybody so silly? Why don't you try to find someone your equal?"

Yet, what my mother feared most was my leaving her. I remember getting an invitation during my fifteenth summer to attend a church camp weekend at a lake near Birmingham. Rarely was I included in such affairs, since I never could provide a date and consequently would be a loose wheel in paired activities. I was terribly excited and wanted to go with the intensity of the passed over. When I told Mamie, I assumed she would be happy, since she pushed me into social activities, saying I needed to spend time with people my own age because she and Daddy were so much older. But when I announced my invitation, her face fell. It seems she had planned an all-day excursion to Elmwood Cemetery, complete with a fried chicken picnic.

These outings were fairly common. We would pack the car with lawn mower, clippers, trowels, spades, rakes, Vigaro or bone meal or cow manure depending on what we were going to plant, and the plants, bushes, or flowers to be set into the ground. Sitting in the back seat of our Plymouth, I often felt like part of the garden supplies. But I still liked going. As on vacation at Fort Walton, time spent at the cemetery was easy and pleasant. Nobody had behaviors for me to adhere to, and working in the ground always brought my mother peace, even at the place where her parents were buried. Though our lot was big enough for eight graves, only my mother's mother and father were there. The remaining six plots were for her and Daddy, Betty and her husband, me and mine. On our work excursions we took lunches and plenty of iced or hot tea, which we ate and drank on an ornamental granite slab bench. These macabre visits to my grandparents' dwelling left me feeling oddly deprived when classmates talked about their wonderful visits to a grandmother or grandfather, complete with laden tables, country air, and cuddly love.

As soon as Mamie told me about the projected trip, I felt guilty. I was proposing going off to have fun with live teenagers, leaving her without her best worker. "How can you be so selfish? But I needn't ask—all of you are the same. If it's more important to you to go and have your fun than to . . . ." I broke in, tearfully, saying, "I'll cancel; I didn't know you had plans for us. I'm sorry to upset you; you know how much I love you. I'd rather dig holes with you than lie around in the sun with some silly kids." She refused to hear of such a thing, announcing stonily that I had to go now that I had accepted. I begged her to let me call and say I was sick with one of my several chest and throat ailments, since by that time I could not imagine having fun. But on the appointed morning, I was sent off with a melancholy wish to enjoy myself.

I lay on the pier, alone, most of Saturday and again Sunday morning, getting scorched from sun bouncing off water. By the time the group dropped me at home, I was already blistering. Unable to sleep lying down, over the next week I peeled off every inch of exposed skin and reeked of Noxema. Mamie cared for me beautifully, having first lectured about my terrible habit of going off with strangers and forgetting everything I knew about being responsible. "Part of my not wanting you to go to this camp was my fear that you'd do something like this and hurt yourself just to be one of the group." "You'll do anything to be liked, you know, and I worry about that impressionable part of you." "Why can't you set the standards rather than lowering yourself to other people's?" I was asked twice more during high school to go on some kind of overnight group outing. Both times I refused.

My junior year I had crushes on two people—Ann, president of the senior class, and Victor, president of the student council. Ann was a Roman Catholic, one of the few in my school, which meant that some mornings she came to school smelling of incense, which fascinated me, and on Ash Wednesday her forehead bore the mark of her priest's thumb—a sure sign to me that she was closer to God and the angels than the rest of us. I began talking to Ann at football games: she was there representing the senior class on the arm of a handsome college freshman active in the Catholic Youth League; I was there selling pop and candy to help my gym teacher. As football season became basketball season, Ann stopped coming with the college freshman and on a few occasions even helped sell pop and candy. When I asked her for a school snapshot, she smiled beatifically and gave me one.

I carried that picture in my purse for years, long after she graduated from high school and long after she killed herself during her second autumn in college for reasons seemingly unknown to anyone. "But she was such a devout girl," or "She was such a good girl," or "I can't understand why such a pretty girl would do such a dark thing" were the things our parents said. My fantasy was that maybe Ann became increasingly lonely for my company. I remember our last conversation: it was late summer and she was going back to college, much to my sorrow. She talked about sin and guilt and punishment. When I tried to say that she did not have to worry about such dour subjects, she flashed her pale blue eyes at me and said, "You can't possibly know what terrible things I've done and can't stop doing— I sometimes think life is just too unfair to be lived!" I never saw or spoke with Ann again. But for several weeks that junior year, I felt I had arrived: the great Ann was my campaign manager (I was running for the student council for the next year, and she thought me the best candidate). She made one amusing if blatantly racist poster for me that showed a Chinese man saying, "You pullee no bonee, You votee for Toni." I rode onto the council on Ann's skirttails.

Victor was not tall or dark or handsome—he was thick without being muscular, had never gone out for any athletics, and had jet black curly hair that was outside the acceptable norms for boy's hair in Fairfield, Alabama in 1953. But he could talk about current events, school politics, and even movies and records. In my high school full of children of United States Steel workers, these abilities set Victor apart. Even his name did that—most boys were called Bob or Bill or Jim, with an occasional Harry or Steve.

At first Victor, like all the other boys, ignored me, but little by little I slid into his consciousness. Flattery and pure adoration provided the oil, and finally he began stiff exchanges in the halls or at student council meetings, which I attended on the pretext of needing to watch how things were done so I could be a better member the next year when he was gone. He even asked me to dance at the junior–senior prom, which I attended with the boy across the street who was a foot shorter and two years younger than I.

Victor did something no one from Fairfield High School had done in recent memory: he went to Harvard. If I had fancied him before, when I learned that he had won a scholarship there, his rating surpassed any scale of measure I knew. He agreed to write me about the Great University and did, though his letters were short and businesslike. But when I won a Kiwanis Club trip to Washington and New York, Victor wrote out of what seemed the blue saying he would come down to the City while I was there and we could go to dinner.

I suffered through the Washington segment of the trip and the bus tour of New York City ending in a visit to the United Nations and a posed picture with Henry Cabot Lodge, who had graciously agreed to speak to us about the work of the U.N. Finally it was six o'clock, and Victor appeared at the Waldorf Astoria Hotel where the Kiwanis Club was putting us up. We went to what I am sure was an elegant dinner at what I am sure was an elegant restaurant. All I remember about the evening was a moment at my hotel room door about one in the morning. I had never before been out so late with a boy; I had never ended any of my scattered dates away from Holly Court, Fairfield, Alabama. Now I was in New York, and a Harvard man and I had walked all over Manhattan after dinner. At each curb, Victor had taken my arm ever so gently to show that he was attentive. Once back at the Waldorf, he did not leave me in the lobby, but insisted on taking me up to my room, "It's so late for a young lady to be in the halls alone."

After I had taken out my key and unlocked the door, Victor took my right hand in his and said shyly, "I've really had a good time, Toni. Thank you for the evening." Then he leaned over and kissed me on the mouth—a thoroughly 1950s American kiss. I never told anyone back home about that kiss, and only my family knew of the date. He wrote two or three short, impersonal notes about classes and springtime in Cambridge, then all correspondence stopped, and he went out of my life. Too ashamed to ask for any explanation, I reached two negative decisions: I simply did not know how to maneuver relations between the sexes; it did not pay to get too close to anyone, since they could so quickly and easily vanish.

The other important men in my life during this period were my high school principal and my music teacher, both considerably older than I. Early in my sophomore year, we got a new principal—Henderson Walker, or Hank to his friends. A little taller than my father or Leon, he had sandy hair slightly waved on each side of a deep part down the middle. His eyes were clear blue with just the beginning of laugh lines at their edges, and a smile often lit up his face. I think it was this essential happiness of person that first attracted me, since the men I had known worried a lot and the boys were mostly angry.

One morning during his first week at school, I got a pass to the library and went instead to the main office to "see Mr. Walker." I never expected to do that, but shortly after I sat down to wait, he came out himself and asked me into his office and shut the door. Such privacy and respect quite went to my head and I could only say such balmy things as, "Welcome to our school, Mr. Walker," and "If there's anything I can do to help you get acquainted, just ask." After days of hearing about almost nothing but the principal from me, my mother agreed to ask him and his wife to dinner. I wrote out the invitation, and they accepted.

From that evening on, Hank and Dot (they insisted I call them that, though of course not "Hank" at school) became fast friends of mine and my family's. He took particular interest in my brain, encouraging me as no one had except Mamie. Any time we passed in the halls, Hank made a point of asking me about my classes or family. Occasionally, he drove me home in his canary yellow convertible, which was the envy of all the boys in school, until things soured for my hero. Because I was so enamored of him, I must have been oblivious to the growing stir in both the faculty and student body. As it turned out, a lot of people did not like Henderson Walker—he put on airs, was too familiar with students, did not automatically believe the faculty about school events, talked of bringing in teachers with dangerously new ideas.

Suddenly the gym teacher, a close friend of my sister and a frequent visitor at our house, announced one evening that Mr. Walker had been asked by the board of education to resign without delay. He had been accused by one of the boys in the senior class of improper behavior toward him. Not entirely sure what that meant, I sensed it had to do with something sexual. Later, Dot's tone of voice and the discomfort in the air of our living room seemed to confirm this. She had come personally because she, like everyone else at the high school, knew how fond of him I had become; she did not want me to be unduly hurt by hearing students talking about him in the halls or lunch room.

The next day, I went promptly to Hank's office to find him looking drawn and anxious. "I've heard all about the charge, and I don't for a moment believe it, you have my total support and trust, and I'll defend you to anyone who says untrue things about you." My words tumbled out from love and an inarticulate identification with whatever it was people thought about this lovely man who had paid me such kind attention. Hank cried his thanks, saying, "It means so much to have your faith, Toni, you are so special a person in this world. I suspect you may be able to understand all this." I could not and was puzzled by his thinking I could, but I certainly did understand that the first man who had accepted me for who I was without needing me to be more or other was being maligned and driven out of his job by people for whom I had little or no respect.

I kept up with Henderson Walker, learning that he worked first at the biggest department store in Birmingham selling men's clothing, then as part of an interior decorating firm. But he cared passionately about the education of the young and finally found a job in a little town far enough away to have escaped the poisonous grapevine that prevented his working in any school in the metropolitan area. He drove over an hour each way in order to continue his work with young people.

When Mr. Parker, my music teacher, was introducing me to Rachmaninoff, Chopin, and Liszt, he already had a Ph.D. from Indiana University's School of Music—that meant he was extremely good both at theory and performance. I suspect he yearned to be a concert performer but could not figure out how to do that under his circumstances. His father had died, leaving him the sole care and support for his ailing mother with whom he lived and in the front of whose house he gave music lessons so as not to leave her unattended for long.

I remember the smell of that room—faintly medicinal and distinctly stuffy. I studied on an upright, black piano with a marbled surface where the varnish had cracked from too much dry furnace heat forced by the prolonged dampness of southern winters. If there were any windows in that room, I do not remember them—certainly they were never opened to the outside air or light. Since the room was just inside the front door, I assume it had once been a foyer when Mr. Parker's house had been a place of human traffic. Now it admitted pupils for the prescribed forty-five minute lessons.

At the end of our first year together as pupil and teacher, he began asking me to go to movies with him on Saturdays and to Sunday League at the big Baptist church of which he was a solid member. Adoring the picture show, I liked the former, but League bored me with its incessant singing and dreary homilies followed by "fellowship" in the basement. This latter activity consisted of cookies, punch, and stiff conversation.

As months passed into years, Mr. Parker on rare occasions held my hand in the movies or put his arm ever so tentatively around my shoulders as we sat having root beer floats at a drive-in afterwards. Then it happened—he proposed marriage. It was a Saturday in early July after my graduation from high school. We had been to some movie and had drunk the ritual float and were parked in front of my house. Eager to get inside because nothing was happening, I opened the door only to be stopped by Mr. Parker's intense request, "Wait, Toni, not just yet."

"I care for you deeply and for your beautiful playing. I want you to marry me."

Stunned but not speechless, I replied, "I can't do that, Mr. Parker, I'm going to college."

"Oh, I know, and I don't want to change that. I'll just wait until you are finished. We'd be engaged, of course."

"I can't do that, Mr. Parker, I'm going to college." I am convinced that I repeated myself because, in my state of shock, I had no more words available.

"You just have a one-track mind, Toni."

"Well, you just have a marriage-track mind."

With this heaven-sent quip, I left the car and raced into my house to find my mother who would surely comfort me in my hour of total need. Mamie was bathing, so I barged in and sat on the wicker clothes hamper where I had perched as a child. I blurted out, "Oh, Mamie, something terrible has happened—Mr. Parker has asked me to marry him, but don't worry, I refused and told him I had to go to college and that he had a marriage-track mind to expect me to do anything else."

To my further shock and amazement, Mamie began fussing at me. She was not angry at this man, my teacher, for behaving in such an uncalled for way. She was mad at me for being "rude" to "someone as lovely as Billie" (she had long since dropped the "Mr." that I insisted on retaining). She actually wanted me to say I was sorry and that I would reconsider his generous offer. Not since the first day of first grade, when she had urged me to apologize for pronouncing "hearth" correctly when my teacher did not, had I been so deeply upset with my mother's reading of a scene involving me.

I did not apologize to Mr. Parker any more than I had to Miss Leslie all those years before. Mamie talked with him, though I never learned what she said. He and I stopped seeing each other, which caused me to feel only relief. But at the same time, I lost an approved escort. The rest of that summer I simply stayed home or went out with my family as usual.

My senior year in high school, 1954, was momentous for me and for the South. My father died on New Year's Day, and in the spring, the Supreme Court ruled on Brown vs. Board of Education. I scarcely comprehended either, and only over time could I feel what they had meant to me. In one way, the two events crossed without my bidding. I had planned to go to the University of North Carolina at Chapel Hill or to Duke because they were good southern colleges where I might learn something after eleven years of boredom in Fairfield's public schools. Daddy's sudden death ended that dream, forcing me to attend the state university in Tuscaloosa.

The weather that New Year's Day was warmish, even for Alabama winters. We had not had rain for about a week, so my bones felt less chilled than usual. After a holiday breakfast of waffles and bacon, I had gone outside to play pitch with myself. Daddy came out the front door about eleven, threw the hardball to me a few times, said goodbye on his way to his office "to do a little work while nobody's there." Eventually I went across the street to play with Kenny and Nancy Myers, neighborhood friends. Several hours went idly by, until I heard Mamie's frantic voice calling, "Toni, Toni, Toni, come home, come home." Running down the three sets of concrete steps to the street, I saw my mother standing at our screen door, her eyes wild, wringing her hands, and barely controlling hysteria.

Once inside the house, I felt fear. Daddy was lying on the bed in the backroom, breathing very harshly, and Betty was talking jerkily on the telephone. Between half-sobs, Mamie tried to tell me what had happened: "He came upstairs through the basement ... cutting wood ... breathless ... went to lie down ... now just listen ... what will I do?" At one point, she stopped and rushed to his side because of his increasing difficulty in breathing. Betty said in a taut voice, "I've been trying to find Dr. John, but it's a holiday so he's not anywhere to be reached. I've called an ambulance. Don't go into the room and upset him any more. Stay out here in the hall with me."

I was stunned. No one had ever been critically ill around me before. Mamie had had spells of arthritis, Daddy belched a lot, Betty and I had had an occasional headache, but nothing more dramatic. The idea of having an ambulance come to our house and take my father away terrified me. All the movies I had seen had taught me that ambulances were last resorts, that people in ambulances often died en route to a hospital or shortly after they arrived, amid red flashing lights and rushing nurses and doctors. How could all this be happening to my father, who only a few hours before had chosen to play ball with me on a mild January day?

The ambulance arrived. Two men rushed in, reeking of whiskey, speaking in falsely hushed tones. They lifted Daddy gingerly from bed to cot, covered him with an unnaturally white sheet and a beige blanket, and rushed out into their long, low-lying vehicle. Mamie went with them. Their siren was turned to full volume as they sped down our hill. That sound, utterly different from police cars or fire trucks, became synonymous with death and dying, and was capable of producing a rush of adrenalin and an instantly dry mouth.

Leon drove Betty and me to Lloyd Nolan Hospital, the "company hospital" that Mamie had always shunned as shoddy and impolite. We were forced to go there because, not being able to locate our family physician, we had to follow ambulance policy: take the patient to the nearest hospital to be admitted through the emergency room. As I waited with my sister and brother-in-law, I kept thinking about foolish things: "Here I am inside the hospital right up the steep alley hill from our house; this is where I cut through on my way home from high school for lunch." "In the fall, leaves are prettiest here because they are protected from traffic." "I remember that afternoon when I was ten, when Betty and Leon were courting, and we spent a Sunday afternoon on Lloyd Nolan Hill, picnicking. Leon took a picture of me running with both feet off the ground down the sloping hillside."

Once we had parked and found the correct waiting room, we were told that no one could go into his room. He had been placed under an oxygen tent with Mamie at his side. My mother stayed by my father's side, alone, until a doctor brought her out in the hysterics that signaled Daddy was dead. In that instant, I blamed her for his dying. He had been alive when I last saw him, even talking to me a bit. Now he was dead, and she had been there. I felt she had let my father die.

Numb, I rode silently home in the back seat of our Plymouth. Everyone was silent except Mamie who sobbed and moaned continuously. Neither Betty nor I cried during the funeral preparations, the event itself, the aftermath meal. It was a long time, years afterwards, before I grieved. We all agreed not to mention his name in our waking life, lest doing so should rekindle Mamie's uncontrollable feelings. I was forced to confine Daddy to my dreams. In the most recurrent of them, he was standing at the foot of my bed, looking sad and lonely, never calling out or speaking but letting me know by a raised eyebrow or a beckoning hand gesture that he wanted me to join him. I would wake frightened but expectant—I never found him at the foot of my bed or anywhere else, though often at play or when I was hanging up clothes outside I felt a presence and turned quickly to see if I might catch him before he left.

The first night after Daddy's death, I sat up in his favored padded armchair in the living room, enraged but silent. I listened in shock as Betty sent telegrams to relatives and talked with the funeral director. Mamie spent most of the evening sitting on the edge of my bed, holding on to one of my canopy posts, rocking herself back and forth, keening. At some point, Dr. John appeared with his familiar black bag and bedside manner. He sat with my mother trying to calm her, giving her a shot of something to help her sleep. I suddenly saw Daddy yelling at Mamie about "all your damn-fooled visits to that doctor." He was convinced that they were engaged in some kind of flirtation and suffered periodic flare-ups of jealousy.

My rage was at my father for abandoning me. I needed someone to comfort me, but between funeral arrangements and Mamie's state, nobody had much time. Since I pretended to be in control, I was delegated to answer the door, be courteous to callers, keep all but the family and closest friends away from Mamie. Lots of men, mostly black, all poor and working at menial jobs at the mill, came to pay their last respects to "Mr. Mac," whom they so obviously had loved.

One older black man stands out in my memory. He refused to come up onto the porch, preferring to stand on the stoop with his hat in his hand: "Mr. Mac, he fished me out the jail once or twice, and he wrote out my taxes free, and he signed papers to keep the garnisheer from taking our things up to the house. And Mr. Mac, he took me and George, my oldest boy, to a doctor who'd let us come in the back door and he saw to my boy when the rest of the doctors didn't take coloreds." It was typical of how my father did things that I had never heard this story. As the man spoke, he kept looking anxiously over his shoulder, obviously ill at ease to be talking with a young white lady in the daytime when some shotgun-carrying thug might see him. But he admired my father more than he feared thugs. As more and more men came to share their simple, moving respect for my father, I understood: no wonder he never played with me; he was always too busy doing things for strangers.

The coffin arrived that day about noon, closed, so that I never saw my father dead. My last visual memory was of his being rolled out of the house two days before. As the ambulance attendants had passed me in the hallway, Daddy motioned them to stop. They did, and he said, "My wallet and keys are on the dresser. Take care of them." Flattered and angry to be chosen when he had a wife of thirty-five years and a thirty-three-year-old daughter who might better carry such responsibilities, I made no response. I did not even have a driver's license, and he had yelled every time we had gone out for a lesson, "You're stripping the gears," "You're grinding the brakes." But before the end of the day he died, I had gotten into the relatively new, sea green replacement for our ancient black Plymouth, driven down our hill, around the corner into a narrow alley, and into the even narrower garage in which the car stayed. The following week, I fantasized I was a chauffeur, needing to take a refresher test for a higher degree of license. Sufficiently psyched up, I went to an agency where people tested, executed the basic maneuvers as if in a trance, passed everything, and got a temporary permit followed by a real license three weeks later.

Imagining how my movie idols, Gary Cooper and James Stewart, would act under similar circumstances, I remained stiff and silent throughout the funeral. I hoped that by doing so I would please my father who lay inside a flower-draped box over which our minister prayed interminably.

The only person I talked to during the funeral was a young man named Earl, who came with my favorite relative, Aunt Carrie, Mamie's step-aunt. Earl wore a black patch over one eye and seemed exotic. His voice was lower and slower than those of the other neighbors and relatives. I considered speaking to him because he seemed able to listen. He came over to me as I sat rigidly in Daddy's chair and perched on a footstool nearby. I made no answer to his first "Want to talk, Toni?" but gradually decided to trust him.

"What subjects do you enjoy most at school?" he asked, as if we were at tea instead of a wake. Surprised, I answered. I talked first about my sixth-grade math teacher, Miss Gray, who had read poems at the end of some class periods, who told me I was quick at all my calculations, even long division and equations.

"And a special favorite was chemistry last year because Mrs. Fiquette let us pour one chemical over another to make beautiful colors in the bottom of a test tube. Her son plays football at the university and she treats me like a grownup, like you're doing now. I only blew up my experiment twice all semester. It went all the way to the ceiling once, and strange-colored spots are up there still to prove it. I want to take more chemistry when I go to college. How did you hurt your eye?"

Earl answered quietly, "In an accident years ago that messed up the retina. They tried to fix it but it got worse. Eventually I lost my sight. I bet you must have lots of friends in this neighborhood."

I hedged because I had almost none. Finally I mustered, "Well, there's Kenny Myers from across the street, we play pitch together, and his little sister, Nancy, but I mostly help her with her arithmetic. On Easter, the three of us, along with Ward, a boy whose father is my father's supervisor, have an egg hunt and someone always takes a picture of us in our new clothes." Then Earl said, "It must be wonderful to live with "Tee Tee" (the nickname he and all of Aunt Carrie's children and their children had for my mother). I muttered something in agreement and fell silent again, not wanting to say how lonely and isolated I felt without Daddy.

Earl got up from the footstool and built a fire in the fireplace. We sat there together until finally I felt like lying down. Next day, I ate a tiny serving from the mounds of food brought by neighbors and friends. How could people sit and consume plates full of cold ham, cold chicken, endless hot dishes, lukewarm overcooked vegetables, rolls and biscuits, and every imaginable kind of pie and cake topped with vanilla ice cream? "Mamie won't have to cook for a week" kept going through my mind; maybe all this was a gift to her. But the scene seemed ghoulish, and I refused to participate. My father had died, and I resented the world's going on as usual. Earl understood and told me it was all right not to eat or sit at the table with the group. When he and Aunt Carrie left, I felt empty all over again.

I stayed home from school for three weeks, not wanting to talk or hear commiseration. Two or three fellow students dropped by the house to say how sorry they were and they hoped I would come back soon. When I eventually did return, every time a hall bell rang, I fairly jumped out of myself. That late winter and spring were my last in high school, and some events were mandatory: I was to deliver the valedictory address; attend a gala senior prom where I would only dance twice; pass the one senior exam from which I was not excused because of high marks. Six weeks before graduation, I contracted a severe case of whooping cough and stayed home another month, unable to speak more than a few words without hacking convulsively. Grinning and bearing it like the little soldier I was sure Daddy wanted me to be, I got up from bed to attend rehearsals for the commencement exercises. On the appointed night, I rendered the commencement address without a single cough, only to be racked with spasms for the next hour. Mamie, Betty, and Leon tried hard to be festive at the small gathering of friends for champagne in our dining room. Aware only of the hollowness of the occasion, I felt bitterly alone.

In the first year after Daddy's death, I put one foot in front of a semitruck only to pull it back in the next moment, gained thirty pounds to hide myself, dreamed that Daddy was at the foot of my bed, and withdrew even further from my family. Mamie's need for silence meant my need for talk went unmet. Because she had by then convinced me that it was not appropriate to discuss private affairs outside the family, I did not speak of my father to anyone for two or three years. When college classmates asked idly, "And what does your Dad do, Toni?" I replied, tight lipped, "He's dead." No further inquiries were made, and my isolation was insured.

Into the Cauldron

While I grieved for my father, the NAACP formed a strategy for integrating southern schools. Fearing the murder of their children if they sent them to grade school or even high school, they focused on state universities as a beginning. For whatever reasons, they picked the University of Alabama first, followed the next year by the University of Mississippi. For whatever reasons, they picked a female to enter the University of Alabama, followed by a male at Mississippi. What that meant to me was that while I prepared to go fifty-five miles down the road, a young black woman named Autherine Lucy was making her own very different preparations to arrive at the same campus at the same time.

I was more fragile at the end of that summer than I knew. My father's death had left me feeling outside the primary relationship between my mother and sister. If I was in touch with my own sexual or erotic feelings, I did not let that reach my consciousness. On those rare occasions when I had a date, the boy avoided all but absolutely necessary physical contact. I attributed my failure at heterosexual social life either to my weight gain (boys preferred girls with large breasts, tiny waists, and no hips—I had medium breasts, a thick waist, and ample hips) or to my intellectual acumen (boys preferred girls who could converse lightly on a variety of subjects—I knew too much about too many things).

That summer, I had engaged in a barbaric institution known as "prerush." Over 70 percent of the students at Alabama belonged to sororities and fraternities and my mother was insistent that on this occasion I be in the majority. Prerush began in June before a person's freshman year and lasted right up until we packed our bags to go down for rush, a week before school started. It involved being invited to coffees, lunches, swim parties, and teas. It was supposed to be a more relaxed atmosphere than the near-frenetic round of parties during rush week. At the gatherings I attended, I usually felt bored and awkward. But two unforgettable events occurred, one of which might have helped bring me out as a lesbian. The first of these was reported to me by my mother and involved a conversation she had had with a friend whom she told about a sorority's suddenly dropping me after several warm invitations. The friend informed Mamie of the reason: they had found out about my being Jewish. Understandably surprised, since I had been going to the Episcopal church all my life and had never met anyone Jewish except a couple of store-owners with whom my mother routinely flirted, I asked her about this newfound heritage. She told me that I was indeed one-eighth Jewish, that her German great-grandmother had, with her husband and family, fled some early persecution.

The other moment was my initial visit to Pi Beta Phi, a sorority with a high reputation at the University of Alabama. They had asked me to a small luncheon in the home of a young woman who lived in the right part of town, where we used to drive on Sundays to look at houses with big yards and high, thick hedgerows. I went to the lunch assuming I would feel the same as usual—too serious, awkward, incapable of social small talk. That was not the case. One of only three rushees, I was surprised to find myself excited to be talking with the members. One woman in particular, Carolyn, was studying to be a civil engineer so she could design bridges. She was tall and angular, wore severely tailored clothes, had a low voice the sheer sound of which thrilled me. She asked me what I thought about things, places, books, and people in the news. The women in that room talked about ideas and their careers, and expected me to do the same—heady stuff for someone whose family discoursed primarily in abstractions and whose peers talked of football and lipstick shades. I did not want to leave—her or the lunch or that group who seemed unlike any girls I had ever met. I wanted to belong to that sorority more than anything, except perhaps to have been the son my father could not have. Though I had never seen or heard the word "lesbian," I felt newly vulnerable to these intense women who focused their attention on me.

After I had been to the Pi Phi's night party on the last day of rush—an event tantamount to pledging—the membership had a nasty fight. It seems I was in competition with a genuine southern belle who lived on the south side of Birmingham: she would bring them a good address and sweetheart pins from three fraternities, including Sigma Chi; I offered intellect, seriousness, and loyalty. The faction of which Carolyn and the other summer luncheon companions were part walked out of the meeting, but the invitation went to the sweetheart. My heart broke for the first time in my life. I loved those women, at first sight and passionately, and I was angry with my parents for living somewhere that made me less than acceptable.

I dropped out of rush, refusing to accept an invitation from my second choice. If I could not belong where I most wanted to, then Mamie would have to adjust to having her daughter be an independent, the term for those few poor souls who could not get themselves pledged to some Greek group. At that moment, I might have agreed that my mother was a failure for not being able to have debutantes for daughters. Later, during open rush (an event staged for those unfortunate enough not to be pledged during rush week), I relented under pressure from Mamie and my own loneliness. I joined a group that wanted me more than I wanted them, with all the ambivalences of such a choice.

But I determined to be friends with Carolyn's group and began speaking to them whenever we passed on campus. They invariably looked down or away until one day I stopped Carolyn near the student union and forced her to tell me what was going on. "We had a big split that last Saturday night and couldn't win for you, but we so much want you to be part of us and don't know how to ask you." Without any hesitation, I began spending more hours at the Pi Phi house than at my own sorority. We talked about physical education, bridge building, law school, medical school, college teaching. One by one and inevitably, these stunning women who so spellbound me graduated. Several married, asking me to be a maid of honor. I recall how sad and pained I was at each wedding, how much champagne I drank, how abandoned I felt by each exit. Years later I would read letters by Emily Dickinson in which she spoke of someone in "boots and whiskers" taking her women friends away from Amherst, Massachusetts, to a state called Holy Matrimony. I understood perfectly her feeling that her precious circle was dying off, one by one. The women in whose weddings I participated were being similarly stolen, going to places far from Alabama, the Pi Phi house, and me.

Bruised and unsure of myself, I needed comfort, a friend, a buffer, a hero. She presented herself in the person of the new dean of women,

Sarah L. Healy, newly arrived from Michigan—a state I knew was up near the Canadian border. Though I could not have said so then, I fell in love with Mrs. Healy at the first freshman orientation meeting. She talked about "women," not "girls"; she said a university could not be our parents, that we had to begin to take responsibility for our own lives; she tried to soften some of the restrictions on female students, such as being in dorms by 7:00 P.M. on weeknights, a puritan rule that successfully prohibited use of the library while trying unsuccessfully to prohibit sex. I attached myself to Mrs. Healy instantly.

During the opening days of school, I was vaguely aware that a "Negro" student had been enrolled. I had read about it in a newspaper article but not paid much attention. Once I had my room in the dorm, however, it was an unavoidable topic. Students talked about her in shocking ways, calling her crazy, an hermaphrodite, retarded, a nymphomaniac, just plain uppity. They had fantasies that she would attract all eligible dates, sleep with teachers to pass her courses, have diseases they would magically catch by walking in the same quadrangle. I learned that she was not in any of the dormitories but was housed at the only black motel in Tuscaloosa, some ten miles from campus. I learned that it was the dean of women's responsibility to drive her back and forth to campus and that endeared Mrs. Healy to me even more. It meant she did not think like my dormmates. I imagined that, since she came from Michigan, she had played with black children too, a possibility that made us blood sisters.

In 1954, Tuscaloosa, Alabama, had two major industries besides the university: a large paper mill and an even larger rubber plant. Both places resisted hiring blacks and feelings were raw among the lower-class white men who worked there. They earned far less than any national minimum wage, had no union, could find no other job if they lost this one. They knew that integration would replace them with better-educated black men. They were fighting for survival.

On the day classes were to begin, the managements at both mills declared a paid holiday for all their employees—an unprecedented move in that town's labor history. When I walked out of my dormitory, fresh in my skirt and sweater and little white collar that kept slipping askew, with new books for courses that I prayed would challenge my mind, I was met by a sight I have never forgotten. Lined up at least four deep, along the main street of campus, were approximately fifteen hundred men from the paper mill and the rubber plant. I had never seen so many men at once, and my instant emotion was fear. They carried a variety of weapons—bricks, bottles, baseball bats, rocks, sticks, billy clubs, brass knuckles, wide boards. I froze in horror when I saw their faces. They snarled, showing yellowed teeth or blank spaces where yellowed teeth had been. Their eyes, squinted almost shut, glared with hate and anger. Their mouths spewed obscenities that cursed deities, human elimination, and women. I was terrified as I made my way toward English 1A.

At first I did not know what they were doing there, though other students seemed to. All those men were there to protest Autherine Lucy's attendance. I felt they were there to "kill a nigger" for knowing how to read when they did not. As I stood behind them, waiting too, though not sure for what, it dawned on me that these thugs were waiting for Mrs. Healy's car to drive by, since she had gone to get Miss Lucy. I felt angry and protective, so I began to watch the same direction the men were. I saw her car turn into sorority row, where we were all milling around. It was unmistakably hers—the big, silent Olds 88, white with forest green trim, license number 1A 2097, a magical car in my eyes because it belonged to my hero. As it drew closer, I noticed a black woman in the front seat with Mrs. Healy. At home, our maids always rode in the back seat, even when no one else rode in front. I had asked why on more than one occasion, only to be told that that was the way things were, that everyone was fine with it, that I should just go out and play.

Autherine's presence in that front seat incensed the men more than anything else. They also were furious with the "white bitch northerner" who let her sit there. They shouted the same obscenities at both women. Suddenly a big dirty man near me threw his brick at Mrs. Healy's car; it missed the back window and glanced off the fender. I threw my English 1A book at him; it missed his ear and glanced off his fat shoulder. I lit out across campus to the Episcopal chapel, ran in, and found a corner pew where I sat and shook for an hour. I had acted without thought, and my stunned brain and body were filled with excitement and terror. I acted to protect the white woman I adored. But no one would have known that, least of all the fellow I almost hit on the ear. He would have branded me a "nigger lover," when more accurately he was dealing with a fledgling dyke.

Though nothing more serious occurred than a broken window in Mrs. Healy's car, classes were totally disrupted by the white working men. By late afternoon, we huddled inside our residence halls, peering out windows. The deans of women and men issued an emergency bulletin cautioning us to remain inside, due to "unusual circumstances" on campus. We all laughed at deans who could think we had to be told to stay inside. No one wanted to go out into that hotbox. The fifteen hundred men hung around even after sunset.

Next morning, the campus was quieter, most of the white plant workers having returned to work. But the diehards took the day without pay and came back, still with their hideous faces, their homemade weapons, and their hate. Classes were scheduled, and we walked in groups to feel safer. I was calm enough to wonder what would happen if one of the men made a move toward Miss Lucy. There was one of her and still a couple hundred of them. All two hundred could not possibly beat up on one black woman, and I knew from reading *Julius Caesar* in high school that mobs need targets once they unleash their emotions. If this mob began to act, it would inevitably hurt white students. They were all men, their language was nasty about women, Autherine was a woman, I was a woman. I believed that if they ever got started, their rage would spill over to white women students rather than to campus men.

That day I recognized something central about being a girl in the world. I felt closer to Autherine Lucy than to my white male classmates, and I felt afraid because of my anatomy and gender. I cried out of what seemed fear but must also have been the relief of identification. Though it would be twenty years before I used the word, I probably became a feminist that day.

By the third day of class, the men from the paper mill and rubber plant were gone from campus. Mrs. Healy continued to drive out to the motel in the morning to collect Miss Lucy and back again in the late afternoon to deposit her. I had prayed a lot during those three days, and now I felt that my prayers were answered, since Autherine was going to classes and Mrs. Healy was not hurt. But nearly every day I heard snatches of ugly conversations among students or between students and faculty about how unfair it was to all of us to have to put up with "her." No one ever called Autherine Lucy by any name, and I flashed to my alley playmates, wishing I had at least learned their first names. I never interrupted those bigoted exchanges to state my own views about having a black classmate or my feelings about what was being said.

In the months that followed, I saw O. C. Carmichael, the university president, forced to resign because he would not lie about Miss Lucy. During that first violent week, some of us learned the board of trustees pressured him to expel her because of the tensions set off in the town by her presence. Dr. Carmichael told them flatly that the town would have to figure out something to do with its tensions. Then the board told him to say that she did not do well enough on various aptitude tests to be admitted. Again Dr. Carmichael refused, pointing out that Miss Lucy's scores were better than the whites from rural school districts, and that, after all, Alabama prided itself on open admissions for "all the sons and daughters of our fair state."

Finally, in a fit of desperation, the board unanimously ordered the president to issue a press release saying that, though Miss Lucy had the intellectual qualifications, she had shown up as mentally unbalanced on the psychological tests we all had been forced to take during orientation week. Dr. Carmichael stood his ground, went to a special meeting of the trustees, and said that as long as he was president, Miss Lucy would be a student, since there was no conceivable reason to ask her to leave except that she was black.

The board took him at his word and sent him a hand-delivered letter, giving him forty-eight hours in which to resign or else be summarily fired. They said that his views were "incompatible with state policies and local custom." Dr. Carmichael took only twelve hours to decide: he sent a curt reply, announcing his resignation effective January 1st, adding that he could not in conscience carry out "state policies and local customs." That happened two days before school closed for Christmas vacation. A small but vocal band of students, of which I was one, was very sad to see him go. We went to the president's mansion with its elegant pair of curved staircases, its second-floor balcony, its French doors. We wanted to sing carols for O. C. and his wife. As I stood on the finely ground gravel of the driveway, shivering from damp southern winter cold and from the loss of this strong male figure in my life, he stepped out onto the balcony with Mrs. Carmichael. They sang with us, and then he spoke, sadly and warmly. He told us the truth: he was sorry to leave his post because he believed education was the only hope for improving race relations; he had not wanted to give the board the pleasure of firing him, so he had resigned. He had not hedged about why he was leaving. He would miss us. They cried, and so did we.

I cannot remember when Autherine Lucy stopped attending classes, but it was not long afterward. The NAACP advised her to drop out during fall semester, while the board of trustees set about its vicious campaign to get her off campus, and to reenter in mid-January when the courts would have upheld the Brown decision. The Alabama Supreme Court supported the autonomy of the university and its trustees, saying they had acted in the best interests of the student body. I wondered silently about Miss Lucy's best interests.

I only saw her a few times, but the memories remain sharp. Once she was walking alone up the steps of the library. Once she was getting into Mrs. Healy's front seat late one afternoon, to be whisked back to her cell for the evening. Once I passed her on the mall and smiled broadly but kept on walking to class. There was no student or faculty outcry to keep her in school. There was never a word about her exit in the school paper (the *Crimson Tide*), the *Tuscaloosa Journal*, the *Birmingham Post* or the *Montgomery Herald*. I asked Mrs. Healy toward the end of my freshman year, which would also have been Miss Lucy's freshman year, what had happened to her. Mrs. Healy looked into the distance, I thought back toward Michigan, where I was naively sure things like this never happened. Finally, in a tired voice she said, "It just didn't work—the university and the state aren't willing to obey the law yet."

The trustees installed a new president who signed a letter saying that Autherine Lucy was mentally unfit to attend classes and, therefore, for her own welfare, the university was suspending her "with no prejudice for future success."

My remaining undergraduate years included virtually no contact with blacks, but two experiences off campus burned their way into my brain to lodge for many years, unresolved and unassimilated. Both took place on Sunday afternoons in the public park next to the Birmingham Public Library, where my sister worked as head of the popular literature department. Both took place when I was nineteen.

It was the summer of 1956, a year or so after the Supreme Court decision. The NAACP felt the time had come to integrate more than downtown department stores, which, after all, wanted money even from blacks. The organization decided to focus on outdoor places where whites went to relax and be cool. They chose a large shady park next to the library's main branch. The previous year, they had systematically infiltrated the library itself. I remember Betty's story of her arrival at work on the morning after the court's decision. All chairs had been removed, stored no one knew where, whisked away in the night by evil spirits. The white people in Birmingham hated more than anything to sit down next to blacks. I was shocked that people who ran a library would behave the same as drugstore-counter owners. Betty reported that not a single white patron complained about having to stand up to read the *New York Times* or the latest novel or travel book or story about baseball's hall of fame. They would rather be inconvenienced than sullied. The chairs miraculously reappeared about a week later, and the tiny number of blacks who went to the library got to sit down if they chose.

My sister had to work one Sunday afternoon a month, and I often went with her. One Sunday we arrived about 12:30 and I noticed a group of people milling around on the fringes of the park. Since I seldom read newspapers or listened to the news on radio or TV, I had no idea that this was the Sunday chosen by the NAACP for black families to bring picnic lunches to that park. After Betty opened up her room, I went into the children's literature department where I usually read. I chose that spot because it had a side door that opened onto the park, where I could sit in the sunshine or stroll on the paths. That day I went outside almost as soon as I was settled at a table.

What I found froze me in horror. About thirty black people—fathers, mothers, and children of walking–talking ages; no babies, teenagers, or really old people—were having a group picnic after church. They all wore suits, best dresses and heels, the children in miniature versions of the same things. A crowd of rowdy whites, not nearly as well dressed or behaved, had gathered to shout and heckle. One of the men (I later learned that he was Martin Luther King's brother, A. D., the minister at a local Baptist church) started singing, "What a Friend We Have in Jesus" and was immediately joined by the rest. They sang and ate their sandwiches and potato chips amidst the booing and cursing around them.

The whites grew more abusive as their numbers mushroomed. I was scared but could not go back into the library and shut it all out. I stood, mute and paralyzed, as the minutes crept by. I wanted the black people to go home before somebody threw something at them or hit them. Unable to fathom why it mattered for them to have a picnic where they were so obviously not wanted, I also wondered why they had brought their children where they could not protect them.

Suddenly the crowd fell silent, and I heard sirens in the hot afternoon air. Police cars began arriving, first in twos and soon in platoons. I counted fifteen cars and knew there were more down the streets. At first, I was relieved, since I thought the police had come to ask the whites to move on and let the black families finish their picnic.

When I saw police jovially slapping white men on the shoulder, my fear returned. Still unable to move, I stood on the outskirts of the action and watched the big, fat police officers, their dark blue uniforms stained by huge half-moons under each arm and triangles down their backsides, open their car doors and let out unmuzzled German shepherds. Before I could register what was happening, the dogs were unleashed, and the police were shouting, "Sic 'em." The dogs raced toward the well-dressed, hymn-singing blacks, who jumped up and ran. They tried at first to stay together but then broke into little units, catching up smaller children who could not run fast without stumbling. Children cried, and women wailed to the deaf police to have mercy. Black men yelled to "call off your dogs" and Reverend King appealed to the white authority. That man was Police Commissioner Eugene Connor, commonly known as "Bull" because he was thick necked and tough and stubborn. His own men, all white, feared him. Reverend King made his way through the crowd of cheering whites and found Bull, shotgun on his hip and a big plug of chewing tobacco in his jaw. I could not hear their words, but Connor's only gesture before he had four policemen drag Reverend King into the nearest police car was to spit a healthy stream of brown liquid at the black minister. It landed somewhere below his knees, wetting his impeccably creased black trousers.

I saw dogs sink teeth into a woman's buttocks and rip her lovely dress. These angry German shepherds snarled at children's feet dangling from their parents' arms. The children became hysterical, a few even seemed to pass out, falling utterly limp in their protectors' arms. The dogs drew blood from ankles, calves, and, in the case of one rather large man who must have stumbled from lack of breath, a face. The whole event did not last more than half an hour. All the blacks were eventually cornered by the dogs and held at bay until the leering police arrested them. Some of the men stood firm with furious dogs all around them, and when a white cop touched them, always violently, they would relax into lifeless forms and let themselves be dragged off. This dead weight made transport harder for the already sweating police, and I was glad.

As they were carried to waiting cars and jail cells, the black men smiled and sang hymns. One came close enough for me to hear what he said as he faced a triumphant white mob, its dirty work being done by law enforcement officers: "We are obeying the law here, and you are breaking it. God will reward us all accordingly." He repeated this meekly but bravely, like a litany and a warning. I believed him and prayed hard for the next few weeks that God would see that I was not being cruel to those picnickers. I felt guilty and ashamed because, just as with Autherine Lucy, I had decent emotions but no will to act. My silent presence seemed assent.

When it was over, bits and pieces of picnic lunches lay strewn over the park grass. I went inside and only then let myself know how scared I felt, sitting in my straight-backed library chair, quiet and serene on the outside, shaking within. At six o'clock when Betty came in to fetch me, I said nothing about what I had seen. There was no news of it anywhere, and no one I knew talked about it.

Years later I learned that national TV had taped the scene, and people all over the country had seen Alabama's finest police force once again restore law and order, assert state's rights, and deny humanity to keep the race pure. Large dogs bit me in nightmares for the next few weeks, and until fairly recently I feared dogs and never wanted to live with one. I also hated police and cowards like me.

The next time Betty worked her Sunday shift, I went with her again. A large crowd of already angry whites circled the park adjacent to the children's room of the library. Betty seemed not to notice them. We went in, and I settled into my usual chair near fairy tales and mythology. But I went out into the park as soon as the doors opened to the public, noticing that virtually no one had come in.

There they were again—a group of very dressed-up black families, sweltering in the summer humidity but sitting proudly on bright tablecloths for their after-church picnic. Some of the adult faces were the same as the month before, and once again Reverend A. D. King was their leader. They must have come earlier this time, since the level of hostility was already pretty high by the time I arrived. There were more children. Had someone in charge thought their presence might appeal to the white women who taunted them? If more little children were along maybe even white police would think before turning loose dogs trained to be vicious. All these thoughts flew through my mind as I stood within the safe shadows of the granite building. In the middle of my fear, I felt strangely drawn to the scene and the blacks who were making it happen. I thought they were brave and I thought they were foolish. I watched the scene in the park as I would a horror movie, feeling relief at some deep level that punishment was being visited on someone besides me. I became a voyeur, not merely a spectator. I felt no allegiance to the white bigots who tormented the blacks; my sympathies were with the victims. But a contorted sense of relief, born of my unacknowledged privilege, was undeniably present. I was not glad that these quiet, peaceful people were being persecuted and hurt, only that it was not I.

Shortly after I took up my post, I heard the familiar sirens close and insistent. Fire trucks, rather than police cars drove up. Where was the fire? The only passenger car was Bull Connor's private, unmarked one, which arrived last. He emerged, minus his shotgun, and began to talk very quietly with the firemen, who in turn began to unroll their hoses and screw them to several hydrants nearby. They turned on the hoses, full force, and walked slowly toward the blacks, who were eating their sandwiches and singing hymns. I have no idea how many pounds of pressure are behind water that comes out of a fire hose, but it is enough to knock over a full-grown man. The group panicked as it had not done the month before. The barrage of water was somehow more terrifying than the dogs. Or maybe it was simply unexpected.

If the firemen trained their nozzles on adults, Bull caught them up short and yelled, "Do what I told you!" Then hard streams of spray tumbled the children, dressed in their Sunday best, head over heels. They were knocked up against tree trunks. They were driven down sidewalk paths, the skin on their legs or arms or faces grated off by contact with cement. They were sprayed directly in the face, which choked and blinded them. Their mothers went crazy at the sight and at their cries of terror and paralysis. I hid my eyes.

This Sunday's horror show was shorter than the first one but did more bodily damage and caused more spiritual pain to the blacks. Men tried to run in front of the hoses to absorb the water's force, but the firemen worked too fast for them. Mothers tried to throw themselves over children's bodies, but again the firemen proved too skillful. Those years of training hoses on a fire's center had been perfect preparation for this afternoon. Within fifteen minutes, they had satisfied themselves, turned off the water, neatly rolled up their hoses, climbed back into their mammoth trucks, and driven off, led by Bull with his hidden siren going full blast. No white person had made a single move to stop this atrocity, including me.

I retreated to the library, much more shaken by this experience than by the earlier one. When I left the scene, a small group of weeping, enraged blacks were trying to calm terrorized, water-soaked children. They swore at bands of whites who laughed and spat out phrases like, "That's what you jigaboos get for coming here and trying to take over our place. Why don't you just stay where you belong?" At first I was glad to hear the victims fight back at least in words, but when I realized that those curses included me, I felt guilty and scared. Six years later, while a graduate student in Madison, Wisconsin, I read John Milton's sonnet, "On the Late Massacre at Piedmont." This poem expresses the poet's rage at hearing of a battle in which people he saw as barbarians "rolled mother and infant down the rocks" of a cliff in order to win the day. The park scene leapt into my mind, and I had to stop reading and go for a long walk.

The second incident made the white papers on Monday morning, and I read about a "minor skirmish" in the park, "quickly handled by Police Commissioner Connor in his usual efficient manner." The story claimed that the only injuries were a "few skinned knees and stubbed noses." I never told anyone what I had seen.

At the same time that racism was becoming a tangible reality to me, I was struggling to keep my own special creativity alive. When I realized that I would not attend Chapel Hill or Duke because my father's unexpected death eliminated the requisite financial security, I let myself get excited about at least one aspect of the University of Alabama. Roy McAllister taught piano in the music department. A wonderful teacher and performer who studied every summer in New York with Madame Nadia Boulanger, he also happened to be my brother-in-law's brother. I had gone to a few of his recitals and been attracted to his patrician nose and deeply wrinkled brow. He and his family had visited us on several Sunday afternoons. On one of these occasions, Roy and my mother had fallen into a violent argument about the relative superiority of Rubenstein and Horowitz. Mamie was sure that Rubenstein was the finer because of the soul that so obviously poured from his hands. Roy found that soul marred by technical errors and preferred Horowitz, whose execution he found flawless, never mind that he played with less emotional investment. In the midst of their fight, Roy yelled something like, "Oh, you only speak from uneducated taste, whereas I'm a serious pianist and know the difference." Leon rushed his brother out of the house as quickly as possible.

This fracas occurred several years before my arrival on campus, but it may well have remained in Roy's mind; it certainly lingered in Mamie's. Naive in the ways of such feuds, all I thought about was having him as a teacher. When he agreed, though reluctantly, I was overjoyed. My weekly lesson was on Thursday at 12:30, and I looked forward to my hour even though I was being reintroduced to Miss Plosser's purists, Bach, Scarlatti, and Clementi. Roy's intensity pervaded the very air of his studio. Whenever he played a particularly difficult passage, I was excited by the contained emotion in his veined hands.

I very much wanted to please Roy, but that almost never happened during the year and two months I studied with him. From his point of view, work devoted to my advanced English class or my premed chemistry labs two afternoons a week signalled a lack of seriousness about the piano. Often, he interrupted my attempt to render a three-part invention with an impatient "You've been doing something besides practicing piano this week." But one day I played several pieces Bartok composed for his children in such a way as to win unadulterated praise. When I finished the fourth tiny étude, Roy paused before saying in a tone I would never hear again: "Well, Toni, Bela himself wouldn't have found fault with those." For days, I played that sentence in my mind as I walked to the library or fell into sleep.

Most days, however, we labored through the hour, he wincing at my obvious rustiness, I vowing silently to do better next time. At the end of our last lesson in May, Roy sat me down and tried to be fatherly: "I want you to spend the summer seeing how you really feel about the piano—try to set priorities, let yourself know how you feel when you play well and when you don't. We'll talk about it in the fall." While that summer after my freshman year is shadowy, I know I did not do any of those things. I never thought of talking about it with anyone, not even my roommate with whom I talked about most things. The topic seemed too intimate, like my sex life or my dreams—parts of me to be kept utterly private for fear of ridicule or rejection. In September, I returned to Tuscaloosa and told Roy I wanted to continue and that I was determined to practice more diligently.

That same fall, a friend of my sister, whom she had met at the library where he went for books about resorts on the Mediterranean, had returned to college on the GI bill. Wealthy and aimless, Tim Phillips told army stories about leaves in the Yucatan where he picked up Rita Moreno in a rented red sports car. He began driving me back and forth to campus, since my family trusted him. We enrolled in the same physics class and signed on for the same lab periods. Not liking labs, we talked openly while the assistant wrote equations on the board. After my glaring failures at dating all through high school, I was vulnerable to any friendly male. I went along with whatever Tim suggested, turning away from Toni the serious student, who had performed so beautifully for so long. Afternoons we rode around town looking at fancy houses, and, in defiance of college precautions, visited one of the several black barbeque outlets after dark.

Needless to say, my resolve about piano practicing faltered. As I was stumbling through a Bach three-part invention in early October, Roy jumped up from his armchair and yelled angrily: "You're betraying your talent. I won't go on watching you do that. You're good enough to become a concert pianist. I want you to decide by next week whether you're willing to work for that. If you are, fine, I'll help all I can. If not, I can't go on teaching you. Leave now and make your decision."

Concert pianists had come to Birmingham, and Mamie had taken me to hear them. Because I had seen females on the stage—the male/female teams of Vronski and Babbin and Lubaschutz and Niemenoff had played in town—I even understood that a girl could become such a person. Beyond that, I knew nothing about what Roy was asking me to decide. I told myself, "Concert pianists would not be home very much, might not even have homes. I want a house full of children and friends and holiday warmth." The seven days slid away.

When I walked into Roy's studio the next Thursday, I said with honest regret, "I guess I'm not going to work to be a concert pianist. But . . ." I was not allowed to finish my sentence expressing real love for the piano as a part of my life short of a major career. Roy snapped, "I thought as much. Well, it's pointless to sit down and go through another painful lesson. This is the end of your study with me. Good day."

That was on a Thursday about 12:45. On Saturday, I went down to the river flats with Tim, where we sat in his front seat with the car light on, playing gin rummy and drinking half a fifth each of warm bourbon. Before that moment, the only alcohol I had tasted was Mogen David, served in tiny, faceted wine glasses at Christmas. The bourbon burned as it went down but smoothed some of my raw nerves.

That evening was the first of countless spent on the river bank or similar spots. Though Tim continued to recount scenes of his picking up and flirting with models or actresses all over the southern hemisphere, he seemed completely oblivious to my body. His wanting to spend so much time with me suggested that something about me pleased him, yet we never got any closer than we could have in my living room in Fairfield. In fact, Tim seemed to prefer my mother and sister as ladies to whom he could pay court. I kept saying "yes" to his invitations, at first out of simple loneliness, but soon out of a fascination with how effectively alcohol deadened my feelings about not studying the piano any longer. If Tim used me as a convenient chum who provided entree into our house, I used him as a supplier of decent bourbon.

After a fall and winter of four nightly visits a week to the river flats with Tim and a bottle, I recognized a fearful dependence on alcohol. Spring was a little late in 1956, but when it came to Tuscaloosa, I could not distinguish the yellow-green buds on the trees that filled the quadrangle. Since watching them unfold had always been special, I panicked at the haze that kept me from them. I tied that hazy vision to my drinking and with characteristic speed, between eleven in the morning and dinner, I decided to stop. Since alcohol seemed inseparable from Tim Phillips, I concluded that I must also stop seeing him. When he came for me at the appointed time, I leaned in his open car door window and sputtered, "I'm not coming with you tonight or any other night; I'm giving up liquor and you." In the remaining months of his stay at the university, I remember only passing greetings when we found ourselves in the same place. My mother and sister inquired about his absence, and I lied, saying he had lost his heart to a sweet sophomore and had no time for mere friends.

Tim was the first male whom I found attractive and who wanted to spend time with me. Though we never so much as held hands, I turned our card-playing drunks into a fantasy sex life. My sorority sisters believed that I was finally doing the "normal" thing, and some even became concerned about the amount of time I was spending with "an older man." Up to this point, I had been valuable as someone whose grades were guaranteed to drive up the house's average. I did nothing to correct their impressions about the nature of our relationship, and when I suddenly stopped seeing Tim, I got a lot of sympathy about the "break-up." They included me in plans for movies or jaunts to the nearest fried chicken hut, attentions that went some distance toward filling the void created by Tim's banishment.

Awakenings

As I made my way through college, I became progressively less sure of myself except as an intellectual. My thirty extra pounds reinforced my conviction that I was not sexually attractive. Simultaneously, I had several close male friends, all of whom were gay. As a voyeur of their love lives, I learned about infidelity, rejection, passion returned and spurned, enthrallment to the beloved. They conveyed an image of sexuality shrouded in secrecy, threats of exposure with dire consequences, and the certainty of each great passion's lasting no more than a few months at best. Their stories never shocked me, and I took the seriousness of their feelings to heart. My sympathies were with them as suffering victims of a cruel society that refused them daylight relationships and expelled them for doing what every coed believed was part of a normal campus weekend. These young men's stories were my first knowledge of love between persons of the same gender.

Though as I moved into my twenties I was not surprised to learn of my male friends' sexual activity with people like themselves, I certainly made no connections to my own life. I knew of no women who loved other women; I had never seen or heard the word "lesbian." Nevertheless, I developed close friendships with some of my own sorority sisters and with those magical women in Pi Phi, and had my first extended friendship with a woman.

We met in English 1A, taught by Miss Locke, a staunch supporter of smart women. An achiever like me, Jean spoke long and clearly about Conrad and Keats, so I started walking out of class with her, prolonging our conversations. When we moved into the same sorority house, we chose to room together. Though most beds were housed on a vast sleeping porch, our room had a cot on which we spent idle hours, rubbing backs, dozing, talking about the meaning of life, crying or laughing about some event in our day.

In our romantic poetry course, we read Coleridge's "Christabel" and decided we were very like the two women in that gothic tale of evil and forbidden fruits. Our nicknames became "Chris" and "Gere" (the other character is called Geraldine), and we developed a private language around them and that poem. At another point, we listened constantly to a popular song called "The Green Door," whose refrain was, "What's going on behind the green door?" Our sorority sisters harbored various feelings about our three-year friendship, ranging from envy to downright spite. When we went into our room, closed the door for hours, and ignored the social life in the adjacent lounge, generous members worried, and the rest were infuriated. Once we came in from classes to find a sign tacked to our door. THE GREEN DOOR, it read in large, angry letters. We further enraged and alarmed our sisters by leaving it there, embellished with pencilled flowers and sketched-in windows. What went on behind that magic door excited me and left me without frustration since I never dreamed that I might want to take my amorphous feelings in any specific direction. We talked long and hard about poetry and plays, about why people did what they did, about our own dreams. We gossiped about our sorority sisters, sure that we were the most sophisticated among them.

In some way Jean and I were innocents: two girls who had led sheltered lives, groomed to become proper southern ladies, wives, mothers, churchworkers. Since the basis of our attraction was mutual intellect, it was only after I had made love to a woman that I fully grasped the complexity of what we had. Later such nonsexual primary friendships would leave me miserable, confused, and angry. But with Jean, I knew a warmth and closeness, an ability to rely on her that had been previously absent from my life.

During her senior year, Jean found an older man who had been a pilot in the Korean War. She dated him, went steady, married, had two daughters, and eventually, twenty-four years later, divorced him. When she asked me to be a bridesmaid, I of course agreed. Her decision left me feeling afraid and lonely: I was about to lose someone precious. Any day, at the slightest provocation, I cried. At one of the rehearsals, I met Jean's cousin, Wayne, who was to be a groomsman. Several years younger than I, Wayne was tall and skinny and full of acne. But he was Jean's cousin, so I liked him. When he offered me a ride home, so that the couple could be alone, I agreed. Before that night was over, we had engaged in some pretty heavy petting. We continued doing that, in spite of my mother's growing anxiety about my seeing him. Wayne and I had very little to talk about. He was anticollege, while I was busily applying for scholarships to graduate school. But I felt closer to Jean when I was with him, so I was willing to put up with boredom and a certain distaste for his boniness and bumpiness.

Shortly after Jean's wedding, I graduated. Having nothing I particularly wanted to do, I accepted a scholarship to complete a master's degree in nine months. I liked the free money and the challenge, since everyone said a master's degree took at least twelve months. Deciding on Vanderbilt as my academy, I made plans to drive to Nashville. It was the fall of 1958, and Wayne had decided to go to the University of Alabama and try to learn. He proposed that I come to Tuscaloosa before I headed north. Cut off from all my emotions except a dull missing of Jean, I went along with his plans. I lied to my mother and left for Nashville seven days early, ostensibly to "help with rush week." Though I officially stayed with a woman friend who lived in town, except for one sorority party, I spent most of my time with Wayne in his already messy apartment hardly big enough for him. Since we still had almost nothing to talk about, I read a lot while he pretended to be settling in, a process that involved moving piles of clothes and books from one side of the apartment to another. I fixed lavish dinners and tried to feel romantic about my escapade, but much of the time I just felt nostalgic, remembering long back rubs and endless talks I had always had with Jean. I kept wondering why Wayne could not be more like his cousin.

When he suggested that I stay the last night before my exodus north at his place, I offered no resistance. Understanding his request to include intercourse—a step we had always carefully avoided—I mustered the courage to ask him to take precautions. He answered, "Oh, yeah, I have some condoms in my dresser drawer."

Suddenly I was ten again, standing in my sister's room a few months after she and Leon had gotten married. As I opened her underwear drawer to put in some clean laundry, my eye was caught by a box that had a Greek warrior's head in profile and his body in armor. It read, "Trojan condoms," a phrase that filled me with some unnamed excitement. Sensing that the box had to do with Leon's being in our house with Betty, since I was sure the box had never been in my sister's drawer before, I took it out gingerly and opened it just enough to see a bunch of rubbery tan things that puzzled me. I never asked Betty about them, since I did not want her to know I was rifling her private things.

Wayne and I did indeed have intercourse, or what he called that. It lasted no more than fifteen minutes and took place in the pitch dark. I was disappointed: I had long wanted to see a man's body and had some notion that he might want to see mine. Wayne seemed utterly ashamed and in a great hurry. Consequently he was awkward and rough about the anatomical details that led up to his release. The instant that occurred, he was out of me and into the shower. No words were exchanged then or the next day about what had happened; no questions were asked about how I felt (this was, after all, my maiden voyage, and he knew it). As I lay awake in the moonlight, listening to late summer crickets and Wayne's interrupted breathing, I thought of novels I had read about first love and high passion. Inside my head, voices vied for supremacy: "You ought to be ashamed of yourself—not waiting until your wedding night." "I'll bet Harold Smith would have wanted to be gentle and playful before and after, maybe even have lain on the bed and talked about how magical it all was." "What a letdown—why does everybody make so much of something that hardly even happens before it's done with?" Next morning, an awkward silence hung in Wayne's apartment as we collected strewn clothes. I hurriedly threw clothes into my suitcase, saying, "Oh, don't bother with breakfast, I'll pick up something on the road." We both carefully avoided any exchange about what our being sexual might "mean." As I drove away to graduate school, Wayne mumbled something about having "forgotten" to put on his condom.

My rage lasted all the way to Tennessee and for the next three months. It was joined by terror when, days after my period was to have begun, I realized that I might be pregnant with Jean's cousin's child. That was 1958 in the South and abortions were done in back alley walk-ups by unlicensed, seedy "doctors." I did not know a soul in Nashville and could not think how I would find such a butcher. All the money I had was a modest weekly allowance; I knew the process was expensive. For the two months I did not menstruate, and the few immediately following my eventual bleeding, every young male I saw, in class, on the streets, in church or the grocery store, reminded me of Wayne and his awkward, silent, thoughtless attitude toward something about which I felt inherently positive, which I had anticipated for years.

In the months preceding my going to Vanderbilt, I had persuaded my mother that I was old enough at twenty-one to live in one of the official residential houses for female graduate students. We were about ten women of widely divergent backgrounds, studying everything from English literature to speech pathology and pharmacology. The woman who wanted to be a pharmacist was Kolinde Schroff, born in Bombay. She wore saris made from exotic materials: cotton for everyday use; a voile-like material when she wanted to look formal; silk for elegant celebrations. On her birthday, she asked several of us to wear a sari to the park where her party was to be held. That park was on the edge of town and housed an exact replica of the Parthenon, an edifice of which Nashvillians are terribly proud. Feeling distinctly international and luxurious, I glided along the grass in a teal blue sari flecked with gold thread. I felt more graceful than I could remember, and distinctly less vulnerable to men yelling compliments or obscenities from their car windows.

As we were dishing up the ice cream, a police car stopped near us. Its two occupants left the car and began sauntering toward our gathering. "What can they possibly want with us? We don't have beer and aren't making noise to disturb any of the families here." It seems we had crossed some invisible line of acceptable white attire—the officers said we were in "inappropriate" dress and would have to leave the premises immediately or be arrested for vagrancy. We agreed even as I remembered another park on another Sunday when police had forced people deemed inappropriate off the grass reserved for whites willing to conform to codes.

Kolinde cooked her own food in our communal kitchen and soon the house was redolent with the odor of cumin. I loved the pungency, but most of the other women complained that "Kolinde's food stinks." She smiled sweetly and kept right on making her curries. In all my vocabulary work, I had never come across words like turmeric, cumin, coriander, cardamom. Now I was not only learning to spell them but to distinguish their special aromas and particular tastes. And rolling them off my tongue—turmeric, cumin, coriander, cardamom—gave me distinct pleasure.

Kolinde was very dark brown with jet black hair worked into a single braid that reached down to the small of her back. She and I were half of a group that formed early in the fall and became inseparable.

One of the other two women was studying speech pathology even as she was preparing herself to become a Methodist minister's wife; the other was in animal psychology, which meant to me that she did studies on Siamese kittens whose feet were kept in test tubes to prevent them from having sensory experiences.

One Friday night in late October, we four decided to go to a movie. It was a major event, the first time we had stolen so long away from our studies. At the ticket window, we lined up with the speech pathologist first, me second, Kolinde third, and the psychologist last. As Martha Jo and I waited for Kolinde and Beth to move up, it happened. The young woman inside the ticket booth said in her deepest Tennessee accent, "You have to go to the line that's for coloreds. This here is the white line." She was talking to my friend Kolinde from India. Kolinde fell mute, so I stepped up and said, from the depths of my racist heart, "Oh, you misunderstand, Miss; Kolinde's not a Negro, she's from India." Unimpressed, the young woman repeated herself. We whites felt insulted for our friend. Martha Jo and I forced the ticket seller to give us back our money, saying, "If Kolinde can't buy a ticket here, we don't want to go to your old movie."

I was humiliated that Kolinde should be mistaken for an American black but oblivious to the racism that lay behind that response. Not understanding about hierarchies of oppression or competitive rankings within groups of color, I wanted to separate my friend from the ticket seller's prejudice. Because I still had not analyzed my attitudes toward blacks, I failed to learn the lesson presented at the box office, just as I failed to grasp the implications in the phrase "colored people." Kolinde was some color, not white; as such, she was inadmissible.

Nashville is the home of several colleges, among them Fisk University, one of the few all-black universities in the South. I had heard it was a good school, patterned after Vanderbilt, its students "clean middle-class Negroes from professional homes." During the fall semester, the English department at Vanderbilt got an invitation for graduate students to attend a foreign film festival at Fisk. The first thing that caught my eye was the alliteration. I decided to go, since I had seen such films in Birmingham and was curious to hear languages and see faces different from my own. Four other classmates wanted to go, so we planned to have dinner together before driving across town to the school.

The series began on a Friday with an open house before the film showing at 8:00 P.M. Curious about more than the foreign films, we decided to get there about 7:30 and meet some of the students. We talked animatedly at dinner about how exciting it would be to meet "educated Negroes," since we had known only servants who had little or no schooling. Because of late afternoon classes, we met at the cafeteria in school clothes: skirts and sweaters, socks and loafers for the three women; blue jeans with nondescript shirts and pullovers for the two men.

We arrived at the administration building on the Fisk campus at precisely 7:30 and walked into the designated hall. We were the only whites in a room of over a hundred blacks of all ages. The series was open to the community, and everyone was in formal attire: men in dinner jackets, bow ties, polished patent leather shoes; women in long dresses or short cocktail length skirts with filmy silk blouses, spiked heels, and gloves. They were all drinking punch from crystal cups, eating petit fours, and chatting.

I felt tacky because I looked tacky. I felt visible because I was. As we were standing on the outskirts of the group, cringing inside and wondering if we could escape before anyone saw us, a tall, handsome stranger walked over and introduced himself in tones I had never heard from anyone in the South. I later learned that he had spent a year at Oxford and now taught philosophy at Fisk. He laughed off our muttered embarrassments, brought us into the circle, put a punch cup and a little cake in our hands, and introduced us to the assembled company.

After what seemed hours, it was eight o'clock. We were ushered to seats, and the lights went down, hiding our gaucherie. I breathed for the first time since entering the room. I have no recollection of the movie because I spent the hour and a half trying to make sense out of what had just happened. What I knew most strongly was that I had been treated entirely differently as an outsider than I had ever seen blacks treated by us. No one turned angry dogs or fire hoses on me; no one called me degrading names or ordered me to leave. I was so moved by their civility and warmth that I went to all the movies in the series, wearing clothes that could serve for formal or informal occasions. I met women and men with vastly more interesting lives than my own or my friends'. I talked about racial politics and learned something about how educated blacks perceived the white world of Nashville and Vanderbilt.

Spring semester, the English department at Vanderbilt organized a film series of old American movies starring great actors. No invitation was sent to Fisk graduate students. I felt crazy: I had been taught from earliest childhood that the code of the white South was chivalry, civility, and hospitality; I learned that in Nashville, Tennessee, the persons exercising that code were black.

In addition to expanding my awareness of racism and coping with my terror over a possible unwanted pregnancy, I spent my early months at Vanderbilt trying to concentrate on Chaucer, Shakespeare, English ballads, and a history course. I also met a man different from any I had known. Adam liked to talk and, furthermore, was articulate on any subject having to do with art or culture. I was determined to avoid silent men, since the last one had almost cost me my future. Adam was tall, gently handsome with a fuzzy beard and a crew cut, soft-spoken, and shy in some way I instinctively trusted. I fell in love and spent that year at Vanderbilt pining for what I could not have. At our initial meeting, he had been quick to tell me about his fiancée in Louisiana: "Anna's wonderful—she plays the piano masterfully—we're totally committed, I want to spend my life with her, we are going to marry just as soon as I get my master's degree and a teaching job to support us." In an odd way, Adam was safe: I could fantasize to my heart's content, risking no more unwanted babies or painful hit-and-run incidents in dark apartments.

We spent endless hours together, and a loneliness I had known since my father died gradually eased. We climbed church towers to find dead pigeons in the belfry; we drove out into the country around Nashville to ogle sleek horses and smell bluegrass; we spent whole nights in the Episcopal church student lounge, talking intensely until we fell asleep on two long couches facing each other across a large expanse of carpet. Only once did we come close to unleashing erotic or sexual feelings. We had been at a late party and were both a little drunk. At the party, we had improvised at an upright piano, making a special kind of love. Riding home in the back seat of a friend's car, I sat on Adam's lap because we were too many for the space. As the driver swerved around a corner, our mouths touched and stayed longer than the maneuver warranted. During that suspended moment, I knew I would marry Adam if he asked me. We never spoke about that night, and we never repeated it. But it erased a nasty taste that rose in my mouth when I thought about my two or three unsatisfactory attempts to be sexual with men. My man-hating softened, I let myself experience vague and specific sexual feelings that never went beyond fantasies but that served to connect me with my body in ways that would eventually help me become a lesbian.

I left Vanderbilt for a teaching job in Mississippi, at an Episcopal girls' boarding school. I went there ignorant of two important facts— one about me and one about the town—both of which I would learn within weeks of my arrival. I did not know when I began working at a school attended by 150 girls, ages fifteen to twenty-two, that I was a lesbian. And I did not know that where I would live for two years was the last place to fall to General Grant.

Sure and Certain Knowledge

As I drove from Birmingham southwest into Mississippi, I marveled at how lush the country was and how soft the wind that came into my car window seemed. The closer I came to my destination, however, the more anxious I became. Eager to begin what I believed would be my career, I was worried about being so young. Barely twenty-two, I fretted over the fact that my students, never younger than fifteen, would sometimes be as old or older than I.

These worries vanished as I turned into the long boulevard leading up to my first job site. The school was situated in a Civil War memorial park in a sprawling colonial building where faculty and students lived, ate, studied, went to classes, had sexual fantasies, spied on each other, and fought for privacy. My room was on the third floor; the window nearest my bed looked out onto a large cannon pointing directly at me. Because there were no movies worth seeing and only one decent place to eat fried chicken, I spent a lot of time driving or walking in the many-acred park. I learned that each state fighting in the Civil War had been awarded a section in which to erect a memorial to the event. By allowing northern states to have space, the town fathers could pride themselves on their liberalism. I discovered, however, that blacks rented shacks in the sections assigned to the North, while wealthy Mississipians held large tracks of land in the southern portions. Streets were unpaved in the northern sections but mowed and planted with day lilies along the shoulders of southern sections. The war was being prolonged at the levels of civil engineering and landscaping. It felt ludicrous, since in a moment of largess, designers had jumbled up northern and southern states. The result was that I could drive on smooth asphalt for the two miles designated

111

for Alabama, only to fall into mammoth mud holes while maneuvering Vermont's five hundred yards.

During the two years between 1958 and 1960, when I lived in that park, I saw very few black people and met none. They were never on downtown streets when I shopped and seldom were seen outside their park dwellings during the daytime. I never found out where else the town was allowing them to live. Not even the school's kitchen or grounds crew were black. The longer I listened to local residents, the more logical the blacks' invisibility became. The town still talked about General Grant as a monstrous firebrand. I was taken to river bluffs from which the brave men of Mississippi had defended their land and other miscellaneous possessions (wives, children, darkies, cattle) for 131 days. They were finally defeated by cleverness—a Yankee trait. It seems the general concluded that he would never scale the bluffs from the river, so he sent battalions around back of the southern troops, surprised them, and won. That in itself was seen as cowardice, since no "real man" sneaks up on his enemy.

Because the town fell on July 4th, every year merchants took down their American flags and installed black ones as a sign of mourning. Not understanding this symbolism, but knowing of the use of such flags by European anarchist groups, I once asked a drugstore owner if that was their meaning. He walked away enraged, constrained from attacking me only by virtue of my being a "southern lady." I decided that in such an atmosphere black people in 1959 stayed under cover because they could only remind the white townspeople of General Grant and the collapse of slavery.

That first job was the hardest I will ever have. I was the English department. That meant I taught three high school classes, in addition to freshman and sophomore courses in the junior college wing. As a perfectionist, I believed each student should write a theme a week. So every weekend for the two years I worked there, I graded and commented generously on some seventy or eighty papers. Many students found their voices in my classes and went on to good colleges, all out of the South at my urging.

The students stayed in my classroom after school to talk about eternal verities and other equally unmanageable topics. And they worked hard at reading, memorizing, writing about literature by all the major white male authors. I did not teach a single female writer. Out of class, we spent idle hours walking in the lovely woods surrounding the school or shopping in the tiny town on Saturdays, when students were allowed off campus without an official chaperone.

My car was the subject of one of their many projects. It was a baby blue Volkswagen, the first car bought on my own, though I had only made one payment before my arrival. The girls decided it had to have a name and for days worked on possible options. Finally they settled on "Beatrice Portinari," which combined their fascination with my story about Dante and his ethereal love, muse, idol, and their loose Latin coining of a word to mean "that which carries McNaron," "porti-nari."

One of the high school seniors, April, began spending late afternoons talking about music and nature and how much she adored whichever writer we were studying. She was tall and willowy with silky-looking dark brown hair that hung down around her shoulders. Her deep set brown eyes looked questioningly at me until I was not sure what to do next. She liked French almost as much as English, and gradually I began reading French with her, telling myself I needed to keep up my skill since I was on my way back to more graduate study.

When her teacher assigned Saint-Exupéry's *Le Petit Prince* as optional reading, April jumped at the chance, suggesting that we read it together before compulsory evening chapel. After a day or two of reading at adjacent desks in my classroom, I proposed that we retire to my room on the third floor where we could be more comfortable. Once there, I realized that the way to do that was to sit on my single bed, since there was only one chair at the small desk provided for letter writing. So tall, willowy April and I began translating a story about a strange and wonderful attachment between a little boy who has fallen from the sky and a fox, a story about taming and being tamed.

Since my dormitory room faced west, our late afternoon sessions were framed by breathtaking sunsets, which we interrupted translation to watch. Kneeling on my narrow bed, we stared out my little oval window, commenting on colors and rays and the beauty of it all. We tried to ignore the cannon on the hill. After one such hiatus, April lay down on my bed instead of sitting back on its edge to continue Saint-Exupéry. "Looking at those last rays of sunlight has made me drowsy," she said. She napped for the fifteen minutes before chapel, while I sat uneasily in the lone chair watching her. Unfamiliar pleasurable feelings were periodically erased by waves of fear. What did it mean that I looked so tenderly at this student who trusted me—or she would not be napping on my narrow bed in the growing dusk? None of my gay male friends' stories entered my mind as I searched frantically for some mooring onto which to pin my strange emotions. It never occurred to me that April might be having similar feelings or even be acting in ways that elicited mine. Since I had never asked her about her past, I had no idea of her sexual history, though she was not at all surprised or awkward when we first made love.

At the end of fifteen minutes, I realized that I had to awaken her or run the risk of missing chapel and being turned in. Attendance was taken of both students and faculty by the dean of women, Agnes Crane. She stationed herself at the back of the church with a clipboard and several alphabetical lists. If a girl missed once without an excuse, she was called in to chat with the rector. If she missed a second time, she was denied her shopping or dating privileges for three weeks. Three times and her parents were called for consultation preparatory to asking her to leave. If faculty were absent, Agnes cornered us somewhere inappropriate like inside a cubicle in the ladies' room. Standing over April as she slept, I broke into a cold sweat. I called to her softly but she seemed not to hear. When I knew that I was going to have to touch her, I gingerly shook her left shoulder with two fingers and saw her eyes open slowly and a shy smile spread over her face. My impulse was either to enfold her in my arms or to run out of the room. Doing neither, I hurried us off to chapel where we arrived as the rector was saying the Sanctus. Agnes erased check marks on two pages, and I registered that she not only knew we were late but that we were late together. I felt instantly cautious, angry, and protective.

Within a week of her initial nap, April and I had lain down side by side on my single bed. Sleepy from translation, she had once again reclined for the half-hour before chapel. Tired myself from a long night of paper grading, I joined her, not consciously suspecting what could so easily happen. Again April seemed to drift into a sound sleep, while I lay wide awake, my mind filled with thoughts and my body with new desires, not present when I had slept with Wayne or even when I had felt passion and tenderness for Adam. Over the next month, our progress on the bed went from long soulful looks to seemingly innocent hugs to a day when we kissed. As a girl, I had experienced mild discomfort at 1940s movies when Clark Gable and whoever was his current flame filled the silver screen with their French kisses. Their lips seemed too parted, too moist, too hungry, especially his. But when April and I kissed, all I felt was excitement. Not surprisingly, we became lovers shortly after that first kiss.

Neither of us felt awkward or shy about how to make love, but I cannot remember what we actually did or how that felt. I remember my experience with April as incandescent, although I have no language with which to describe it.

Our initial setting was the logical place: my bed. But not even faculty doors in the dormitory had locks. We began to feel anxious and to interrupt our delight when we thought we heard footsteps outside or someone turning the door handle. Once we were barely able to spring up and rearrange our clothing before a student came in to ask me about some poem by Alexander Pope. She had not bothered to knock, and I felt the same way I had as I saw Agnes Crane erase her check marks in chapel: watched, suspected, guilty without quite knowing of what. After that narrow escape, I determined to find a more private, preferably lockable place for us.

But before I could locate such a haven, I was called into the rector's office. The head of our school eventually became presiding bishop of the Episcopal Church of America. That morning in 1958, he tried to preside over my dismissal, but I refused to cooperate. He told me that a student had come to him with a "sickening story" of having seen me the previous evening kissing April in the back of chapel. My immediate response was, "Call her in and have her say that to my face." Maybe I had read of such melodramatic scenes in novels and remembered the stoolie's collapsing in the face of the virtuous accused. Whatever my model, I was reversing the scene: I was asking a young woman in one of my classes, where I insisted that students name whatever reality they saw in literature, to look me in the face and deny that she had seen what she had indeed seen. April and I had taken to staying at prayers until everyone else had finished. Then we met quickly in the foyer for a few words, some small gesture of endearment, and a goodnight kiss.

The rector agreed to the meeting but stipulated that April be present as well, hoping that she would betray us. While he sent for the informant, I rushed to the student lounge, which was in a separate building fondly called the Play House. Finding April smoking with her choir friends, I pulled her aside and told her of our plight, that she would have to submit herself to the interview with the rector and the as-yet-unknown informer. Once we gathered in his office, the student looked at me, burst into tears, and stammered something about being mistaken or just exaggerating again. Stymied, the rector's anger flared, his face reddened. He sent us all away, shutting the door loudly behind him.

The rector continued his accusations over the next year. Steeled against what was to come, I would enter his office and hear the door shut firmly behind me. I waited for him to lock it, since his office did have that capacity for privacy. Usually we were alone, though sometimes Agnes was there with her ubiquitous clipboard. Twice we were joined by the dean of academic affairs, Henry Hyde, who not only liked me but thought me a superb teacher. The rector opened each of these grillings with the same phrase: "Toni, I'm going to have to ask you to leave if you don't change your behavior. You're corrupting the young and I can't allow that." His fantasies of how I was doing that must have upset him a great deal because, by the end of this brief opener, his face would be covered with ugly red blotches. My responses were pretty uniform, too, ranging from "I don't understand what you're talking about" when he was general in his condemnation, to "But you have no evidence and so you can't fire me" when he mentioned April specifically.

Once when the rector was particularly vicious, Henry intervened, reminding him of my excellent work with the students, bringing hard evidence in the form of their devotion to literature, their memorization of endless lines by numerous poets, their long, cogent papers written and copiously responded to every week. He also reminded his boss that I was the only English teacher they had, and it would be impossible to replace me mid-year. The rector sputtered and fumed but backed off for that interview. My gratitude to Henry was expressed in renewed efforts to do my job superbly; my students thrived while I consistently gained weight, drank too much, and slept poorly.

My initial confrontation with the rector heightened my sense of urgency about finding a private place for April and me to meet. A place presented itself within the next week. My classroom was across from the library in the basement of the main building. It opened onto a narrow corridor that led to piano and chorus practice rooms. Sounds of students playing Chopin or Bach and of young voices lifting hymns of praise comforted me on evenings when I sat alone at my desk grading yet one more student theme. In that corridor were two doors: one to a toilet and the other to some unknown space. Inside the second door, I found a tiny room full of trash, part of an oil furnace, and a small metal box just inside the door in which lay a lead key. A security system comprised of several of these little boxes was strategically located around campus. Evenings, an aging watchman patrolled the grounds, checking in at each watch box by inserting its key into a round clock slung over his shoulder. I never figured out how that activity could possibly alert him to anything amiss, but the watchman was quite faithful. In order to determine his interaction with the empty space next to the bathroom, I observed him for four consecutive nights. His habit was to reach around the corner of the door, bring out the key that he inserted into his clock, perform the requisite ritual, and then return the key. During this period, I also registered his schedule of rounds, so I would know precisely when he would need to be able to reach into our room.

At no point in his proceedings did he do so much as shine a flashlight into the abandoned space, so I decided to make that little room our everywhere, though it had neither lights nor a window. Every night for two weeks, I went directly to my classroom after supper, ostensibly to grade papers. Part of each session was spent filling my two wastebaskets plus the ones in each empty practice room with as much trash as I dared without raising the janitor's suspicions. Finally, the room was empty of debris. I cleaned it as best I could, installed a padlock on the inside, gave April the second key, and hoped for the best.

When I felt all was under control, I invited April in for our first evening in privacy. I bought flowers, though it was too dark to see them. There, in that literal closet, in constant fear of the curious or fatal knock, my gentle and loyal first lover and I talked and cried and made love.

By and large, my scheme worked, though we had a few narrow escapes. The worst was the appearance of the watchman fifteen minutes before his appointed time. We were lying on our clothes making love; I was experiencing as I always did the sheer luxury of that, compared with our contorted squirming amidst skirts, hose, garter belts, underthings, blouses. I recall April's having just laughed softly at something I said about her body's resembling a flower—we both referred often to the other in terms right out of the English romantic poets. Suddenly the door was pushed hard, the padlock jangled ominously; after a few seconds, the watchman pushed even harder, assuming perhaps that something had mysteriously gotten wedged against the door. I motioned for April to grab her clothes and get behind the door. I threw mine on, talking to him all the while about having bought a lock for the room so I could have a little hideaway from all the students wanting to sit in my room and talk after hours. By the end of this outlandish tale, I was more or less dressed and could let him in. He pushed open the door, little aware that right behind it stood a stark naked student who might at any moment break out into a sneeze or cough or laugh or uncontrollable cry of sheer terror. His motions with the lead key were reluctant, as if he sensed my lie. But he finished clocking our station and must never have spoken to the rector about this strange occurrence or even about my use of the room.

Once he left the furnace room, I waited to hear the side door open and close on its slightly rusty hinges, indicating his exit from that part of the building. Then I drew April from her hiding place, and we collapsed into tears and laughter. That near miss happened in February, and I never really relaxed again, though we continued to meet when our schedules allowed. We never spoke of our escape any more than we spoke about any part of our relationship. But the scene of our touching and kissing and of my discovering something new and powerful about myself in a dark hole intended for garbage haunts me.

My closest friends at the school taught art and music, and were very good at it. I remember the art teacher's invitation to her dormitory room for late night tea, where she looked me hard in the eye and asked, "Is there anything I can do to help, Toni?" I was not able to answer her. Too much was understood, too little had been articulated. The effort fell flat, and we both sat awkwardly with our cups and our mutual pain. I found out, after neither of us taught at the school any longer, that she had been fired from her previous job for exactly the same "offense" as my own. Even more frightened of the real topic between us than the art teacher, the music teacher simply tried to love me and show support. No one of us ever said a word about what was going on. When I first read Adrienne Rich's "To a Woman Dead in her Forties," I wept twenty-year-old tears for the three of us trapped in that hothouse environment, singing, painting, and speaking about poetry, unable to touch any of our personal scars or to name any of our real joy.

Because it is still easier for me to blame a man or men than it is to acknowledge the depth of patriarchal thinking in all of us, I want to talk about Agnes Crane. She and the rector were old church friends, and she and the academic dean hailed from the same town in Arkansas. She had five grown sons, though no longer any husband. Her energies went into flirting with the male staff and fussing over "her girls," as she called the students. My popularity undoubtedly caused her pangs, since she had been chief confidante before my arrival.

Even before April and I became lovers, I had discovered that Agnes could not be trusted with any confidence. Once I shared my early impressions of the college freshmen, usually young women unable to attend prestigious schools but embarrassed to go to a local public junior college. One of those freshmen confronted me shortly after my talk with Agnes: "Mrs. Crane says you prefer the high school girls because they are quicker and more verbal and because they adore you. Is that true?" Though twenty-one-years old, I felt eight again, coming home from school or play to hear my mother questioning me about a confidence I had just risked sharing with a playmate's mother or a teacher I thought I could trust.

From the moment in chapel when I watched her erase checks by my name and April's, I guarded myself in Agnes's presence, understanding that she was against me in some intangible and significant way. About a week after my first scene in the rector's office, she waylaid me after supper and insisted that I "come have some tea" in her room. Her room was filled with photographs of her children at every age, engaged in every conceivable ultramale activity: little boys on ponies; slightly bigger boys in their Little League ball uniforms; teenagers playing football; older boys holding up large dead fish or sitting in speed boats grinning into the sun. No image of her husband existed. Our decorating tastes were antithetical, with Agnes's running toward pinks and frills while mine leaned toward wood or rough-textured burlaps and corduroys. Being in her apartment reminded me of home; every surface was covered by ornaments. I felt once again that I had to keep myself as narrow as possible or I would upset some valuable and appear clumsy.

Agnes was all smiles and solicitations, asking about my classes, my family, friends back home. The crunch came early: "And is there someone special back in Birmingham waiting for your letters and visits?" I knew she did not mean my mother or best friend, Jean. Agnes was fishing about the men, or more hopefully, the man in my life. My sparse "no" concerned her. What followed was a tortuous recital of the need for heterosexual bonds and most especially for children to "steady" us women and "give us a focus." I listened politely, noticing the wings of sweat fanning out under each arm of my blouse, wondering when I could go. April was waiting in my classroom, and we only had forty-five minutes until the student curfew bell sounded. I finally excused myself "to prepare my classes," but as I was opening the door, Agnes sidled over, put an arm around my shoulders, and assured me that I could tell her anything that was bothering me. Smiling weakly, I thanked her, saying nothing was troubling me. As I left, she said for the first time a sentence I was to hear often during the rest of that nightmarish year: "Toni, you'll understand all this better after you've had five sons." At the time I assumed she meant I would be fine if I were just like her, since that was the size and gender of her brood. More recently, I have wondered if she was admitting to some love for women in her own background, which she forcibly stamped out by producing a brace of boys.

In the months after that awkward tea, Agnes made me her project. Evenings found her skulking around my classroom, offering ever slimmer explanations for her presence. Suddenly my room became attractive to her, and she would burst in without even a soft knock, saying, "Oh, I was just up here [on the third floor] and thought I'd stop in your room for a view of the river." Cannon you could see from my window—the river, only in the dead of winter when all leaves were off the trees, and this was early November. When I became as cool as I dared, she backed off and convinced lonely students to spy on me. I bore Agnes very hard feelings for her infringements, probably displacing my own guilt about my earlier trick with the student informant. We were all caught in a web that necessarily comes to surround personal lies, secrets, and silence. The necessity for my relationship with April to remain hidden was bound to mean complicity, unseemliness, and base actions on all sides.

The most hurtful part of the dean of women's campaign was her determination to force me to see the ill effects my friendship was having on April. Always tall and thin, she had lost weight by spring, what with trying to live a regular student life and her clandestine one with me. The strain of juggling and lying showed, and I worried. Though I bought special treats that would help her gain weight, no amount of malted milks or candy did the trick. My lover simply began to look peaked by late March. Agnes noticed, of course, and thought she might reach me through April, since her more direct efforts were failing. I remember one especially grim interview where the only topic was: "Have you noticed, Toni, just how bad April looks?" As she listed the signs—loss of weight, circles under her eyes, increased cigarette consumption, jittery nerves and poor temper, inability to sleep well—I felt myself sinking under the sheer onslaught of data. I agreed to having noticed some of these symptoms but insisted that she had occasion to see April in more settings than I: "After all, Agnes, you're her dorm mother, and I am only her teacher." Both of us knew my comment was a particular lie.

After that dreadful scene, I had a long talk with April, trying to be sensible, saying that she was not the cheerful, happy person she had been in the fall. I suggested we stop meeting in the dark room. Flatly refusing to stay away and assuring me that she would cut down on cigarettes and get more sleep, my lover stuck it out until graduation day. We had talked in the final weeks of school about my coming to visit her in Georgia, where her family lived. Setting a date for the end of summer, we agreed to write twice a week and to call periodically.

Graduation arrived and all the parents and siblings of the seniors invaded campus. They brought trade to local motels and hotels but put a strain on the school's kitchen staff, who had to feed a couple hundred more mouths. I was anxious to meet April's parents; she had written them about her "keen English teacher," saying we had become friends outside class. They had responded either with positive remarks or neutrally, so I felt I had a good chance to be liked. Her father taught English literature at a southern university, and I assumed her mother would be like my mother's friends in the neighborhood and at church. I felt no qualms about conversing with either of them.

What I omitted from my fantasy was the extent of the rector's anger. As I would learn from Father Hyde, the rector felt it his duty to have a private chat with April's parents before they met me, telling them in unimaginable terms about my dire influence of their daughter, urging them to get her home as quickly as possible and to discourage further contact with me. Unaware of this interview, I approached the meeting with a strange eagerness. The academic dean did the honors, saying something very complimentary about me. I extended my hand to April's father, only to find it dangling in space for the first time in my life. I was shocked and crushed. Her mother was cooly polite in a way southern ladies are taught to be in awkward social situations. Only her little brother smiled. He had not attended the private meeting and so did not know I was a monster.

Excusing myself as quickly as possible, I fled to my third-floor room and wept bitterly. I drank too much that night with my friends in art and music, and left for home the next day depressed and fearful. I wrote April immediately, trying to be casual, hinting that maybe my summer would be too busy to get to Athens after all. I waited in agony for her reply, only to wish it had been longer in coming once I read it.

She wrote briefly and stiffly: "Thank you, Toni, for all you've been and done for me this past year. I really appreciate it and you a lot." Then came a brief paragraph that confirmed my sense that the entire note had been dictated by the man who had found it impossible even to touch me. "My father forbids me to receive or send any more letters to you under the circumstances. All my phone calls will be monitored, and I am to have no visitors from All Saints' this summer while I regain my health and color." It was signed, "Sincerely, April."

That letter was more devastating than the year of office run-ins with the rector because it seemed a betrayal of me and of the reason for our suffering. I spoke to no one about my pain and spent a lonely summer that ended in a six-week vacation with my mother, up the Atlantic seaboard to Washington, New York, Quebec, and the Gaspé Peninsula. Every day I thought of April and the warmth and closeness we had gone to such lengths to achieve and maintain. To have all that snatched away left me isolated and bereft. I would return to the school and its distinctly southern ghosts for a second year and be as coldly aloof from students as I had been accessible. I would be celibate because it was simpler than finding my passion only to have it denied me. Someone had slammed a heavy door in my face, and I did not want a repeat performance.

On the surface, my second year in Mississippi was quiet. I taught well, left my classroom when my last class was over, and retired to my room to read. I had been given space where only faculty lived; the doors had individual locks, and students were not welcome. The authorities allowed me in, ignoring their own waiting list, in hopes of "containing" me and keeping me away from "their girls." I was happy with the privacy; it helped me live a hermit's life fit for the pervert the rector's lectures, Agnes's condescension, and April's father's disgust had named me. I was best kept away from impressionable youth unless a literary text and a lot of distance lay between us.

All that year I continued to gain weight, to drink far more than I should, to stay up late grading endless student themes I had assigned to guarantee myself no free time. The art and music teachers and I continued our Friday night vigils at the local chicken emporium, but I concentrated more on the food and bourbon than I did on conversation. The one purely positive fact of this year was my confirmed sense of myself as a teacher. I loved my work, no matter what whirlwind of pain and confusion raged around me. I remembered my four months of practice teaching at the end of college. Working in the local high school, I discovered my gift for catching and holding students' attention. Refusing to wear high-heeled shoes ("After all, how else can the students distinguish between themselves and you?" our supervisor intoned), I found countless ways to stand out as the teacher. Even boys who generally booed when it was suggested they read Shakespeare came to my sessions prepared and eager to talk about why Brutus could not just feel good about killing Caesar or why Pip had to be brought to his senses after he comes into his inheritance. I was one of the lucky ones, as I would come to understand. Not only did I enjoy my work, but I had found it on my first try.

In the midst of my malaise, I met Harold, a senior at the local public high school. His English teacher asked me to tutor him in poetry and playwriting. He actually wanted to be a painter, so I was less helpful than his school had hoped.

He began coming over several afternoons a week to sit in my classroom, just as April had. Since his presence helped me to display an acceptable self, I left the door open for all to see. By the time I met him, I was lonely, so I also welcomed our time together, especially when we went to a movie on those rare occasions when something worth seeing played at the local picture show. He sketched me once in colored chalks, and I carried that drawing around for years. I must have figured in Harold's erotic fantasies because one night, under the porch chandelier, he leaned over to kiss me. I did not resist but rather thought, "I hope Agnes Crane and the rector are looking." While I may have used Harold, I also had great ambivalence toward him. Still confused and mute about my own sexual development, I was flattered by his attention. Finally, after all those years of trying to date, I seemed attractive to a boy. Part of me had always assumed I would marry and have children, so Harold's adolescent courting "fit" my expectations better than my previous year's underground passion with a woman. The fact that he was satisfied to hold hands, be affectionate, and occasionally kiss coincided with my need to give and receive warmth while avoiding sexual passion.

At the same time that this young man was drifting around the edges of my life, I was helpful if not friendly with the girls I taught. From verbal clues, I guessed that several had understood all that had happened the previous year and wanted to befriend me. Unable to tell them anything, I was distant with them. One senior in particular, Nella

Day, tried to talk with me after class about writing and poetry, but I snubbed her. She was very bright, lived in the Southwest with wealthy parents, and had scars on her face from too many x-ray treatments prescribed as an acne cure. I liked her and knew that I could depend on her.

Most of the students were willing to forgive and forget whatever feelings of neglect or jealousy they had harbored while I had ignored them for my lover. In fact, the senior class dedicated the school annual to me over the fierce objections of the rector and Agnes. It must have galled them to have someone they considered a pervert honored in so public a manner. I cried when the students presented the first copy to me at assembly and marveled when many parents expressed appreciation for my insistence that their daughters work hard and for my belief in their abilities and creativity. In particular, Nella's father thanked me effusively, inviting me to visit if I could get away during the summer. The contrast with the previous year was startling.

As I packed to leave my first job, a knock came at my door. I opened it and found Nella standing somewhat shyly outside, asking, "May I come in and say goodbye, Miss McNaron?" After some standard remarks, she said she hoped I would accept her father's invitation. I held out my hand to shake hers only to have her smile and embrace me. That summer we wrote every other day and talked several times by long distance. At the end of August, I went to the Southwest on my way to Wisconsin from Alabama over loud protests from my mother that it was miles out of the way. I knew Nella and I would become lovers during my visit.

She was a good choice because she was open about her love of women and because she obviously relished her body and my own. I first heard the word "lesbian" from her. Before that, I had known only what I felt and understood that society deemed it wrong. We sustained our relationship over the next two years, while I went to graduate school in Madison and she attended a good university in Texas. The day my doctoral prelims were over, I got into a friend's old Nash Rambler and drove nonstop to see her. I stayed near campus, visited a few English classes and met her professors, toured her dormitory. The rest of the time we made happy and continuous love in my motel room.

As I was about to leave, Nella shyly told me that April had gone to school at her father's university under his watchful eye, been selected sweetheart of some fraternity, became engaged to the captain of the football team. That was the last I ever heard of my first lover.

I paid a second visit to Nella at her home. It was financed by her father who insisted that I accept his help since I was on a meager fellowship. Wanting very much to see my lover, I accepted this bizarre offer. The visit went along without incident until one morning when Nella, her younger sister, and their mother decided to motor to the nearest town to shop for clothes. Not included in this outing, I planned to read Tennyson for my next week's classes. Mr. Day (K. C., as he insisted I call him) asked me to lunch at his dining club, where women could come only as guests of the all-male membership. But before we went to that club for elegant plates of chicken salad, fruit slices, and a parfait, he tried to have intercourse with me.

Feeling the specialness of the occasion, I had dressed in my nicest dark blue skirt with a blouse embroidered along the neck and sleeves. When K. C. pulled into his drive before lunch, I gathered up my gloves and purse, eager to be escorted to so fine a place by so fine a man. But once inside, he wanted us to chat a bit, since his reservation was not for forty-five more minutes and it took only ten to drive to the club. He went into his daughter's bedroom, motioning me after him. Standing too close to me, K. C. suddenly drew me into an awkward embrace, and I felt the pressure of his big hands urging my body backward toward one of the twin beds. Feeling simultaneously terrified and safe in his strength, I offered no struggle. After considerable fumbling with my clothes, he moaned, "Let me put it in." I refused, and he did not force me; he settled for rubbing my vagina with his fingers. After what seemed an interminable period, he stood up so I could get off the bed and arrange myself. He had never even taken off his lightweight summer jacket or loosened his tie.

What I remember most clearly is how red K. C. got and how deeply his breath came and how much hoarser his voice was than usual. Stunned, I had let him fondle me. Part of me even thought I had achieved some new level of acceptability if a mature man was attracted to me. If he comprehended the relationship between Nella and me, part of the price of his acceptance was granting him this seamy favor. When we were both presentable, he drove us to his club where I met several of his cronies. He felt no need to tell me to keep our secret since he assumed I would never mention the incident. I never spoke of it, indeed stopped remembering it until about ten years ago, when, listening to a woman talk about her uncle's sexual abuse of her, I suddenly was propelled back to that morning, full of shame and rage.

Nella and I separated before she graduated from college. I lost track of her until recently, when I located her in a nearby midwestern city, living with her successful doctor husband and their one biological and two adopted children. Children had been the stumbling block to continuing our relationship: she desperately wanted them. She preferred women for her emotional and sexual pleasure, but being a mother seemed more important than either of these. So we parted, and she found a kind man with whom to live out her life. Once, in about 1984, we saw each other briefly when she and her husband were in Minneapolis for a medical convention. After a strained but civil lunch and before a tour of my house, Nella asked me somewhat cryptically if being with women was "enough," if I might not be "lonely."

Advanced Studies

*A*fter a long, solitary drive north in my second Volkswagen, forest green this time and packed to the roof, I arrived in Madison bone weary. My blind date and old friend from Tuscaloosa, Joe Wheatley, miraculously was getting his Ph.D. at Wisconsin and had eagerly agreed to ease me into the local culture. When he met me, however, it was with changed plans—he could not host me around town that first weekend because he needed to drive to Mundelein, Illinois, where his lover taught high school. I was to stay at his apartment while I found one of my own; I knew no one else. Not wanting to abandon me completely, Joe had asked a good friend to stand in for him. So it was that I met Barry, a short, fiesty man who held radical political and literary ideas and had small tolerance for those who did not.

Barry offered to take me to some of the local beer gardens on State Street, the heart of the student quarter. Grateful for companionship, I quickly agreed. At about eight o'clock we set out on what would be an amazing evening. At our second stop, I had barely accustomed my eyes to the near total darkness when I saw a sight that stopped me in my liberal tracks. Seated at the bar was a couple: she was white; he was unmistakably black. My expression must have given me away because Barry touched my elbow and said, "So what's up, Toni? You look like you saw a ghost."

The ghost was from my southern background. While no one in my immediate family had ever railed against mixed-race dating or couples, the very air I had breathed for twenty-four years had been fouled with that nameless terror, "miscegenation." I thought I had rid myself of my racist roots by speaking positively about Dr. King, by loving Josephine dearly, and by driving north. "I've never seen a mixed-race

127

couple, Barry, and it's just a shock, I can't help it." I could not say more since opening my mouth to say anything made it clear that I was about to be nauseated; instead I rushed to the ladies' room.

Before that evening was over, I had drunk a lot of Wisconsin beer and told a comparative stranger my feelings about the South—all negative. Several times I had to say the word "Negro," since we were talking about black–white relations and "black" had not entered our vocabularies. Barry told me toward the end of our talk that I had to do something about my pronunciation. Defensively, I snapped, "But I'm very careful to say 'nigra' as my mother taught me—she forbade me as a young child ever to say 'nigger'—it would have hurt our maid's feelings."

Patient for one of the few times in my experience of him, Barry informed me that in the North, people who wanted to be understood as antiracist said "negro"; if anyone at the university heard me say "nigra," they would brand me a redneck bigot whose father probably belonged to the KKK. For the next few days I practiced in front of a mirror making my mouth form the longest "e" imaginable. By the time I was in conversation with other graduate students, I had mastered the magic vowel that could save me from disgrace.

Though I continued to see black students on campus, none ever took graduate English classes with me or was in my freshman comp courses. Gradually I learned that many of the dark faces were African, exotic and therefore less threatening to the status quo than American Negroes. Eventually I understood that my discipline would be one of the last places such students would ever risk being found, since "correct English" was a weapon used against them. Moreover, in my three years of doctoral study, I was never asked to read any literature by black writers.

Going to Madison, Wisconsin, had felt like a deliverance from things southern. I had received chamber of commerce materials that included proud statements about the city's history of liberal politics. Brochures boasted a wide variety of persons at the university (40 percent from foreign countries) and a metropolitan atmosphere without any metropolitan problems. Progressive schools nurtured the whole child, and Jews and Christians had a long tradition of working together harmoniously. One sentence even went so far as to advertise Madison businesses as refusing to discriminate on the basis of race, creed, color, or religious affiliation.

I arrived in this shiny place in early September, 1961, and, following an old custom, bought a newspaper. Madison was in the midst of a full-scale housing war. Blacks were moving into posh neighborhoods, and residents were up in arms—the very same arms I had seen so often back home, never mind if the objections were phrased in multisyllabic, polite terms. Hired counsel for the white residents had drafted a petition delaying the integration of residential areas until more studies could be conducted to show the impact on children and real estate values. Midwestern rhetoric was opaque rather than inflammatory, but I still felt tricked. Madison did not want "coloreds" in their parks or restaurants or libraries, but having let them into those places, they were up against a wall of their own making. From such a vantage point, these liberal midwesterners looked sadly familiar.

During the years I studied there, I was putting down new roots in a part of the country that would become my second home. I tried to have friends my own age, something that was quite foreign and not a little scary. Also, I used those three years to weigh men and women in terms of my own sexual direction. By the time I left, I had moved away from marriage fantasies and into a life centered around women.

Like most graduate students in English, I read late into the night after spending evenings in some part of the library stacks. I wrote endless short reviews of critical articles, did longer papers at the end of each semester, and took what seemed interminable tests staged every three weeks or so throughout the year. Recreation often centered around bratwurst and beer, the cheapest way to eat and drink out. I even remember going to St. Patrick's Day parties where genuine green beer was ladled from the bathtub of our Boston Catholic hosts.

Unlike most of my peers, I still attended church. In fact, the only other friends who did so were the Roman Catholics among us for whom Mass was still important. I found a small Episcopal church within walking distance of my apartment, where not only was there Communion every Sunday but each Wednesday at seven in the morning, and every day during Lent. Going to all these services, I quickly discovered that I had found a so-called "high" church, where the only real difference between us and the Catholics seemed to be obedience to the Pope.

My love for ritual was so satisfied that in gratitude I taught an adolescent Sunday school class. Though we seldom read the Bible, we talked a lot about situation ethics and how to be both moral and sexual.

They seemed to like me, and the class grew from three or four a week to an unprecedented ten. In addition to the usual flowers and candles, this church was permeated with the faint odor of incense, used for early morning Communion on Wednesdays and for high holy days like Ash Wednesday and All Souls'.

The priest preferred to be called "Father" and was known to hear confession without the anonymity of a closed booth. When I later learned that the good father was sexually involved with two of my friends, I tried valiantly to reconcile this behavior with his extreme piety. Failing, I shrank from the church altogether, attending only on Sundays and occasionally during Lent. But I stayed with my class of teenagers until the year was over, thinking they were the least appropriate target of my anger at this man's hypocrisy and misuse of position.

I loved taking classes in a great sprawling building on top of a steep hill. By the second week of school I understood that Bascom Hall was the locus of campus agitation. Protests in front of "my" building occurred at least weekly. Graduate teaching assistants protested their treatment at the hands of tenured faculty and organized a union; undergraduates picketed over everything from poor dorm food to the Bay of Pigs invasion; we all attended rallies decrying the U.S. military presence in far-flung places.

But the single event that brought out almost the entire university and caused classes to be cancelled was the assassination of John F. Kennedy. It was about 4:30 P.M., and I was at Cecil's Shoe Shop. Cecil was a fixture around campus, beloved by me for welcoming me to his shop and talking to me when I felt lonely. At least twice a month, he insisted on taking me to breakfast at the local diner; on Saturdays when he went fishing, I minded the store. Each spring, Cecil brought me morels from a special woods known only to him.

This particular November afternoon, we were listening to a country western music station while we talked leisurely. Suddenly the program was interrupted by a man speaking in a shaky, frightened voice: "The president is down! The president is down! We don't know more, but he's been shot in the head in Dallas. Oh, no; oh, no; oh, no ..." Cecil and I looked at each other, too stunned to speak. We stayed by the radio, silent, waiting for more news. The next comment was the final one, "John F. Kennedy is dead; our president is dead from an assassin's bullet in Texas."

I wandered around back onto campus, eyes unwilling to focus and head beating. When I passed other students and faculty whom I recognized, we had absolutely nothing to say. No one seemed to know what to do, so we gravitated toward Bascom Hall. A priest had been pressed into service and was conducting a silent vigil for Kennedy's soul. I had no qualms about his soul but was terribly worried about the country's and felt sick within my own. We stood around even when it began to drizzle, reluctant to leave the cold comfort of the group.

Next morning I went to a friend's to watch the funeral. All day I sat frozen, staring at the black-and-white images proving that the first public figure about whom I had ever felt passionately was gone from my life—vanished as surely as all the private ones before him. At lunch and dinner time, I put sandwiches into my mouth and drank tea or strong ale; I left the screen only to go to the bathroom.

For the rest of that week, no one went to class, and no one cared that we didn't. The faculty was probably relieved not to have to go on with business as usual, since most were liberal Democrats. I called my mother long distance, and we quietly cried together for a long time. I drank too much beer and ate too little food. I avoided Cecil's Shoe Shop, unwilling to stand in the space where the horrible announcement had found me.

Though Wisconsin's undergraduates had energy to protest outside the English building, they seldom wanted to take risks inside. Many of the students I taught had come from secure upper middle-class homes, lived in expensive dorms, and were preparing themselves to be medium-range executives or their wives. I was used to students who worked long and hard, who inquired about everything literary. Most of my freshmen wanted to do the least possible to get by. But then, so did I, since my primary purpose for being at Wisconsin was to get the ticket necessary for admission to the professoriate. I taught with only half a heart, though I taught well enough by everyone's standards.

All freshmen composition instructors were required to teach the same novels—one year it was *Barchester Towers*, hardly exciting fare for eighteen year olds; the next, *The Forsythe Saga*. Try as I might, I could not make my students care about dotty country parsons and their female relatives or generational development and intrigue, even when they involved money and power. My self-styled blasé radicals were bored to tears.

In addition to teaching the same literary texts, we were supposed to use standard handouts on construction and grammar as we molded better expository prose writers. I can still remember those handouts, carefully prepared by the woman who ran the program: printed on variously colored paper, they seemed deadly dull to me. One series, on a washed-out blue background, had a string of statements in each of which was embedded some syntactical or grammatical error. In the exercise, students were to spot the mistake and revise the sentence accordingly. Sometimes, I did not know what the mistake was; other times, it seemed so obvious as to be insulting. The worst aspect was the content: not quite at the "See Spot run" level, it was certainly no more advanced than eighth grade. Not only were my freshmen self-styled radicals, they were also self-styled chic. My blue sheets were sure to evoke their scorn.

In a gesture partly of defiance and largely of desperation, I said as I distributed the sheets: "I have to hand these out. Use them as scratch paper if you like." Though I gained some small degree of credibility with my classes, I went around for the next week in utter dread that the program director would find out and call me in on charges of insubordination.

If my life as a freshman composition teacher was less than successful, my world as a student made up for that. I had chosen Wisconsin because of the presence in the English department of a woman named Helen C. (for Constance, one of the dearest New England virtues) White. Miss White had an international reputation for her work in medieval and seventeenth-century literature, and I wanted to write a dissertation on John Donne. When I was accepted into the graduate program, I was ecstatic: not only could I flee the South, I could work with my academic hero.

My first semester, I enrolled in three classes and taught two sections of freshman English with fifty attendant weekly themes to grade. Finally I was in a learning situation in which I had to perform at levels not automatically easy; the pressure excited me. I was determined to prove to the university registrar that my southern A's were genuine. In my acceptance letter, he had written: "Though your record at the University of Alabama is excellent, 'A's' from southern colleges are viewed as 'B's' until you demonstrate that you can receive the same marks at Wisconsin." Though I slept very little that term, I made all A's and was never late in handing back freshmen themes.

Miss White herself taught the graduate lecture course on meta-physical poetry. Twice a week, I sat spellbound as this six-foot plus, large-boned woman dressed invariably in purple burst upon the lecture hall and opened her file folder. As she spoke with knowledge and passion, interweaving lines from poems with facts and anecdotes about the various poets' lives, informing everything with stunning critical insight, I hardly breathed. When the lecture was over, she closed her file folder with certainty, smiled benignly, and strode out as if she knew she had just given a stellar performance. So completely did the work of the metaphysicals enter my consciousness that I once actually went out onto the mall after reading Andrew Marvell's garden poems and embraced a tree. Later, when I discovered Henry Vaughan's mysticism, I convinced myself that I too had seen "eternity the other night like a ring of pure and endless light." Richard Crashaw's extravagant stanzas seemed a bit too baroque for my taste, though I valued his insistence that his relationship to God be erotic like St. Teresa's. John Donne and George Herbert won my heart. Donne knew sin intimately and treasured love above almost everything; Herbert's simple faith caused him to worry about usurping God's role by creating lyrics even if they glorified the deity—a conflict I found terribly moving.

On the first day of Metaphysical Poetry, Miss White said that different forms of literature were classified into something that started with a "g." No one at Alabama or Vanderbilt had ever spoken that word; I puzzled over whether it might just be a northernism. Unable to spell whatever Miss White had said, I wrote in my notes what I thought resembled its sound; that night I spent a very long time with my dictionary until I found "genre." Though this was an extreme case, I often encountered totally new concepts that stirred me to know more. *Hermeticism* was one such term, and I was greatly disappointed when Miss White leaned over the podium and said, I was sure only to me, "Now, students, don't ever toy with hermeticism—either embrace it entirely or leave it alone—it can be dangerously attractive to the dabbler." It was not until a few years later, when I first taught Marlowe's *Dr. Faustus*, that I more fully understood what she had been cautioning. But, loyal to her every word, I did not pursue the hermeticists.

Miraculously, since she had her pick of each year's graduate class, Miss White agreed to be my dissertation advisor. Her exact words were, "Now, Miss McNaron, you have already been out in the profes-

sion as a teacher. I want you to finish your dissertation and leave
school just as quickly as you can. That will be my main goal in looking
over what you write—to help you become your own mistress." Good
advice, though I frequently longed for fuller commentary on my
chapters.

I wrote on John Donne's sermons—all 170 of them. After using the
library's copy of volume 1, it became clear that if I were going to
complete my project I would have to own my own books. There were
seven large volumes, costing over thirty dollars each in 1963. My
dissertation fellowship barely paid for food and the rent on my
apartment, the entrance to which was from an alley later named
Clymer Place. I wrote a pleading letter to the publishers, outlining my
straits and asking for the privilege of paying small amounts over many
months. It was the sixties and they agreed, sending me all seven tan
volumes with gold lettering on the spines. When they arrived, I
promptly installed them on my primary bookshelf and began making
copious pencil marginalia.

The professor who touched me most deeply, after Miss White of
course, was Alvin Whitley, expert in romantic poetry and vintage
sherry. Because my M.A. had been on Keats, I was deemed "prepared"
in the Romantics and hence barred from his courses. But I visited on
the days he talked about the odes, and I was sure that he identified
completely with the melancholy young genius, that he believed his life
was equally doomed and so had remarkable insights into the meaning
of the works. Whenever I read or teach the odes, I still picture Alvin
standing in front of us in his black three-piece buttoned-down suit.
With the slightest lisp, he delivered piercing truths about these great
poems.

He could also be piercing about undergraduate frivolity. On one
occasion, a young man came into lecture late—something sure to
infuriate Alvin. Rather than taking an empty seat in the front row, the
student crept up the risers to the row in which his assigned seat was
located. As he was sitting down, somehow the change in his pants
pocket began falling out. Coins clattered onto the wooden floor, and
several rolled loudly down steps until they finally stopped, one of
them almost at Alvin's feet. He had stood utterly still during this
excruciating scene and when the last copper was silent, he looked up
at the devastated young man, smiled a lethal smile, and said, "Bring
your tambourine?"

When I heard that he had come to my rescue during the evaluation of my doctoral preliminary examination, I was deeply touched. I did not quite pass the eighteenth-century exam. No wonder, since I found that material the least stimulating of any for which I was responsible, and since I had not understood one of the two questions asked. As a reader of the nineteenth-century exams, Whitley knew my performance there. When the readers met to assign final marks, my failure was reported. In a conversation with the reader of the medieval essays, Alvin had learned that mine was perhaps the best of the lot. He argued that my excellence in his century, together with my extraordinary comprehension of the middle ages, should offset my weaker handling of Pope, Swift, Fielding, and epistemology. The committee bowed to his suggestion and gave me a low pass for the entire exam, requiring no retakes. Because I knew all this from a confidential source, I never was able to thank Alvin.

The other men who taught me seemed trapped by something I could neither see nor comprehend. One paced from one edge of the podium to the other throughout every lecture on the early moderns. Another had never quite adjusted to civilian life after having served as a major in World War II. A third sweated profusely from a bad case of alcoholism. The only happy one was my Anglo-Saxon teacher. Newly from Harvard, he had bushy red hair and a tall chunky body, reminding me of an oversized teddy bear. I caught his enthusiasm for Anglo-Saxon poetry and culture, feeling that if I had taken my *Beowulf* requirement sooner, I might never have made it into the seventeenth century.

Though Wisconsin's English department had several distinguished male professors, it boasted a troika of powerful women at a time when most universities employed them primarily as secretaries. Miss White was one; the other two were Madeline Doran (authority on Shakespeare and Renaissance poetry) and Ruth Wallerstein (giant in late seventeenth-century prose and poetry). Several years before my arrival, Miss Wallerstein had been driving her sports car in the Alps when she had a fatal accident. Rumors had it that she may have intended that accident because a great romance (with another woman, we constantly wondered?) was ending. Miss Doran had flown to the scene to claim the body since no one had been with her, and there seemed to be no available kin. Miss Wallerstein's presence hovered over the other two grand dames, and she came into their conversation often. When either Miss Doran or Miss White spoke of her, their tone of voice sank to a lower, more intimate level. Though they never called her "Ruth" in front of us, their devotion was obvious and marvelous to witness.

Miss Doran was about ten years younger than Miss White and a sterner presence altogether. Shorter by several inches, she had dark hair with gray wisps at the temples. She wore it pulled back severely from her face. Her eyes, also dark, drove into you until they turned away in some kind of animal terror, like a startled deer or a rabbit caught in headlights. Her style of dress was tailored and fairly drab—the antithesis of Miss White's marvelous shades of purple, lavender, and pink.

Though I shied away from Miss Doran's Shakespeare seminar, I sought her out for readings of Sidney and Spenser as I began preparing for my Renaissance prelim. Her office walls were wrapped in books, many old velum volumes of secondary and tertiary figures from the sixteenth century. Beside her large wooden desk and her own chair on rollers was one straight-backed chair placed for the student lucky or brazen enough to get beyond the door. Miss Doran led an almost reclusive life in a little house located on the grounds of the university arboretum. She was a passionate bird watcher who reputedly arose at dawn to station herself with binoculars on her secluded deck, waiting for the day's parade of winged creatures.

Like Miss Wallerstein, Madeline Doran was also supposed to have had a great and failed romance, the gender of the other party remaining a subject of speculation. By the time I knew her, she was well insulated from students, seeing only such long-time associates as Miss White and a sweet beanpole of a man working in the late middle ages. Several of us latched onto a story that she and Miss Wallerstein had been close and that after the alpine catastrophe, Miss Doran had sunk into a personal decline.

My visits to her office had an intensity that fairly seared my nerve ends. I would go in timidly with my question about *The Faerie Queene* or *Arcadia;* Miss Doran would begin responding with total concentration on the question and me. As she talked, she inched her chair ever closer to my face until by the end of some exposition she might be within a foot of me. Suddenly, she would return from somewhere purely intellectual, realize her proximity, and literally wheel herself back to her side of the room, making clear as she went that further exchange was unthinkable. Sensing her discomfort, I would hastily end the interview, leaving her with tiny beads of sweat on her upper lip and forehead—beads that reminded me of Christ's agony in the garden of Gethsemane. Like him, Miss Doran was struggling with some phantom capable of diverting her from her determined purpose.

In my last weeks in Madison, before going to the University of Minnesota where I had accepted an assistant professorship, an extraordinary event occurred—Miss Doran invited me to lunch at one of the several Italian eateries on State Street. She had a small antipasto salad but insisted that I get some of the splendid spaghetti for which the restaurant was famous. We talked awkwardly during the meal, since I certainly felt it inappropriate to ask her anything, and she shied away from personal inquiries. Most of our comments ran to birds and flowers—safer subjects than ourselves. Just as she was figuring out the tip, she looked up at me with her startled deer eyes and said so quickly I almost missed some of the words: "Toni, when you arrive at Minnesota be careful, don't try to change the system; it's like a broad brick wall, and if you do, you will only hurt your head." Before I could respond, she had scooped up the check and was fleeing the cool, darkened interior for the brightness of a late May afternoon on the pavement.

Many times during my first years in Minneapolis, I recalled those urgent statements. I knew there was a personal story behind them that I would never hear. I also knew she was profoundly right since my increasingly frantic efforts to change the structure and workings of my department, college, and the larger university were leaving me depleted and lonely, often with a headache that I numbed with generous quantities of bourbon.

When Miss Doran retired, she spent time in California with her ailing mother; when her mother died, Miss Doran spent time in her retreat house with uninterrupted bird watching. At some point, she published a book of nature essays reminiscent of Loren Eisley. When I read them, I wept for the wasted passion in her life. Some human being could have been made joyous in the aura of Madeline's magnanimity. No wonder her lectures about the concept of greatness of soul that flourished in Renaissance Italy and England moved us so. Like Alvin Whitley, she thoroughly identified with her subject, talking about herself the only way she knew how—in deep code and through someone else's text.

Miss Wallerstein was lost to me by death, and Miss Doran was largely absent, I thought, through her fear of what attachment might mean. But Miss White had a warmth and accessibility that quite amazed me. I decided the reason lay in her active spiritual life—she wrote novels (under a pseudonym) about such saintly figures as Francis of Assisi and had received the Roman Catholic church's award for outstanding service by a lay person. As I ferreted out how someone as worldly as she seemed could remain so devoted to a church whose doctrinal positions were far from her own, I comprehended something that proved invaluable: Helen White took from the church what she loved—the spirit of prayer, the example of Jesus, the sheer aesthetic glory of the liturgical calendar—and let the dogma go.

It took students very little time to figure out why she was nicknamed Purple Goddess. All her clothing was either purple or a color that went easily with it: flowered blouses in magentas, ochres, pale greens; entire dresses of soft lavender wool set off by a paisleyed scarf of red violet and navy; luscious purple skirt suits accompanied by spotless white blouses with Peter Pan collars. Once I steeled myself to ask why she seldom deviated from her color. Her reply missed the point of my question, perhaps intentionally: "Well, my dear, it's so much easier just to get out of bed and take something from the closet knowing it will match." I wanted information on why that particular color, not an argument from expediency. My own theory ran to one of two connotations: purple is the color associated with women-loving women; it is the color used in liturgical churches (and monarchical governments) to connote royalty. "Goddess" had been added because of her stature—she resembled an Amazon gliding from office to class to the ladies' room nearby.

I remember going into that ladies' room on one occasion and spotting Miss White's unmistakable black brogans in the stall next to me. I held my breath, excited to be so intimate. Rather than speaking through the partition (which would have been invasive and, besides, would have let her know that I was making a careful study of her footwear) or even hurrying with my own activity so that I could just happen to be washing my hands when she was, I sat very still and listened while she let herself out of her cubicle, ran water to wash her hands, pulled out and used a paper towel, perhaps touched her cornsilk white hair at its edges or arranged her clothing before meeting the public, pulled open the eternally squeaking door, and vanished.

Yes, I had a crush on Helen White. She was the most exotic woman I had ever seen off the silver screen. To come into such close and frequent contact with one's hero is usually not desirable; our need for giants demands distance. But I wanted ever more personal closeness and went to exorbitant lengths to get it. For instance, Miss White always walked up Bascom Hill on her way to work from her small apartment off State Street. After weeks of trial and error, I determined almost to the minute when she began her ascent. I began arriving at the beginning of the sidewalk precisely as she did, acting surprised to see her, falling into step beside her. I still can hear her even breathing as she took the long, slow incline deliberately, pausing midway to tell me about the architecture of the Law School or to show me the periwinkles as they progressed from glossy-leafed shoots to a luxurious ground cover full of tiny blue–violet blooms. Occasionally Miss White would give in to my repeated offers to carry something—two or three reference books from her library at home, a plastic bag housing her brogans for wear inside. (When it snowed, she wore short booties with the merest hint of a heel.) Once or twice I even carried her overnight bag, brought to work because she would taxi directly to the airport and fly away to speak at some conference or to a major university where she would consult with others of her rank and station, though I was convinced there were no such individuals.

The Purple Goddess protected her doctoral candidates from bureaucratic harm and other forms of academic harassment. One summer she found work for the not-as-bright husband of a brilliant woman working on the influence of things medieval on metaphysical poetry. Another summer she helped me stay in Madison by hiring me to alphabetize her library. Every morning I arrived at her apartment promptly at nine. It consisted of a smallish living room, a dining area used as a library / workroom, a tiny kitchen in which she ate breakfast, a tinier bathroom, and her rather large bedroom with its single bed always unmade. Some days I felt bold enough to make it, wash her dishes, bring in fresh flowers for the table—I fantasized being Helen's partner, taking care of the one who took care of so many of us. When I did these domestic things, I always got a little scribbled note in her miniature handwriting. I kept these tiny sheets for years, inflating them to the status of billets-doux, reading and rereading their few words of gratitude and warmth: "You're so sweet to tidy up"; "I prefer my bed made but am just too lazy to do it"; "My dear, you are too kind." A few mornings she left out crackers and a clean tea cup with a note to fix myself midmorning tea; once she prepared a light lunch of cheese slices and rounds of caraway bread, lovingly covered with waxed paper.

When all the books (literally hundreds) were in perfect alphabetical order within specified categories such as "medieval romances," "pre-Socratic philosophers," "Donne criticism," I could no longer prolong my visits to my idol's private quarters. On my last day, I cleaned the entire apartment. For her part, Miss White had left the last of a series of checks for more than my hours warranted. When I had protested early in the project, she had written feeble excuses: "Oh, my dear, I must have misread your figures"; "Oh, yes, well, we'll fix all that in the next check, won't we?" When it became clear that she had no intention of paying me what I had actually earned, I decided that she had probably invented the entire scheme to have a gracious way of giving me money. My suspicion was confirmed when I received a late night call two days after I had finished my work. It was the Purple Goddess saying, "Now, my dear, I'm so sorry to disturb you, but could you come over in the morning and find some books for me? You have my library in such wonderful order, I'm terribly afraid I can't locate what I need, being so disorganized as I am." In a flash I knew that the activity had been for my benefit not hers, that she would probably have to revise the order to find what she needed quickly.

We devotees endlessly speculated about why Miss White was "Miss." The more conventional among us were sure that her deep participation in Catholicism encouraged her to be a kind of secular nun. The more romantic believed she had probably had a "great love," and when he jilted her, she had shut off her sexual self, sublimating that energy into writing and teaching. Those of us who stood outside heterosexuality had a different version. If there had been a great love, it most certainly had been a she, perhaps even the elusive Ruth Wallerstein of the alpine car crash. My private fantasy was that sometime in her far distant past, Helen White had invested too heavily in some female graduate student who had then left her for career or husband or both. This story reflected well on me, since I fancied that Miss White felt some special bond with me. Certainly I would never forsake her if she would only speak the word to draw closer.

While I am relieved to say that the word never came, Helen White did save me on one crucial occasion. During the second year of my studies, just as I was formulating my dissertation topic, my mother became seriously ill. Under and between the lines of her letters, I heard her wishing me closer. More overtly, my sister told me Mamie's health was worsening, that Mamie missed me, that my absence was increasingly hard on Mamie's nerves. Bowing to a guilt I already felt for leaving home in the first place, I wrote that I was applying to graduate schools closer to Alabama so we could see each other more often. Since that process entailed getting letters of recommendation, I of course asked Miss White for one.

In no time I received a note from the departmental secretary asking me to make an appointment with Miss White at my earliest convenience. The minute I stepped into her inner office, I knew she was serious. After telling me she would be glad to write a strong letter, she sat quietly, pensively, indeed I even thought, sadly. Not daring to disturb her, I waited uncomfortably. Finally, she turned her swivel chair until she faced me and began telling me an autobiographical story. She was from Boston, one of four children (two girls, two boys), none of whom had ever married. She described her mother as the matriarch of the family and her father as rather shadowy. Gathering herself up in her chair, she came to the climax: "Well, my dear, there came a day when my father called me into his room and said, 'Helen, leave Boston now or you'll never get away and you'll end up like me.' I understood him to mean that all of us were so involved with Mother that, without a physical break, we would simply submerge ourselves. I left that fall and have thanked my father ever since. I could not have done what I have without his words. [There followed a long silence in which I watched her struggle with some complex range of emotions.] Toni [my heart leapt inside me, for she'd never called me by my name before—"Miss McNaron" or "my dear" had served], I've told you this because I fear for you now. You love your mother so very much, but if you say yes now, you may never say no. Of course, I'll do whatever you ask about your future."

When she finished, she sat staring out her window. The effort of sharing her life, even at this great remove, had obviously tired her. I think her silent response to her own words made as much impression on me as the words themselves. But I was not strong and that evening I phoned home to tell my mother and sister that I would come closer if it were necessary. My mother rose to the occasion: "Honey, I want you to stay there. My health is improving and I just know you will get far better instruction at Wisconsin than you could at the University of Texas or Colorado [places I had been tentatively accepted]. Now promise me you'll call them and cancel your application."

I made a feeble protest that I did not mind returning, which in turn let Mamie insist that I stay. We both saved some face. I hung up in tears of relief and sadness that my life was taking me further and further away from a woman whose love I both wanted and feared. As I sat on my bed across the one room of my apartment, looking at the decaled refrigerator, I remembered Miss White, gazing wistfully out her office window. That night I lay awake listening to the hum of that refrigerator, feeling grateful to my mother, who had decided that it was important for me to stay in Wisconsin without guilt.

During my last year there, I was freed from teaching by receiving a much-coveted dissertation fellowship. As Miss White had promised, she hurried me along with the writing: "You need to finish and go be an adult somewhere," she told me kindly. When the chapters came back with such brief comments as "Fine; keep going," I sometimes resented her pushing. When she did make a marginal note, I valued it far more than I might had she been more copious in her responses. My favorite came in her spidery hand on the first page of my second chapter: I had remarked that language could be used to mask as well as to reveal; she had written in the lightest pencil: "Very well put and wise too."

My last fall in Madison, Helen C. White asked me to accompany her to the local grocery late one afternoon as we both were leaving school. She had agreed for the umpteenth time to entertain a small group of honors freshmen at her apartment. Every year, this internationally famous scholar chatted with eighteen year olds while serving them cider and cookies. This year's crop was due in a few hours, and she had neither food nor drink.

Ecstatic, I assented, and we hurried down Bascom Hill to her place where she swapped her ancient leather briefcase for a large string bag she had picked up in Italy on her last visit to the Vatican. Once at the little grocery, she set about with dispatch, and in no time had three boxes of mixed cookies and two gallons of cider paid for and ready for transport. She put the bottles into the string bag first, then the more delicate cookie boxes, and turned to me: "Toni, my dear, can you just take one of the hoop handles and I'll take the other?" So I grabbed the left-most handle in my right hand, while the Purple Goddess took the other in her left, and we walked briskly up University Avenue the five blocks to her apartment. I was supremely happy to be so fully involved with her, even if in so mundane an activity. We said little but were drawn together as the evening closed around us. Once at her building, she took her bag in her own large hands, smiled warmly, murmured a good night, and slipped inside.

Though ostensibly working toward a Ph.D., I found myself plunged into a period of intense emotional growth. I struggled to form friendships with peers, fell seriously in love, and received my last marriage proposal. Having learned in Mississippi that I was neither a sexual nonentity nor a sexual failure, I could no longer pretend unconsciousness. My first job had also taught me how it felt to be rejected and in danger because of my erotic feelings. So crushes on Miss White or fantasies about Miss Doran were safer than having lunch with some woman in my James seminar toward whom I might develop an unmanageable attachment. I made easy connections with the men in my classes or with whom I shared an office. With women I maintained polite distance.

The men I gravitated toward were usually married or gay, hence less likely to have romantic expectations of me. The exception was Michael O'Hara, close friend of my favorite people, Jim and Mary Kilroy. I met Jim in a graduate course my first semester and soon he had invited me to dinner at their apartment. Mary was one of the sweetest people I had ever met, and we often saw each other for long talks over several cups of tea. When they had to rush to the hospital one predawn morning because their second child was insisting on making an appearance, I was the person they woke to come stay with their first.

To one of their dinners, they invited another friend, thinking we might like each other. Michael was a Catholic whose mother's family had come from Italy in the not-so-distant past. He was volatile and easily wounded. A bit shorter than I, he had beautiful dark brown eyes that looked out under heavy black brows. Opera and Victorian prose writers were his great passions, with good food and Boston University, where he had been an undergraduate, taking a close second. A worrier, on one occasion he ordered tickets for a famous string quartet a year in advance.

The four of us spent many slow hours over Italian dinners talking about God and literature. I felt secure and calm with Michael, not romantic, though I must have given my family to think that I did. In a letter written in response to my concern about possibly leaving Madison to be closer to Mamie, Betty wrote that she was so happy that I was in love with such a nice-sounding young man. I seem to have been worried that I would lose my last opportunity to find a husband I loved and made Michael central in letters because my relationship with him was "normal." What I needed most was someone with whom to talk about my increasing passion for an older woman at the university, about the confusion that was causing me. Betty assured me that other suitable men would present themselves since I was embarking upon an academic career that guaranteed interesting and sensitive colleagues. I was considering whether someone teaching at a major university could live with a woman lover and keep her job.

When it became clear that Michael was also misreading the time I spent with him and was thinking in terms of "our" future, I stayed awake calculating my options: I could marry him, have a pleasantly companionable life, and be safe and cared for; I could be honest and move more wholeheartedly into my lesbian self, even though that carried with it all manner of unforseeable troubles and punishments.

Trying to act differently from my past, I discussed this major decision and my dilemma with Joe Wheatley. Himself engaged in a closeted, commuter relationship, he talked about the futility of suppressing "homosexual leanings" if I had them. He cautioned me against using a man and marriage to buy social respectability, tempting though that was to many of "us."

Joe and Mary Kilroy were true friends through it all, exerting no pressure on me to fall into Michael's arms, although they would have liked nothing better than to be our witnesses at a quiet little ceremony at the local Catholic church. After a month of deliberation, I decided to tell the truth. This was rather ticklish, since Michael had never formally proposed, though we both knew he meant us to marry. He was disappointed and probably angry, and avoided me for a long time after our stilted conversation. Several years after we had both left Wisconsin, I heard he had married, and when next I saw him at our professional meetings, he seemed simultaneously uncomfortable introducing me to his wife and smug to have one to present. I wished him all success and meant it.

Nella and I had split up because she wanted children more than anything, and, in 1961, that was not possible within a lesbian relationship. After smarting under distinct feelings of inadequacy and remembering my contorted attempts to become my father's son, I had begun to adjust to single life. At the same time, I was falling in love with the most interesting and unusual woman I had ever known. We both were connected with the university, though in quite different capacities; we were separated in age by more than fifteen years; and she was still in her marriage. I simply did not care how complicated things were or might become; I was powerfully drawn to her. Not since I had played Liszt and Rachmaninoff had I been so absorbed. The fact that we had to be clandestine felt unfair to me, but the frustration was minor compared with the intimacy. This relationship had all the power of a fully realized attraction, but the seeds of its eventual doom were implicit in her reluctance to sever her marriage bonds—when we first became involved or many years later. To speak more specifically about our time would be self-indulgent, since she would wish fiercely to preserve anonymity; not to acknowledge her at all would be false to the overwhelming emotions I originally felt.

Though our eight years together were anything but placid or easy, I felt more alive and in touch with what I now understand to be my essential self than at any time in my life. I learned to appreciate the outdoors and the life of the mind as we drove out into the Wisconsin country, spent long weekends in northern Minnesota, and roughed it in the Pacific Northwest. Our conversations ranged from Elizabeth Bowen to Democratic politics, from which perennials could survive midwestern winters to how a kind god could allow children to die and countries to wage war.

Perhaps it is fair to say I grew up in my relationship with this woman. The process included betraying and feeling betrayed, a recognition of just how hard a virtue clarity can be; but it also affirmed me as a vital, physical person whose thoughts and desires could stimulate and please someone with remarkable faculties for self-exploration and engagement with the world.

Around the edges of these two intimacies, I developed a special friendship with a woman named Katherine, whom I met in a class. A graduating senior, she seemed far more worldly and self-reflective than I. As had been the case with my college roommate, Jean, so many years before, we began by liking the same British writers—Thomas Hardy and Wilfred Owen in this case. Gradually we formed a pattern that greatly pleased me: as soon as Professor Wiley, the pacer who grew progressively more caged during the semester, finished lecturing, Katherine and I went for tea. The longer we did that, the more I wanted to talk about other things, even ourselves. She met my interest with her own, and our friendship developed to a level of closeness that frightened me because I feared I would lose her as I had April. But I stayed put and waited.

As Katherine took me into her confidence about the man in her life, I became keenly aware that I never spoke about my sexuality. No one at Madison "knew" except Jim Stathis, and I planned to keep it that way. Now I felt this woman searching with her eyes and inviting through her trust. Dare I tell her who I was? Would she not vanish in disgust or at least retreat to the safety of war poets and the Wessex landscape?

While I was agonizing over whether to disclose, Katherine was introducing me to her old friend Jane, with whom I wound up sharing an apartment my second year in Madison. Always expecting the best from people, Jane was often disappointed but never lost heart. We lived together for a year in genuine amicability, splitting chores, shopping, cooking. She loved my southern grits and fried ham with red-eye gravy; my favorite was her English boiled dinner: big peeled potatoes, some cheap cut of beef, a few carrots, and a whole green cabbage simmered for hours in nothing but salt, pepper, and water.

When she and her fiancé married, I drove from Madison to Elmira, New York, taking them something far too expensive for my budget— a large Orrefors vase—but feeling glad for my sweet friend and her happiness.

One of Katherine's favorite things to do when Jane and I were roommates was to come over for supper and then fall into hours of deep talk at the end of which she'd be too tired and it would be too late to go home. She would then curl up on our couch and stay over for breakfast. Once while Jane was visiting her parents, Katherine proposed that we have one of our evenings. I assumed she meant just dinner and perhaps an abbreviated talk, since without Jane's presence, she would not choose to stay over.

After a dinner of fish bought on sale and delicately poached, steamed broccoli topped with warm mayonnaise, and fudge ripple ice cream with coffee and tea, we settled in the living room to discuss Buber's notions of I-Thou. About midnight, we were too bleary eyed to care about the distinction, and I suddenly blurted out, "Katherine, I've wanted to tell you something for a long time—I love women and can't seem to find men appealing anymore. I know it may be wrong to you with all your Christian background, but it's the truth."

Not waiting for her response, I began to pick up cups and fetch her jacket—it was March and evenings still got cool. Looking surprised and a little hurt, she said, "But, Toni, I always sleep over when we have these marathons; can't I do that now? And, besides, I can't just leave after the gift of your telling me about yourself—we have to talk, I want to know more, my 'Christian background' just makes me love you more for being so honest. Sit down and let's keep going."

Amazed at this acceptance from a heterosexual woman, I sat back down and cried. Katherine held me, which puzzled me even more: she was not afraid of physical contact even though she knew my deepest secret.

Knowing I was a lesbian seemed to let Katherine talk even more freely about her own love life—something I had not expected, since she was in love with a man. I had no understanding then that being specific about myself made it easier for her to do the same. We grew closer, and when she moved away to attend Union Seminary, I genuinely grieved. I gave her a hardback copy of one of her favorite theologians, and she gave me a delicate nightgown. Falling just below my knees, it was pale lavender with a scooped neckline edged by a tiny bead of lace. The card read, "For a dear woman who deserves all the softness she can find. I love you, Katherine."

I cried and cried over that nightgown. In 1958 when I had discovered my sexuality, all I knew about lesbians was that psychology books said we all wanted to be men. I did not want to be a man, but without any other ideas, I was no longer sure that I was a proper woman. By presenting me with that nightgown, Katherine affirmed that, in her imagination at least, woman and lesbian could be one. I had always worn either pajamas or longish t-shirts, believing diaphanous sleepwear was reserved for some other kind of woman. Though at first the gown crept up around my neck during the night and felt very sparse all the time, I slept in my gift with pride and curiosity.

Long after Katherine's gown was frayed at the edges, I persisted in wearing it. Then for years I used its fragments to dust my most precious possessions. Finally, the material melted into almost nothing, but the meaning remained intact. I had been seen, heard, and loved anyway—my healing had begun.

Alone

How to love my mother without getting lost: I struggled with that dilemma from early childhood. My efforts at independence and privacy worked best when they took place out of Mamie's geographical sphere. Try as I might to define privacy at 5130 Holly Court, I invariably found myself drawn back into communal space where my mother held sway. Yet, from the moment I went the fifty miles away from Birmingham to Tuscaloosa, Mamie supported my movements further and further away, coping with whatever sense of loss she felt. So the final story is a complicated one.

It is too simple to say she wanted me to stay at home—of course, she did, but she also wanted what was best for me out of her great love for me. Letters frequently said something like, "Multiply how much you miss me by 100 and you may approximate (nearly) how much I miss you—but my love and my thoughts are with you constantly." On my birthday in 1960, she wrote:

Waked up this morning at seven o'clock and thought of my baby, as I do every morning—But—this was a very special morning. At seven o'clock twenty-three years ago—you were born—I was filled with a sense of relief from pain—and a feeling of anxiety as to your welfare—*But* when they brought you to my bed—and told me that you were a *perfect* little girl—and put you in my arms—*my first contact with you,* so precious—so warm—and so completely dependent upon me—*that was pure delight!!!* You know what a joy you have been to me—I realize what wonderful daughters I have, and I am very grateful to you both—How could anyone who loves as deeply as I love my babies and is loved as deeply as I know they love me—not believe in eternal love—and a Divine Being?

For my part, I wanted her approval at the very same time I wanted to be my own person. When I first went away from home to the University of Alabama, Mamie and I agreed to write one another every day, even if only a brief note. Most of the time I kept my part of the bargain, but when I did not, I got a frantic phone call from Fairfield asking if I was sick or tired of writing. I always assured Mamie I was just overwhelmed with schoolwork, avoiding the real issue—sometimes I did get tired of writing. Often I scratched off a hasty note late at night just to have something to put into an envelope. Looking back at some of her letters, I understand that she must have done the same: often I have a single sheet of relatively small paper, in her largest hand, telling me she is too tired or sick or busy really to write, but "just want to get a word off to my Baby before the day ends."

By the time I began my Ph.D. work, we had come to a tacit agreement that three letters a week were enough, though Mamie still commented if one was late. My correspondence must have been longer and more interesting at that time, because her letters are full of obvious replies to things I have initiated: discussions of movies, books, politics, the complexity and power of human relationships, and lots about spirituality. Though her poor health and worries about not being asked to do enough substitute teaching to earn the money she needed pepper this correspondence, for the most part my mother seems fully participatory in an inner life and in the world around her. She tells me of concerts attended, plays and movies seen, art galleries visited—all with a relish she seemed to have for new ideas as long as they occupied some public space and did not require direct changes in her daily life.

These letters are also full of cautionary notes about my hair, my finger picking, my long-term weight problem, my grammar and spelling, my general state.

Fall 1962: How is your hair? Rolling it? I had a topaz rinse put on mine and it looks lovely—not brassy—just "highlights."

Spring 1962: Gary, my poor, stupid little pupil—picks his fingers which reminded me of you. I'm afraid that your poor fingers have suffered during *this* [I was preparing for my German exam]

—Won't you use the Nivea and Band-aids? I'll be glad to pay for them—Don't think a *teacher* with *no fingers* would be very apt to acquire a good post. Really worry about your fingers—Understand (really I do) how nervous you are—but couldn't you develop *another* habit—not biting your mouth for Heaven's sake [I had done that until a doctor terrified me by telling me that if I persisted, I would have to have the sides of my mouth and perhaps my tongue removed]—that would *mutilate* something beside a part of your anatomy—Please try, honey . . . .

Fall 1962: All of the eating that you write about *must* be putting pounds to your already overweight body—Why don't you do without one meal a day—I know it is hard but I hate to see my lovely Toni gain *so much* weight. Please try—I am going on my starvation diet again—Want to get down to 139 before you come home for Christmas—think it is impossible but I shall try.

Spring 1963: (*Your* saying, darling) remember the gerund takes a possessive pronoun? [I must have used "you" in my previous letter].

Late winter 1958: "Pushed up" [I had used this phrase in a letter] is a very poor choice for an English major getting her Master's—and Watch your grammar—vocabulary—rhetoric—syntax—wish *we* were near to help with that—Your *knowledge* is remarkable—your perception—ability—keenness of mind—expression—ability to write—*but I do find fault/criticize/condemn/disparage/disapprove/lament* your grammar and rhetoric.

Spring 1962: Poor Easter eggs *died* instead of *dyed*.

Spring 1963: I *will* see, young lady, that you attend to your lovely teeth when I get there [written shortly before her visit to Madison the spring before she died]. Do you want to wear dentures? Makes me angry to think that I did everything and ate everything that would prenatally be of value to you and now you are *abusing* the very thing that I was and am concerned about—teeth . . . and *gums* (hate that word)—but your lovely soul and spirit, are a joy to behold.

Mamie's vigilance about my appearance often drove me away; I felt her concern as nagging and did everything possible to avoid certain subjects. I also eventually tried to avoid going home, since in her house I was under her rules. The summer after my first year in Madison, I went home for about a month. After a year truly on my own, I was not looking forward to resuming my place within the family; to protect myself, I militantly outlined what I had to do to pass my preliminary exams coming up the next March. "It's absolutely *imperative* that I cover everything in medieval and the Renaissance this summer or I'll never be ready by next March. That means rereading and making study notes on the most important of *The Canterbury Tales*, plus outlining Malory and 'Sir Gawain' and the Pearl poet. And that's just for the fourteenth century. Then I have everybody from Barnaby Goodge to Thomas Hooker to review for the sixteenth. So I just don't know how I'm going to be able to get it all done in time." Mamie agreed to my modest request to retire to study one hour in the morning and another in the afternoon, showering me with, "Oh, honey, I'm so proud of you; you're at such a triumphant point on your intellectual journey. I don't know anyone else's child who has done what you have." Just underneath this effusion, I felt her hurt and sense of neglect. She also wanted to say, I was sure, "Since you're home for so short a time, can't you just suspend study—after all, it's eight whole months till that test; can't you study on your time and not mine?"

I had long suffered from the oppressive heat of southern summers, finding it impossible even to read for more than about twenty minutes at a time because sweat ran down my legs and arms, and I stuck to whatever I sat on. Using this as a defense, I set up a study space in our basement. Most days, as my hour neared its conclusion, I would hear the upstairs door softly and slowly open. Determined to have my agreed-upon time, I would act as if I had not heard the squeaky hinges. In a minute or so, Mamie's footsteps would then ease down the first two or three steps. There would be a long pause, while I continued with my head bent studiously over one of my several outsized texts, and then she would say, "Toni, your study time's over and I won't see you again till Christmas; surely you don't begrudge this little time with me."

One of the most significant things my mother and I ever did together was to take that unique vacation, just the two of us, during the summer of 1959. I had finished my first year of teaching in Mississippi, where there had been nothing to spend money on but Friday night dinners and the one movie worth seeing that year—*A Room at the Top.* Since room, board, and laundry were included under my contract, I banked the majority of my salary. I proposed to Mamie a driving trip from Birmingham over to Atlanta and from there up the Atlantic seaboard to Williamsburg and Washington, D.C. After a week in New York, we would drive to Quebec City and then due east to the tip of French Canada, a place called Perce because it boasted a huge rock from which an arch had mysteriously fallen out during the late nineteenth century. A few miles out into the sea there was Bonaventura Island, home to thousands of ocean birds, even the elusive puffin. We would be away almost six weeks; I had never been alone for that long with my mother.

Williamsburg's reproductions of products and people from the revolutionary era bored me after the first hour of sauntering along falsely cobbled streets, and trying to drive around D.C.'s monuments and government buildings when I had never been near a freeway made me frantic. But New York was a sheer delight. My mother's enthusiasm for antique shops and Broadway plays knew no bounds. No inch of Seventh Avenue escaped our scrutiny, and we saw ten plays in seven days. We sat in the front row for *West Side Story,* and Mamie was enchanted by the young men dancing so close that their sweat fell from the stage into her lap. We seemed to understand the inside jokes at *The Tenth Man,* sat glued to our seats through electrifying performances of *Five-Finger Exercise* and *Toys in the Attic.* We even braved our way to the off off Broadway original production of Genet's *The Balcony,* staying afterwards to speak with the actors who came out from behind the arena stage to mix with the audience.

In Quebec I put us up at the Chateau Frontenac, paying exorbitantly for room service at breakfast, complete with a waiter who brushed off the tablecloth in between toast bites. Mamie relished every minute of our stay because it reminded her of her Selma girlhood with its grandeur and elegance.

In Perce, we relaxed. Absence of neon came as a welcome change from the Big City, and we walked on the beach for hours every day, picking up magic shells or just watching the tide creep up the sand toward our bare feet. If we felt energetic, we toured one or two of the ubiquitous shops displaying local artisans' work—images in every conceivable medium of seagulls, cormorants, puffins, and the big rock with the hole in its middle. Our hotel was a throwback to an earlier, more leisurely era—spacious rooms with huge bathtubs, a dining room with glass windows on all sides so no one missed the gorgeous view at any meal, a porch across the entire back facing the ocean and filled with outsized cane rocking chairs. Guests were assigned their own table for the duration of their stay, so Mamie and I got to know our waitress and were advised to wait and tip her after our last breakfast in the dining room. The food was primarily French: beautiful vegetables augmented by piquant sauces of mysterious composition; perfectly broiled and absolutely boneless fish; bread so crisp on the outside you could hardly get teeth through it to the still-warm softness of the middle. The desserts made even Mamie envious—giant éclairs with the least rubbery dough we had ever tasted; layer cakes whose fillings were sweet but not in an American saturated way; homemade sorbets and ice creams that soothed away any slight perturbation from the day.

One of the high points of our week in this place at the edge of the world was an afternoon trip out to the famous pierced rock and the bird sanctuary. Little boats motored small groups of tourists to within a few yards of the face so we could see bird nests and colonies. The trip out was leisurely enough and the display of bird life spectacular: miniature gulls nesting on ledges so narrow they seemed no ledges at all; bigger gulls with their young still screeching frantically for food; cormorants hanging onto sheer rock; even a puffin or two comically holding fish in their bills, just as on the postcards in every shop in town. As the boat swung around to head back to the dock, winds suddenly came up causing waves to spill over the edge of our tiny craft. A nonswimmer, I panicked, sure we would capsize any minute. The driver kept assuring us, "This is nothing, ladies and gentlemen, sit back and enjoy; we'll soon be tied up, snug as a Canadian bug." Before we reached such safety, our boat was half-full of sea water, and the helmsman looked more worried than not. Mamie seemed to love it, however, holding her hand out to catch the spray, licking her salty fingers, comforting me with words about our "seaworthy" boat and her superb skills in the ocean. That night we ate the speciality of the house, telling ourselves that we had earned it from our adventure on the high seas.

We both loved our time together, but when either of us talked with friends about this trip, we tended to recount the worst aspects. For Mamie, those were my getting lost trying to get out of Boston (and driving over the Mystic River Bridge five times until the man in the toll

booth recognized us) and her conviction that I wished I were somewhere else with someone different. My story involved asking for a
morning alone after our first night on the shore of the St. Lawrence
River en route to the Gaspé Peninsula. We had been together virtually
every moment, in hotel and motel rooms or my tiny Volkswagen bug.
I needed some breathing space. Though Mamie accepted my withdrawal, she subjected us both to a day or so of hurt silence. Perhaps
neither of us could acknowledge how wonderful it had been to sneak
away from responsibilities and stare at rows of serene gulls for hours
or eat French delicacies at every meal.

My motives for taking my mother on that trip were complex.
Having just completed a difficult first year of teaching, punctuated
most dramatically by my growing fear about what it meant that I
wanted to make love with women, I needed not to spend three months
sitting idle in Fairfield. But as much as I needed that movement, I was
led to propose our getaway from some deep sense of loneliness for my
mother. The facts are that my mother spent a great deal of time with
me when I was growing up and was extremely generous in giving me
things and opportunities that enriched my life tremendously. But I
always felt outside, that her relationship with her husband and first
daughter, my father and sister, overshadowed my chances for genuine intimacy. To "have her to myself" for six weeks seemed a rare and
important event, worth the inconveniences it might cost me.

The summer before she died, Mamie came to Madison with Betty.
She stayed with me in a friend's home; Betty audited a summer session
class and chose to live in a dormitory. For my part, I was trying to get
history courses out of the way quickly, so I had registered for two,
which proved an almost disastrous miscalculation. I introduced my
mother and sister to my friends who were uniformly charmed by
Mamie and impressed by Betty's verbal prowess and eclectic knowledge. Most afternoons, they sat at teas or elegant extended lunches at
one of Madison's luxury lakeside hotels, while I tried to cram pages of
information into my head before dinner time.

I could tell Mamie was not well because of glaring somatic and
psychosomatic symptoms. Several times while on shopping outings,
she was seized by attacks of bursitis or extreme shortness of breath,
forcing us to take her home or to a doctor. Partly out of a terror about
her health and partly from overexposure, I tried to deny the reality of
these "spells." After all, I had been coping with them since childhood

and knew that occasionally they were ploys, albeit unconscious, to get me to do what she wanted. Somewhere deep inside, however, I knew things were more serious this time, and I supported her trying to slow down Betty's desire to experience everything Madison had to offer in the way of culture.

Because of my own academic schedule, I felt mostly torn between wanting to show Mamie my world and needing to find a carrel in the library and study seventeenth-century English history. But we had long breakfasts in the usually cool summer mornings—tea and toast in front of my friend's huge picture window that opened on a beautiful garden. I also remember vividly my sudden fear the day we had all three walked up Bascom Hill so Mamie could see where the English department was. Once the tour was over, we were to walk back down, but her face told me we could not do that. It had turned ashen, her generous application of rouge notwithstanding. Little beads of sweat had popped out through the French powder on her forehead and upper lip, and her breathing had become labored. Betty seemed to be blocking out all these symptoms: was she even more afraid than I? I stepped in, "I'll just go get the car and pick ya'll up and we'll take Mamie right home to lie down and rest before dinner."

At the end of that summer, I drove back to Alabama with them in Betty's Volkswagen. We had planned to have lunch in Nashville with an old friend who was to meet us at a Holiday Inn on the outskirts of town. After a lively meal, as we were ordering dessert, Mamie announced she was having an attack and could not breathe. While Betty rushed to the reservations desk to get a room for the afternoon, I said hasty goodbyes to our friend and went in search of ginger ale. Sometimes, having that over shaved ice helped to calm Mamie's system enough for her to stop hyperventilating. After a few hours of utter quiet in a tightly curtained motel room, she felt better, so we set out at dusk and arrived in Birmingham by nine that evening.

I stayed home for the next week, watching Mamie switch from proposing we all go to a picture show to lying on her bed trying to catch her next breath. When she felt more herself, she lectured me about my susceptibility to my friends, my need for continual vigilance about food and finger picking, and my tendency to speed on the highway.

When I drove away from Holly Court in early September of 1963, waving gaily and expecting to return for another lavish Christmas celebration, I little thought that I would never see my mother again.

Late in the afternoon of December 12th, I had finished a seminar on John Donne, on whom I was beginning my dissertation. I was to spend that evening with my lover and was excited to get home and straighten my apartment. When I walked in the door, she was standing in my dining room, looking grim. I panicked that she had come to tell me it was off because her husband or employer or some other authority had found out and was threatening dire consequences. Before I could ask, she put her hands heavily on my shoulders, looked me hard in the eyes, and said all in one breath: "Betty called me at the office. Your mother's dead. I've made an airplane reservation for a six o'clock flight with a changeover in Chicago. I'll help you pack and drive you to the airport."

All I remember about that trip to Alabama is the changeover in Chicago. I was supposed to have an hour to get from one flight ramp to the other, but we were kept circling over the city interminably. Once in the airport, I had seven minutes to go up the terminal causeway, across the main circular building, and onto another causeway that would take me to the southerly routed planes. It was 1963, and I was in high heels, hose, and girdle. I was carrying a suitcase, overnight bag, and purse, but I ran harder and longer than I had since I used to race around my backyard until I dropped, my wild energy momentarily spent. Somewhere along the way, I became aware of pain in my hands from the weight of what I carried and pain in my feet from running in pointed-toed shoes. My chest hurt so badly and my breath was so short that I felt dizzy and nauseated. But I made my connection, amid various statements of concern from passengers, red caps, and stewardesses. I smiled weakly or thanked them, but spoke to no one, preferring to have three stiff bourbons and ginger ale with no dinner.

My carefully disguised drunkenness was met by Betty's obvious state of shock. I remember how ravaged she looked and my awkward attempts to comfort her. But she would have none of it, needing to stay in control as we drove to the funeral home. As we went, I asked her repeatedly to tell me how Mamie had died. My questions were met with silence, comments such as, "How can you ask me that now?" or sobbing. At the funeral parlor, I was outraged by the piped-in organ music playing maudlin tunes and the dark, flowerless hallways with their trapped gardenia scent. I think I saw the coffin then—closed, not to be opened—again denying me the physical reality of a parent's death.

Mamie's funeral was a replay of Daddy's. Betty fell apart; I held myself together on the surface and dealt with visitors, this time shielding my sister from all but the chosen few. Her husband was in Endicott, New York, learning about a new IBM machine. He arrived unmet at the airport several hours after I did. When he entered our living room, he burst into tears. He broke down again at the cemetery, where I sat dry eyed and stony, full of emptiness and guilt and a sense of final abandonment.

I flew out of Birmingham a few days after Mamie was lowered into the ground, returning to Madison and the care and comfort of my lover. Ten days after my mother's death, I repacked my bags and returned to Chicago for the annual meeting of the Modern Language Association. If I wanted employment that next fall, I had no choice but to endure the interviewing process. Still in shock from Mamie's death, I ran up and down the stairs of the Palmer House hardly aware of who or where I was, much less of what I was saying to questions that seemed too trivial to be endured. My head pounded without stopping during the entire three days, but some protective angel kept me from drinking, and I survived the seven interviews scheduled.

At the interview with the University of Minnesota, where I eventually took a job, Samuel Holt Monk, renowned scholar in eighteenth-century literature, revealed that he was from Selma, Alabama. Through a chain of questions that brought me close to fainting, he determined that he had thrown the *Selma Gazette* onto my mother's family's front porch when he was a little boy. Tears almost surfaced, but I was trying to appear professional and sophisticated. I pushed them back for the second time that month. It would be many years before I let them spill, before I even began to grieve my loss of this primary woman in my life.

Part III

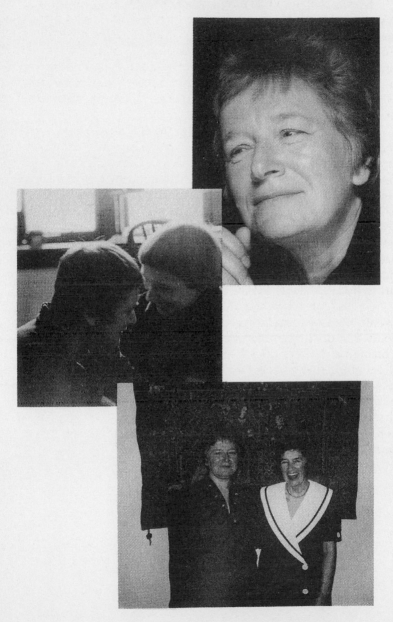

Top right: the author, 1990; *center left:* the author and Susan Cygnet, 1980; *bottom left:* the author and her sister, 1987. Courtesy of Toni McNaron.

Finding Self, Finding Words

The next ten years bleed into one another like Madras cloth in the wash: one ten-week course after another in Shakespeare or Milton or English literature from *Beowulf* to Virginia Woolf with from thirty-five to sixty undergraduates; one passionate nine-month relationship after another with a woman ten to fifteen years younger than I; one evening or weekend after another full of too many bourbons and ginger ale or on the rocks.

On an external level, I accomplished a lot during this muddled decade: I won promotion to associate professor after only three years, billed as one of the bright new stars in Minnesota's crown; I won two competitive awards for outstanding teaching; I became one of the most sought after faculty to serve on policy-making committees. Efforts at writing were less than satisfactory, though I began many projects. The closest I came to publication was the acceptance of a book manuscript on Shakespeare's late romances in which I argued that forgiveness and continuing to live were more valued by the older bard than heroic deaths or the senselessly violent pursuit of vengeance. Mouton, a publisher in the Hague, liked it and was about to put it into press when their budget and my project were slashed. My severe depression over this catastrophe only deepened when I heard that one of my colleagues had probably written someone he knew at Mouton to sabotage my work by claiming it was actually the product of my graduate research assistant. Jack Daniels profited enormously from this reversal, and my writer's block worsened.

Social psychologists are fond of hypothesizing the ill effects of precocity and perhaps that partially accounts for my slump. Certainly, I had sailed through school, college, and graduate school with assorted A's, fellowships, and awards. But it had only been partly a joke that I was best with children and stray animals: I was not adept at making human connections, and people my own age tended to silence me unless I had had several drinks.

As a new assistant professor, I was invited to dinners and cocktail parties held in the homes of older members of the English department. Unable to refuse and unable to take my lover to such gatherings because we had convinced ourselves that we had to live in one of the darkest closets imaginable, I hovered at the drink and food table hoping no one would try to make conversation with so obviously unsocial a being. Inevitably someone did.

"Well, Toni, and how are you finding Minneapolis/your students/the winter/our art galleries/the symphony/your neighborhood?"

"Oh, just fine, thank you," gulping my drink or sandwich in a frantic gesture to buy some time while I thought about what I could say next to the person trying so hard to set me at my ease. I certainly could not return the gambit, since whoever was in front of me had lived in the city for at least a decade.

"Are you making friends, meeting people, or are you lonely for someone special back in Madison?"

Utter panic. My "someone special" was at home studying the MMPI or Rorschach blots or theories of personality development and deviancy while we lived a life my conversational partner might well see as an example of the latter. So how was I to answer so innocuous a question? "No, I'm not meeting people—it takes all my spare time to manage my lies and secrecy, thank you."

Gradually, I began to refuse such invitations, preferring to stay home where I could drink uninterrupted. If I did go to a colleague's for dinner, the pattern was set: I arrived exactly at the appointed hour and either refused any predinner alcohol or sipped something tasteless. Once at dinner, I nursed a single glass of wine while other guests went for seconds and thirds without seeming to give it a thought. The moment dessert was over, I excused myself, offering class preparations or my habit of arising at 5:30 in the morning or a headache from a hard day at the office to my confused and at times irritated hostess. Back in the isolated safety of my apartment, I began to drink in earnest, drinking until I fell asleep or drifted into a blankness that passed for sleep.

By my early thirties, I certainly realized that I was in trouble with alcohol, though that realization made no difference either to my drinking or to my efforts to get help. I promised myself routinely that I would stop on the first of the next month or when the current bottle was used up, on New Year's Day or my birthday. Such promises and their attendant "wagons" lasted anywhere from a day to six months on those rare occasions when I was more frightened than usual about not being able to read as long as I once could or not being able to get letters of recommendation done on time or at all.

Working in the English department during the late sixties and early seventies was poles away from present conditions for incoming assistant professors. We taught three courses for each of three quarters, almost all of them different from one another. That meant that nine times a year I faced new students, strenuous preparations, hefty sets of mid-quarter exams, papers, and finals. We were expected to serve on at least two department committees a year, attend at least one professional conference, and somehow miraculously progress toward being famous scholars in our fields. The longer I escaped into alcohol and remained unable to speak about my personal life, the less well I did at any of this except classroom teaching. For some reason, the moment I entered one of the uniformly dingy spaces in which learning was to occur, I dropped my shyness, lost my fears of being apprehended as a criminal, and spoke—passionately and convincingly—about "The Wanderer," with whom I identified completely as he waked from his lovely dream of some good old days when he sat at his master's feet after having served him loyally to the cold reality of old age and loneliness, or about the Romantic and Victorian poets, who again appealed to my growing melancholia and *Weltschmertz*.

When anti-Vietnam protests reached my campus, I was one of the first faculty to participate. The students struck against a university with heavy investments in the Honeywell Corporation, which was busily making antipersonnel bombs just across town. Out of fierce sympathy, I held classes off campus, hauled my Milton students in my little red pick-up truck from one to another of their nearby apartments. We read *Areopatigica* and grasped censorship in a way not possible in previous quarters. When a graduate student friend and I were maced, I realized that there were all sorts of reasons the authorities might turn against their own—not just sexual difference—and understood coalition for perhaps the first time. Bob and I rushed into the nearest classroom building where other students stood at water fountains with wet cloths for burning eyes. Once we could see again, we decided to proceed as quickly as possible across the bridge that separated us from my parking ramp and the quiet of home. As we were about to go up the stairs leading to it, a large, angry policeman stopped us with, "Just where do you think you're going? Can't you see we've got a situation on our hands with these stupid kids rioting?" After I showed him my faculty identification card and assured him that Bob was my assistant and not a "stupid kid" even though he had very long hair, he grudgingly agreed to our passage. But when Bob put his left hand on the stair rail, the officer became suddenly incensed. In a split second, he brought down his billy club with full force just inches from my friend's hand. When I saw how close Bob had come to having his five fingers pulverized, I grasped just how furious certain Americans were at other Americans.

When students on the Kent State campus were fired at and killed, I marched with outraged students and faculty in Minnesota. When similar events occurred at Jackson State, I watched liberal colleagues straining to feel what had come so naturally when white students were attacked and killed. During this time, I renewed my acquaintance with the only black person I have known at all well since moving north. I had met Anna years before when she took a train from Mississippi to Minnesota to attend a community college where my lover worked as a counselor. She came to our apartment once for iced tea. Though we were all pretty stiff, she and I did talk about Mississippi and her grandmother. When she decided to transfer to the university, I was her initial contact, but we had not seen each other for some years.

A rally marking the deaths at Jackson State was held atop the steps and between the Doric columns of our large auditorium. It turned out that Anna and I were both scheduled to speak: I to demand action from the university about another academic assault; she to demand action from whites. I was cynical, and Anna was bitter. While an assistant vice-president for student affairs was droning on, we made rather loud fun of him from the sidelines. When he tried using black language, Anna and I broke out laughing. For the next few minutes, we talked urgently about what it meant that we had both grown up in the South. We acknowledged that for the moment we were closer to each other than to white or black northerners; we shared a common culture and language even if we were on utterly different sides of southern tracks. That scene on the stoa of Northrup Auditorium remains incandescent in my memory, though my bone-deep racism continues to haunt me.

In 1983 my partner and I were vacationing in London. Friends had told us to be sure to visit the public baths near our flat, assuring us that they were antithetical to their American namesakes. We made appointments for "Ladies Day" and had a two-hour adventure in water and steam heat. My only anxiety turned around the significant numbers of black women who were also there. I had never seen a black woman naked and kept catching myself staring at their bodies. Swinging from amusement at my own fascination to awkward embarrassment, I especially recall an older woman, wiry and strong, with salt and pepper hair on her head, under her arms, and at her pudendum. She talked with us as if we were just some more people at the baths: "Oh, it's just so invigorating to go quickly from the sauna to this cold water. I jump in all at once and swim to feel the most tingling possible. You must try it, really." Other black women advised us about which saunas were the best temperature that day, where it was safe for us to put our towels, and how to sign up for a marvelously nurturing soap massage during which whole buckets of tepid water were thrown over one's back. No whites spoke to us. I was drawn to and afraid of black women up close, unable to relax in their presence, unable to imagine caressing or being caressed by them without feeling either too excited at breaking a taboo or just a little squeamish. Later I admitted to myself that I would have deep trouble making love to a black woman. In that instant, I tasted the southern poison running in my veins at a level seemingly untouched by intellectual, literary, or even emotional change.

My experience of the Vietnam War combined with fledgling conversations beginning to take place about what would later be called feminist pedagogy taught me a permanent and invaluable lesson. I comprehended that the classical lecture format in which one person is supposed to have all knowledge while many others are convinced of their ignorance if not stupidity was academic colonialism. If I was willing to risk my vision and safety protesting such a policy in Asia, I surely needed to rid myself of my own comparable practices.

As so often is the case, I careened from one extreme to the other. In the early seventies, I stopped lecturing entirely, saying to each new group of students, "Coming in here every class and beginning to lecture about things you may not have the slightest interest in hearing is like intellectual prostitution, and I won't do it. I will arrive and wait for questions from you on matters of urgency in this play/poem/

story." Naturally, my students were stunned into deeper silence than usual, and we spent many uncomfortable sessions: after all, I was expecting them to know enough to ask me intelligent questions about a subject they had taken precisely because they wanted more knowledge of it.

Fortunately for us all, my innate passion for the literature overcame my rigidity about having academically pure politics. Though I have never returned to unbroken lecturing, I have come to accept responsibility for all I do know that they do not, and remain accountable to them for using that knowledge to empower rather than mystify.

Drinking enough Jack Daniels or Seagram's Seven Crown (depending on when pay day had been), silenced the voices that told me I was somehow inadequate. But by using alcohol to escape them, I also lost contact with my best self. From earliest memories I have seen myself as intense—the four-year old oblivious to anything but shaping animals out of her feces; the child digging tunnels under the oak tree for an imaginary escape in her toy cars; the ten-year old devastated by the brutish foot that smashed her peep show. But I have also understood sabotage from a very early age, how insidious it is and how cunning. While accenting my spontaneous intensity, I ignored or downplayed my need to carry through, to face the consequences of being bright or sensitive or creative. I let out just enough of my interpretive powers to know that at the heart of my often flawed or unfinished products lay a jewel. I fooled myself for years. Somewhere along the way, I began pulling back from full experience or expression of myself. Others' early responses meant too much: "No one draws pink cows and brown people." "That note is way off key and too low for a girl to sing." "If you touch yourself there, your hands will fall off." "Girls don't become orchestra conductors or forest rangers." "Why don't you go out with some nice young man who is appropriate?"

Bourbon numbed my feelings and left me depressed. I swung between heavy drinking and periods of sensing that I could not continue both to drink and develop my intellectual and creative abilities. The first thing to suffer was my critical writing; eventually, I ceased being able to put any words onto paper. By 1968, I had stopped writing letters to everyone except my sister and Josephine.

Evidence of my demise lies in pathetic souvenirs of attempts at creativity. My filing cabinet still has a folder in it full of lists of projects:

subjects for long high-minded poems; topics for scholarly articles; designs for a better world. The tab on the file reads: "Scraps"; "Fragments"; "First Thoughts"; "Bits and Pieces"; "Inspirations."

In addition to these ephemera, I have drafts of articles, first on Shakespeare and later on Virginia Woolf, written when not actively drinking. These were sometimes even sent away to a journal, only to be rejected. On rare occasions when comments accompanied the nos, readers indicated that my piece had a bright kernel lost in opacity and verbiage. Such essays generally came back when I was once again focused on whiskey, in no condition to revise.

For the last eight years of my drinking, I managed only essential schoolwork. Papers that absolutely had to be returned were read; otherwise, they piled up for months, even years, collecting shame along with office dust. Books were somehow gotten through, though sitting still to read became virtually impossible toward the end of my drinking years. I had to resort to teaching titles of which I had prior knowledge. Most of my time was taken up with academic committee service, for I sensed that if I did not want to be exposed as a raging alcoholic, I had to move into administration, where work could be defined less specifically than in the classroom or in the library.

Two tangible outcomes are the existence of several university documents of major importance and a thriving women's studies department. While unable to write literary criticism, I authored a policy for evaluating teaching on a regular basis; a system-wide statement about academic freedom and its less-welcome corrolary, faculty responsibility toward their students and institution; a plan to give students one more credit than the number of hours spent in the class, thereby recognizing that learning takes place outside the classroom. What I remember most clearly about those documents is typing drafts way into the night, always with a glass near my typewriter. Occasionally I would reminisce about 1959 in Nashville, when I wrote a master's thesis about neo-Platonism in Keats's *Endymion* and lived on farm-ripe tomatoes and Jack Daniels Black. It was summer, and my fellowship had run out at the end of May. While my family gladly would have sent me more if I had asked, my guilt over spending so much on liquor kept me from asking. Once a week, however, I cooked for an evening meeting at the Vanderbilt Episcopal student center, always making more than was needed, counting on the charity of the chaplin who insisted that I "take home leftovers or they'll just get thrown out back."

In the case of women's studies, I was approached by a small cadre of graduate students eager to see us begin offering courses with an avowed feminist perspective. Not only did I assist them in drawing up a document to present to the dean, but when a program was established on a three-year experimental basis, I applied for and was chosen to be the first chair. My three years in office coincided with my last year of drinking and my first two of not. While we made tremendous strides as an academic unit, I struggled inside with a growing sense of desperation. In order to perform the groundbreaking functions set before me, I simply transferred my addiction from liquor to food. One of my last acts as chair was to clean out the massive wooden desk we had been willed by a woman retiring from decades in student personnel, who in her last years had consistently rescued our fledgling program from such minutiae as class scheduling deadlines and faculty appointment papers. In one of the side drawers, I came upon ancient crumbs from cinnamon rolls quickly stashed there when I would hear a student or colleague open the door of the outer office.

In all my years of drinking, I never missed a day's work. But I remember waking up feeling as if I would not be able to get out of bed, stumbling through a shower and strong hot tea, driving too fast to school to meet my classes. Once school was over, I drove purposefully home, thinking only of that first drink. I parked my car outside my house, walked quickly up the steps and into the foyer, opened the heavy oak front door, and made a straight path into the kitchen. Out came a glass into which I poured liberal amounts from my current bottle, maybe adding ginger ale, maybe not. Swallowing as rapidly as possible without choking, I downed number one. Only after that reliable streak of fire had cut down the front of my body was I calm enough to speak to my two cats who had come into the kitchen to greet me, take off whatever coat and shoes or boots I might have on, pick up the mail from the concrete floor of the foyer, and get a sponge to wipe up the trail of snow or mud or rain water that I had tracked on the wood floor and linoleum in my frantic need to drink.

The more deeply I sank into my pattern, the less able I became to make positive choices in lovers or to stay in a relationship longer than about nine months. My partners increasingly became women unwilling to face their own involvement with liquor. Our liaisons began in high passion but usually ended with my feeling victimized by younger women whose attention had wandered. Actually my own attention had never been focused on them. To do that would involve time and risk, and I already knew how much energy it took to maintain myself within my secret. Besides, no person could be counted on to deliver exactly what I needed as often and without fail as my beloved bourbon could, so I chose partners who would not interfere with that pursuit. A year or so before I stopped drinking, some brave lesbians opened the Lesbian Resource Center (LRC), housed in a storefront across the street from a popular gas station. When their newsletters began coming to my home, I was shocked and frightened, since "no one knew." But come they did, announcing pool playing, card games, weekly community meetings, occasional dances, special holiday meals and celebrations. I devoured every word, memorized all the dates and times, quickly located the address, and drove by on community meeting nights. Unable to walk in, I tried to soak up something through my car windows and the center's heavily curtained front. I told myself I did not fit in, but the truth was I knew I would and was scared. Being a private lesbian was one thing but identifying with a cross-section of society seemed quite another.

I began to mail the LRC cash donations in unmarked envelopes, telling myself I would be fired if my bank saw a check made out to such an organization. One Thanksgiving, I received a colorful flyer announcing a feast in lesbian space, asking people to bring food and to come share warm company. Afraid to attend, I nonetheless had become increasingly an invisible part of the LCR's activities. After some brain wracking about how to participate without going, I devised a workable if sad solution. I had a neighborhood grocery deliver a handsome turkey to the center the Wednesday before Thanksgiving, and, as I ate a T-bone steak alone in my house, I pictured a room full of women brave enough to go and eat that bird.

The LRC supported a journal, *So's Your Old Lady (SYOL)*, and, from the occasional copies I had seen, I knew I had skills to offer such an enterprise. Simultaneously, I was becoming aware that a couple of political lesbians had opened a bookstore in someone's basement. I tried to convince myself that I could work on these activities or at least publish in *SYOL* under a pseudonym. Nothing happened for another year except that I worried about the idea whenever I was sober long enough to catch a glimpse of where my life was going.

During the summer of 1974 a colleague told me he had been to a wonderful bookstore full of books by women, located next door to a combination pool hall, bowling alley, and bar. His recommendation allowed me not only to drive by but finally to park my car and go in. I told the two women working there about my *male* friend's excitement, hoping that my flimsy excuse would cover my real reason for being there. One of the women was tall and quite thin, the other shorter, more compact, and intense. Both were utterly silent, forcing me to initiate any conversation. They owned a rather large black dog named Sappho, who insisted on being friendly but whose nuzzling frightened me even more than I already was. By the end of an awkward half-hour, I had volunteered to work in the store two hours a week on Saturdays.

The shorter woman, who turned out to be a cofounder of the LRC, was usually on duty when I worked. I had to laugh about getting in way over my head with my first foray into the "lesbian community." Her name was Karen Browne, and I was immediately attracted to her—politically, intellectually, physically. Each week my two-hour shift stretched a little longer, and we slowly developed the literary side of the holdings, since current stock reflected both her and her partner's training in social science and political activism. We undertook an inventory and devised a system for ordering new books. We also gazed at each other a lot, touched hands of necessity as we worked with books, became a bit easier in one another's company. Only as I was driving home would I realize that I had not been breathing very deeply during my shift.

One Saturday, Karen talked about women who sent the LRC anonymous donations but never lent energy to the ongoing life of the place. I called in sick the next week, ashamed of my cowardice. She risked public ridicule so that lesbians could meet somewhere other than dark bars or private homes behind pulled shades, while I sent in my secret money.

The big change in my life came in the fall of 1974 when I was thirty-seven. Karen had a part-time job at the university and, since we lived within three or four blocks of one another, it seemed natural to ride to and from work together. As I fell increasingly in love with her, I realized I had to end my pro forma relationship with the person living in my house. She was a kept woman—kept by me. I paid for elaborate dinners, a plane trip to Denver and the Painted Desert as a celebration of her passing her doctoral examinations, her room and board in my house, a Cordon Bleu crêpe pan so she could fix her friends elegant suppers when I was working late at school. I even let her bring an

English sheep dog into my house, when I thoroughly disliked dogs. That puppy was locked in the laundry room each morning as she left for long days at the library. The combination of his frantic whimpers and the growing smell emanating from my basement drove me to walk him around the block, urging him to "Do your stuff" outside. My two cats looked at me with startled eyes every time he grew another inch, something that seemed to happen every other day. After all my wool carpets were deeply stained by urine, my lover asked if I would buy an outdoor running pen for her playful pup. In a conversation with a salesperson at Sears I learned that the cheapest run cost $1,200. That evening I announced that we were getting rid of the forty-five-pound puppy who made my hardwood floors shake when he careened from kitchen to front porch. That decision was the beginning of my exit not only from the relationship but from the matrix within which it existed.

The summer before, this same woman had sat rocking in my living room, drinking gin and tonic. Suddenly she stopped, leaned toward me, and said calmly: "I miss the excitement of our first six months, 'cause now I feel like I know all there is to know about you; we're not finding out anything new about each other and I'm worried about getting bored." I countered with: "Maybe we've gotten through vital statistics and can now really start getting to know each other on deeper levels." When I saw that my suggestion was not registering, I silenced my rage by falling off a six-month wagon. Under that rage lay a depth of hurt that overwhelmed me but that I pushed down as I tried vainly to think up more exciting tidbits about my past that might catch her attention. What I wanted most was someone to tell what it felt like to live inside my skin, lonely, hung over much too often, scared of being out as almost anything I really was—Southerner, lesbian, drunk, writer, passionate human being with dreams of a feminist world.

That fall was early and violent. By mid-October, most leaves were down on lawns, in gutters, in the crooks of steps. Late on the night of October 22nd, I was driving my car home from Karen's. The wind was throwing wet, dead leaves all over the street in front of my car. I slowed down to watch those leaves rising on the updraft, only to sink back into a sodden heap and be ridden over by someone on their way somewhere.

I decided to write a poem about the leaves when I got home.
I decided not to sleep with the woman who found me boring
   after half a year.

I decided to a read a book (*Sappho Was a Right-On Woman* by
 Sidney Abbot and Barbara Love), which I had let sit on my
 shelf for over a year, not wanting to know what it said.
I decided not to drink while I read that book.
I decided to stay up all night in my living room so both the book
 and the poem would be done by breakfast.

That night was uncommonly long. Lying about feeling restless, I
found my book, some scratch paper, and a pencil, and went downstairs. I boiled water for hot tea, which tasted bland, harmless, unsatisfying; I wanted a big glass of room-temperature bourbon swallowed fast to quiet the jitters beginning down the middle of my body.
I drank quarts of tea, liking it less as my hands began to shake and my
stomach to draw up into familiar knots that meant my liquor ration
was overdue. But I sat rigid on my couch, reading, fighting against
sleep and panic and pain. About three in the morning, I came to a
sentence late in the book on the right-hand side of the page that burned
its way through my brain just as Jack Daniels had burned my body. In
a long discussion of small ways lesbians lie about how and with whom
we celebrate, the authors asserted that for a lesbian to go to work on
Monday morning and lie about the sex of whom she spent her
weekend with is like committing suicide slowly but surely. I spilled
the tea I was nursing and began to shake from something new; Abbott
and Love were speaking only to me in that living room while the fall
wind whistled and moaned around the corners of my house.
    I left the book unfinished and worked on my poem about wet
leaves in a chance wind—it seemed infinitely safer. What I wrote fast
and carelessly did not qualify as a poem, but it had lines, indented
from the left-hand margin, and it told the truth. I stuck it away in my
study where I would not come upon it for over a year. For the rest of
that night, I sat stone still while my cats slept nearby offering mute
comfort and my mood swung from lightheadedness to terror to
something resembling sanctification.
    Before the woman upstairs arose, I poured all my bourbon down
the sink and threw the empty bottles into my outside garbage can. I left
the gin since it had never been my drink but wrote a note saying I
wanted it and her out of the house by December 1st. Then I walked toward my neighborhood shopping area, feeling sick from no whiskey
for almost twenty-one hours. I found a café open early, where I devoured a lumberjack special: two eggs over easy, hash browns, toast,

bacon, sausage, lots of very strong tea. Later that day, I decided to tell somebody I was lesbian and picked my good friends from whom I had bought my house. I called to ask if I might stop by after work. That seemed to shock them more than my news: I had never dropped in on anyone or wanted them to drop in on me since I drank in secret. In their living room I was offered a drink. I said, "Thanks, I'm on the wagon," a comment accepted without question. After a couple of stuttered false tries, I blurted out my dire announcement. Martin smiled easily: "I love ya," while Martha quipped, "I was beginning to think there must not be any in Minneapolis."

Nothing magical happened when I sobered up. I simply stopped taking liquor into my body. While that was a momentous decision, my ways of dealing with myself and the world remained essentially unchanged. I transferred many of my compulsive needs from bourbon to Karen, putting far more faith in and strain on our relationship than any such delicate connection can bear. Though we continued to respond passionately to each other, sustaining the dailiness of a commitment was not possible, and we eventually set one another free.

Most of the mileposts along my recovery route involved wanting to make things. The first summer after I quit drinking, I decided to paint the trim on my house. For months, I persuaded unsuspecting friends to "come over for dinner and a little outside project." We climbed ladders, hung from eaves, and fought late-summer wasps. There came a moment when everything was done except three small pieces of gutta-percha pipe sticking up above my brick chimney. Determined that it be perfect, I eventually straddled my chimney and painted away these last traces of fading brown. Having enough sense to grasp that getting up on the peak of my steep roof alone might be a bit foolhardy, I waited until an old friend was visiting. She stood on the opposite side of my house from the chimney and held a thick clothesline, the other end of which was around my waist. We both believed this scheme would magically save me if I fell. Sitting atop my roof on a gorgeous Saturday afternoon, I was alive, able to breathe, happy. A snapshot catches this moment: me grinning against a perfectly blue sky, holding my four-inch paintbrush and my funny rope.

The second summer of sobriety, I dug a small garden in my side yard and planted flowers bought from the local farmer's market. Though my garden brought me moments of pleasure, somewhere around midsummer I forgot the plants and focused on the bright cans of cold beer everyone else in town seemed to be holding. The weeds got ahead of me that year, but every year since I have put flowers into the earth. When I finally bought perennials, I knew I was willing to bank on having a "next spring," that I wanted something to bloom from the year before. Those first tulips and lemon lilies were precious investments in my capacity to care for my own creation. Before signing a purchase agreement to sell my house, I inserted a clause stipulating that I could return the next spring to dig up my lilies and take them to my new yard.

For many years after 1974, my creations were primarily nonverbal. One Saturday when I wanted more than usual to drink, I drilled three-quarter-inch holes in very long two-by-fours instead. I needed space for cookbooks and other volumes that were spilling out of my downstairs study, so I decided to build a bookcase in the hall. Shunning the simple, I picked a no-nail design needing twenty holes for dowels on which would rest welcome shelves. I drilled ninety holes because I knew that as long as I was in my kitchen doing that, I would not go to the liquor store.

As a child, I had loved stories in books; my teenage years were consumed by books, since reading smoothed the edge off my loneliness. Once I was deeply into drinking, however, my ability to concentrate inevitably lessened. While going through a treatment program after I stopped drinking, I heard a lecture that helped me understand and forgive my restlessness in front of a printed page. It seems that each time a person gets drunk, several thousand brain cells die and must be replenished. I had to accept that it would take longer for my brain to dry out than it had for my hands to stop shaking. When, during my fifth year of sobriety, I suddenly found myself reading for a whole hour, my joy was exquisite. Almost every night as I lie in bed with my current book, I give thanks for the return of that gift.

As long as I was drinking, I could not afford to invest very heavily in my ideas or their expression, preferring the predictability and cold comfort of a bottle. But, in 1975, I accepted that I had something to say in words, on paper. After about a year of unsuccessful attempts, I stumbled upon Virginia Woolf's *A Writer's Diary* where she speaks of the function of her journal as a place to loosen her writer's ligaments, comparing journal writing with practicing piano scales before tackling more formal compositions. Willing to try her method, I tentatively chose to begin a journey toward my voice—I bought a journal.

Each volume was titled, which now intrigues me as I wonder what

I might have written inside something called, "A Notebook of Spirals," "Fronds & Tendrils," "Webbings," "Knots." At one point in my recovery of my writing self, a friend suggested that I cull from all those journals salient vignettes and publish them. For a month, I read diligently, marking in red along any margins I thought worth excising.

June 13, 1975: Reading exam papers from a course I just coordinated on courtly love—a thought on the word "elevation" in relation to power. Power is played out on the street level, the pavement as Woolf calls it. By elevating woman, men removed her from contact with power. So when Shakespeare says in Sonnet 130, "My mistress when she treads, treads on the ground," he is doing more than mocking courtly love conventions. His mistress seems genuinely in control, not falsely so by virtue of the poet's participation in the courtly love game. The desire to put woman on a pedestal is a way to keep her off the streets, out of the places where power is played out. We might consider the trap inherent in the myth that power corrupts. Like Renaissance-elite males wishing to preserve their position at the top who argued that ambition was evil, contentment with one's lot good, men may have made up the slogan "power corrupts" to deter the truly moral from embracing it. Power only corrupts if its wielders use it badly. Women could use power in new ways and not corrupt ourselves or others. . . . I've felt so well today, yet still can't stop my current eating binge—I have to do something. Each morning I intend, each night I gorge. I need to get physical exercise—I feel chained to this house.

June 10, 1976: Mary Schultz had her breast removed.

Losing Weight

"I'm still a compulsive eater" you say
Even though they've taken your breast away?
Was it white meat, or are we, like ducks, all
    dark?
"I lost in the hospital" you muse
from loss of appetite, you think.
I say your white-masked Shylock sliced his legal
    pound   and then some;

left you lopped and asymmetric/
Latter-day Amazon, take up your bow
against the world of female measurements:
   0–34–38
You sit amongst us eaters, worried that you'll
   binge again
"reward" for losing tissue, skin, and special
   female veins.
Grafting pounds to other places
cannot bring you back your lovely melon,
cannot fill that utter hollow.
So sit and smile your brave, wan smile
and be a bosom cyclops.

I've said I'd make chicken salad for Mary so she won't have to ask others to make so many meals for her. Here I am, in my kitchen, dripping sweat into the bowl—special natural salt—cutting a gelid chicken with big, sharp scissors just like my mother did, covering it and me with grease that will become worse as it warms on my skin. Once all the available meat is in the bowl (tall, super-white metal bowl that held *So's Your Old Lady* money when I read of women's hurts and loves) and some scraps are in my cats, I move to eggs—hard boiled a day ago so the shells fall off from compression in the ice box. Once naked—smooth and super white, like the bowl—eggs go one by one in a childhood gadget that slices them thin and even. Criss-cross I go to make smaller cubes—cold crumbles of yolk stick to my greasy hot fingers and I suck them and revel in that yellow softness on my tongue. Now the celery: greener on the outside cuts, whitish at the center—cut, cut, my knife eats up stalks, making them hard diamond cubes tossed in on top. Suddenly the salad looks like a monotonic mosaic shelf. Mix it up, I think—and do with my bare hands—up to my wrists—the stuff takes me over and my total impulse is to sink my face into the sea of salad and drink it in gulps. Instead I spoon mayonnaise into, around, among ingredients till the whole is viscous, oiled, ready—a mound of chicken salad for a lady with only one breast.

Travels back to my creative self have been slow, filled with relapses into verbosity and abstraction learned in childhood and rewarded by schools. I struggle not to feel either ashamed of where I am at my age or full of grief for the wasted years. Those women who have patiently but consistently urged me to my own speech have given me a jewel that I cannot always accept with open hands but one without which I would still be largely mute.

Every so often, I stumble on some artifact that simultaneously heartens, frightens, and depresses me. These remains share certain features: they do not look familiar to me, yet are in my handwriting; they reveal how much I can draw from a poem or a story when I focus. One of the clearest of these ghostly experiences came in 1983 while I was teaching a seminar on the poetry of Edna St. Vincent Millay, Louise Bogan, and H. D. When I opened my copy of *Helen in Egypt*, I was immediately distracted by marginal comments. Neatly penned in blue ballpoint, they indicated an intelligence keenly in tune with the poet's own. In addition to copious notes, boxes appeared around certain clusters of words having to do with shadows, ghosts, veils, dreams—images that provide crucial linguistic and emotional threads through this epic. I could not recall making the notations, but the handwriting was unmistakably my own. Turning to the front of the book, I found that it had been a birthday present in 1977. Amazed, I realized that though I had been free from alcohol for three years when I read H. D.'s work, I could still engage in an intense project that would then pass out of my consciousness so completely as to seem foreign six years later.

As I continued reading the poem and my work with it, I felt moved by the critical and creative interpretation that was building as steadily as H. D.'s story. The next day, I shared my experience with the seminar, naming those annotations as a sign of my ambivalence toward my creative voice and as evidence of my slow recovery from years of destructive drinking.

The same day I gave up liquor, I began telling people I was a lesbian. Originally that decision was political and therapeutic, but one long-term effect has been on my writer's voice. Gradually I have found and claimed my truest audience: lesbians and feminists interested in women's culture. Once I conveyed this shift in my focus to my department chairman, my writing became surer, livelier, more engaged. My first public speech from this position was on Valentine's Day, 1977, in the guild hall of a local church. Part of a series sponsored by an alternative women's learning institute I helped operate, my lecture was on the poetry of Olga Broumas, Audre Lorde, and Adrienne Rich as it contributes to a lesbian aesthetic. My typescript was more than twenty pages long, and it was good. The overwhelmingly lesbian audience was alert and supportive; for the first time in my life, I felt that my literary training might be put to some use.

As my journal writing developed, I became open enough to include poems and bored enough with my erratic love life to include entries about work, books, and other people who came into my life at a less intense level. Surveying the thirty-six notebooks I have made since 1975, I discover that sometimes I hardly talk of external conditions at all—my journal is a confidential source for self-exploration. At other times, I seem deeply caught up in the world around me.

In April 1978, I went to New York City to read the correspondence between Louise Bogan and May Sarton housed in the Berg Collection of the public library. I wanted to write an article about ways in which letters served as underground support networks for women hungry for other women's ideas. Amidst their discussions of aesthetics I was surprised to find an unmistakably intimate note. Sarton writes asking to extend their developing friendship into a sensual and sexual relationship. Bogan refuses, pleading her disastrous relationship with her first husband. Sarton values her friendship enough to struggle to readjust her feelings. All this is spoken of tentatively and painfully in the letters; my lesbian perspective and my awareness of my own partial alliances lent me a sympathy I might otherwise have lacked. As I read through their often tortured exchanges, I felt respectful and clear about not wanting or needing to distort what was on the pages. Empowered through my own experience, I was able to articulate what the webs of their caring and fighting looked like.

My journal from that month is full of long, introspective entries about everything from the drunks who stopped me as I walked to the library from the subway to the art, ballet, and drama that were integral to my stay. One of my last days in the city was spent at the Cloisters. I gave myself a whole day at that museum I had wanted to visit for years. Journal entries written there contain my responses to the unicorn tapestries. A segment from that visit indicates my growing desire to direct my critical faculty toward my environment:

> #7 is the famous scene of unicorn in captivity in round white fence. Unicorn looks rather dead in #6, then is set up in stasis in #7 as some ideal to be looked at and controlled even if not

understood. It's so clear—these men could never fathom the complexity of the creature they find, hunt, kill, capture—they are so worldly and decadent, the unicorn so magical and pure—there's just no way for them to connect at all. I need to know what I feel, looking at #7. It's sadness at the small space left for the magic beast—she can sit as she does, or stand—no walking—no movement at all. Not only is she inside a fence but tied to an orange tree as well. And in the center of a huge field of flowers, all free in nature. This series is about hunt—war—blood—violence—sex—*men*. The Cluny ones are about the relationship of the unicorn and the lady—look at Robin Morgan's poem once home; go to Paris some day and see the originals.

When I look at my stack of gray-bound books, I remember Evi. She was an editor of *So's Your Old Lady*, whose staff I had finally joined under my own name. Being part of that enterprise was immensely important to me as a writer, since I learned the mechanics of editing a magazine and found the first outlet for my own words.

Before Evi left the group to enter a martial arts collective, she called me out of the office to make me a present of a handmade leather folder in which she kept her own writing. Once I had admired it, asking where she had bought it. Its San Francisco origin seemed to place it beyond my grasp. Now Evi's own beautiful object sat on my lap with a card that read, "So you can unlock your word-horde." Tears sprang to my eyes at her remembering my telling her about my favorite Old English poem in which a man had kept his story silent until his old master told him to unlock his word-horde, to speak the truth within him.

The most important step toward speaking my truth about litera-ture involved my coming out at the university. My career at Minnesota spans twenty-six years, twelve of which were spent in the closet because I felt residual shame about being a lesbian and because I re-mained in an alcoholic haze that prevented me from seeing clearly. During those years, I survived but at great cost to myself. Not knowing how to express disagreements without antagonizing my colleagues, I either ranted or sat in stony destructive silence. In a journal entry following a 1978 department meeting, I wrote:

I am home from a four-hour-long meeting—headache, exhausted, drained, mute, nauseated, all stuffed in. I "made nice" all through, not saying how misplaced I find their values, not asking why there are no women writers on one man's list of canonical humanities texts, not saying that they're slanting the fiction writer search so as not to have to pay the woman candidate any heed. And we are going to promote to full professor a dullard, primarily because of his "time in rank" (five years to my thirteen). *Faces:* ashen, cud-chewing, carved in sneers, upturned lip, droopy eye, duck-tailed hard on devil's face leering, white roach grog dead, sunglassed mole, pearly-curly dandy, soft falling waves and deep hurt eyes, impish pucker covering steely-eyed true sight, balding round faced joker in forever pain, dicktracy chinned gentle, baggy-pants baggy-eyed vapid, short-haired thin, insipid loner, barefoot lad with deep set teddy bear eyes—English department rogues' gallery. I feel much quieter now.

Clearly I had no idea how to handle my workplace or its inhabitants. Equally clearly, there is no description of me, who at that stage in life was greatly overweight and stressed out in the face, had wildly curled hair à la Janis Joplin, owned ten picked fingers from agitation without an object, and pretended to like triple-knit suits, heels, and hose when I only felt at home in corduroys and flannel.

At the end of the seventies I took a year's leave without pay. I had to decide if I wanted ever to return to an institution that invested in research of which I did not approve and in companies that fed the defense machine, and to a department that refused to promote me to full professor no matter how hard I tried to be their version of me. I discovered the obvious: a teacher cannot make enough freelancing to keep body and soul together. I also learned that I disliked intensely having to advertise myself or arrange classes under my own aegis. The surprise of the year came during a visit by Florence Howe to our campus. She came to evaluate the women's studies program, from which I had just retired after three years as its first chair. We met for a long dinner away from campus followed by a visit to my house where we kept talking about the current state of women's studies work in the country and at Minnesota.

When I took Florence back to her motel, her hand on the car door handle impelled me to speak about what was really on my mind. I blurted out my dilemma about where to work, saying at one point, "I want to do something radical and going back to school seems so easy and safe."

Florence turned to me and said as distinctly as anyone has ever said anything to me: "No, Toni, you have it wrong. Going back to the university is much more radical than staying away. Don't you know you are one of the handful of lesbians with tenure in America and that teaching and working with students from an open position is far harder than offering courses in a church basement or park building. Take the power of the podium and use it—go back and endure the derision that will come your way."

I drove home with her words burning in my ears, feeling simultaneous shock and relief. Within weeks, I had made my sabbatical decision: I would return to the English department, but not until I had met with my chairman to tell him my plan to return as an out lesbian–feminist critic and teacher. I scheduled that meeting and announced to a man who had worked his way through an English college on a pugilist scholarship: "I want you to know that I will be giving you articles and syllabi that assume a lesbian–feminist perspective on literature. I want you to evaluate them the same way you do anyone else's work. Only on this condition can I return to this place." He blanched momentarily before assuring me, "My theory of administration is to find out what makes my staff happy and then help them do it."

When I told my best male friend about my conversation, he fairly beamed with some pleasure I could not at first fathom. He told me that my declaring myself had destroyed an ancient plan on the part of some old timers in the department. It seems that he had heard them at poker games when everyone was a little drunk boasting that should I ever have the nerve to complain about their refusal to promote me, they had the perfect rejoinder. They were maintaining a secret dossier of incriminating tidbits about my private life and would happily bring it out to challenge my claims of mistreatment.

Since that momentous and rather breathless interview with my chair in 1979, I have consistently offered courses in lesbian literature, culture, and critical theory. I have visited other classes to discuss such matters when the regular faculty either did not know enough to do so or held too precarious a position to risk it. My colleagues gradually have either accepted my perspective or decided to leave me alone and be civil.

Occasionally homophobia surfaces, as on an afternoon a few years ago. I was standing in the hall talking with a friend. Because my back had recently gone out of alignment, I was wearing a spandex girdle to help me sit during our long preschool meetings. In an attempt to hide as much of it as possible, I was wearing a blousy knit top that hid the pristine whiteness entirely in the front. In the back, a band about three inches stuck out below the bottom of my sweater.

As my friend and I were speaking animatedly, we were interrupted by one of the chronically homophobic members of our department. His opener to me was, "Well, Toni, in training for the Vikings (Minnesota's professional football team)?" Determined to show my disapproval, I rejoined, "Actually, Fred, my back is out, and I'm in constant pain, thank you." Covered with embarrassment, since he views himself as a liberal humanist, he stumbled through belated expressions of his concern and empathy, saying, "I know about backs; mine goes out on me, too." I am quite sure that, had he seen one of my heterosexual women colleagues in such attire, his imagination would not have conjured linebackers.

Florence Howe turned out to be exactly right that night over a decade ago. Occupying space as a lesbian at the university has changed virtually everything about working there. No longer do I come home with terrible headaches or a churning stomach; no longer do I deny what I see in the literature I teach or the theory I espouse; no longer am I useless to students interested in talking with someone who has lived and thought as a lesbian for more years than many of them have been alive. My classroom manner has become more relaxed because I no longer fear a question that will force me to lie quickly in order to avoid some devastating revelation that will cost me my job or at the least a reprimand from someone in authority for "corrupting the young." But the single most lasting benefit has been to me—being open in my work has been a tremendous boon to my finding and using my voice. Since 1980, I have published three books and several substantial articles and poems; I write reviews for *Hurricane Alice,* a feminist journal that I help edit, and for *The Women's Review of Books;* I have worked on this memoir for some six years. I no longer become terrified when I cannot write on demand or every day, trusting now that I am a person who writes and who will always do that. My greatest conflict these days is between paid employment and my desire for more time at home to write.

Everyday Magic

If Freud is correct when he says resolving love and work is essential for psychic health and happiness, then I have finally arrived. The last piece to fall into place, however, has been love, because trust and vulnerability both frighten and draw me. I also am a confirmed introvert, preferring my own company to almost anyone else's, having to force myself to make dates for lunch or walks when I would rather stay home with my animals and read or write or putter around the house and yard. But I also yearn to be known and cared for, to have a special someone to whom I can tell everything without fear of censure or ridicule, to give myself over entirely if briefly to another's wishes.

Thirteen years ago, I made a series of decisions that moved me closer to being able to hold this basic contradiction in solution, like letting oil float on water without demanding emulsion. I remained celibate long enough to review my sexual history and formulate some clear sense of what I wanted in a partner. Simultaneously I entered and completed several therapeutic programs intended to facilitate self-understanding. In 1978, at the end of this period of intense introspection, I began seeing a woman of whom I had known for years.

It began in 1972, when I attended a conference for counseling and guidance workers. My lover at the time, who owned the English sheepdog and nursed her boredom with me, was working toward a Ph.D. in that field and wanted to attend. Having no money, she let her wishes be known, and, as usual, I jumped at one more chance to secure her dwindling attention.

When I expressed a wish to tag along, she could hardly object. At the conference, a panel was held on special counseling needs of gay people. Still closeted at the university but hungry for information and contact with lesbians, I went. In a stuffy room, filled with anxious members of the helping professions, I witnessed a quiet, slight woman speak about the interrelationship between chemical dependency and being a lesbian in a hostile culture. Her words found my heart; when the program was over, I went to the front of the room to thank her. Shaking hands, I felt courageous and asked for her phone number and whether she would like to have tea sometime. Though she agreed, I was never able to complete the requisite telephone call. Twice I tried, once getting so far as actually dialing all seven digits. To my utter relief, the line was busy.

Because the lesbian community in Minneapolis was relatively small, I ran into Susan several times between our initial meeting and our beginning to court. She was at that time driving a city bus after more than a decade of public-school teaching. Every so often I found myself boarding her vehicle, sitting in the seat across from the driver's chair, talking nervously. After about four years of these chance encounters, I joined a group of lesbians that met weekly for dinner and discussion. Susan and her lover were members and I remember paying particular attention when she talked about their life together. I also was especially aware of her the night we abandoned personal consciousness-raising for an old-fashioned swimming party.

In the summer of 1978, two years after our Friday night group experience, we were asked to organize an older lesbians support group. I was determined to set the admission age at thirty-five, since Susan's lover was only thirty-four at the time. After each month's meeting, we found ourselves talking near our cars or arriving before anyone else "by accident." At the same time that her relationship was coming apart, we had lunch—two lunches actually. I suggested a little vegetarian place called the Mud Pie where we sat under a wooden trellis and had enchiladas and fruit juice. Susan took me to her club dining room for an elegant Sunday brunch followed by a spin around the nearby lake in her Fiat sports car. We confessed to wanting to be friends and that attachment grew until by late fall we acknowledged that we were in love. We took long walks along the Mississippi River, scuffing fall leaves, or drove out into the country in her little car with its top down and radio playing classical music, or spoke last thing at night over the telephone. Sensing this connection might be unique, I vowed with Adrienne Rich to "love with all my intelligence."

During the winter of 1979, Susan and I became lovers and after twelve years are still deepening our relationship. Occasionally I recollect with a wry smile the graduate student complaining about there being nothing left to do after six months. Occasionally I also still want to cut and run, finding intimacy just too hard, but I stay put and talk about my fears. Currently, we live in a large three-story house with a singular cat named Slate and a sweet English cocker spaniel called Blue. The past decade has brought enough happiness into my private life that I no longer entertain an old fantasy about living alone, isolated in a tiny apartment where I could die and no one would know it for days.

Household projects have become especially satisfying for us to undertake, and there have been some rare moments along the way. One of these happened during the first few months of our relationship. That winter was harsh even by Minnesota standards. Susan's house had a gently sloping roof on which snow accumulated in vast amounts as we lay snug and passionate in her bed. Having a steeply pitched roof myself, I was unfamiliar with the effects of snow build-up. After a January thaw, her roof began to leak around the insulation vents. To correct the situation, someone had to climb out onto the roof, shimmy over to the vents, and hammer the ice into disposable chunks. While I did this, Susan insisted on holding onto a rope tied around my waist. Remembering my earlier rope episode, I tried to persuade her of the final ineffectiveness of this plan, but she was sure she could save me should I slip. I firmly believed that I would suffocate from its being pulled too tightly around my middle or else pull Susan out the window so that we both would plummet down to the cold ground.

Before the ordeal was over, Susan ventured out onto the roof, admitting to a certain acrophobia. We reversed the rope trick and hoped for the best. Her fear flared up when she found herself further away from the entry window and me than she had intended, and she froze midway between safety and the ice line. Inch by inch, I talked her toward me until she could take my hand and scramble into her house, shaken both by the experience and by her willingness to gamble on my dependability.

From this early fiasco, we have progressed to semiannual hangings of forty-five storm windows or screens, depending on the season; a fall putting in of over a hundred bulbs on a day when finger tips turned blue; laying of bathroom carpet complete with precision cutting around toilet, lavatory, tub, and radiator; a yearly ritual Memorial Day planting of two flats of impatiens in our front garden;

a summer's labor of sanding, priming, and painting all the house screens in light lavendar to match one of the colors in Judy Chicago's Sappho plate. When we fall into old competitive ruts, we have to scream and yell. But mostly we mesh talents, patience, and taste so that we get amazing things done while having a good time.

We first understood how important an element travel would become in our life the spring after our roof adventure. I had planned for some time to take that quarter off from teaching and spend six weeks in England. Three of them were to be spent in London, doing what I liked most to do in that magical city: strolling in Bloomsbury, taking meat pies to the park for lunch, visiting the Tate or British Museum, eating mutton at an old chop house off Bond Street, riding the tube to place names that charmed me and then walking in that district until I felt tired. The other three would find me in Cornwall, at St. Ives where Virginia Woolf spent many childhood summers and of which her earliest memories are composed. I would search out her old family home and lie idly on the beach, listening to the same waves she had so loved. Between this plan and its execution, Susan and I happened. To my amazement, one autumn Sunday as we ambled along the river, talking about my April hegira, Susan said she would join me if I liked. She would spend two weeks in London with me; I would go a week early and find a place to stay. Once we had "done" the city, I would go on to Cornwall for my hermit period.

When we broke out of our parting embrace the day I left Minneapolis, I felt like someone was peeling the top layer of my body off. During my solo week in London, two firsts happened: I felt homesick, and I saw London sober. Each midmorning I lingered over tea, crackers, and cheese at a little shop near the German YMCA where I had taken a room. When it became embarrassing to sit in the same booth any longer, I looked for lodgings, a process that resulted in my renting a two-bedroom flat for ten days. Though it cost more than a hotel room, we could cook and be private in a living room of our own. Several evenings I called Susan and cried into the transcontinental phone for tens of dollars. By the time she flew into Heathrow, I had made a strange decision: I was going to return home when she did, dropping St. Ives from my itinerary. For an entire afternoon before coming to this, I roamed Virginia's streets, sat in her favorite squares, listening for voices warning me about giving up my time alone. Hearing none, I wrote her a poem in which I said, "Your waves will lack my echoes for the present/ I'll not go west to see your childhood shore/ I need to hear my own concentrics." I was choosing to live my own moments of being rather than trying to retrace some of hers.

The day before Susan's plane was to arrive, I cleaned the flat and laid in special provisions: malt wheat bread and sugarless jam from a health food store I located after much searching; fresh scones from the elegant little bakery a few blocks down Queensway; delicately wrapped fruit for our first breakfast; blue and purple flowers for the coffee table. Though her flight was not due until noon, I took an early morning airport bus so I could get a good place at the barrier for incoming passengers. With four hours to while away at Heathrow, I had a second round of tea and toast, paced the waiting area, tried to read but ended up just working at breathing evenly.

An interminable period lapsed between a voice announcing the arrival of Susan's plane at some invisible and unreachable gate and the appearance of a passenger. Since I was pressed against the yellow plastic-covered wire separating arrivals from greeters, I could not miss anyone's walking up the ramp. I watched as well-dressed business men filed off with attaché cases and black umbrellas, couples strolled up arm and arm and bleary-eyed, young families were met by grandparents and older people were welcomed by children and their children. I was sure hundreds had deplaned and still no Susan. As I began to panic, thinking she had fallen ill at the last minute or some other dire circumstance had occurred, I saw a stunning woman striding up the gangway in a broad-brimmed felt hat with a pink band around the brim and a rain garment that was half coat, half cape, all magic. For a split second I thought, "what a terribly handsome creature," feeling instant disloyalty to Susan. Looking again, I discovered the terribly handsome creature *was* Susan. We waved ardently and rushed up either side of the dividing rope until we reached its end and could touch.

Eventually we found ourselves in a traditional Hansom cab on our way into downtown London. In my navy pea coat and short hair, I had been several times mistaken for a man. When we pulled up at our flat, the cabbie said, as I gave him a generous tip, "Thanks, guv'nor."

Since that halcyon trip, we have returned several times to London, cabined in the Tetons, driven through the South to visit my sister and Susan's undergraduate college, lounged at a glacial lake in the Canadian Rockies, trekked around Paris and Florence, eaten lobster off a weathered wharf on the Maine coast, hiked across an island off the tip of eastern Quebec to gaze in wonder at a huge gannet colony, and driven often to the north shore of Lake Superior to watch ice break up in March. A few miles out of the city, things seem to loosen, drop away, leaving us together and close without need for scheduling.

Because our bond is so deep, I am vulnerable to hurt, anger, and disappointment when our moods do not coincide or our needs are not complementary. Occasionally our expectations about some event differ radically. The first Halloween we lived together showed us the disastrous effects of not knowing the other's history. I have never put out candy or popcorn for children, probably because when I was a child, my family did not let me go trick-or-treating. Fearful that something terrible would happen to me, they staged an elaborate substitute in which I dressed in my costume and then rang my own doorbell repeatedly, each time getting some new treat. Their fear was not unfounded, since in the forties in the South, mischievous neighborhood children soaped all our car windows or dragged all the furniture off our front porch and onto our lawn. Halloween did not seem benign or fun to me. Susan's history was much more participatory and pleasant, both as a child who went out in her trusty sheet and an adult who left bags of goodies on her lighted porch if she had to be away during the evening. Contrarily, I either went to a movie or retired to some room at the back of my house, turning out all the lights as I went.

Because we had not shared these Halloween stories, I thought we would go to a picture show, while Susan assumed we would carve pumpkins and hand out goodies. When it became clear that we did not agree, each of us felt devastated. After an exhausting fight that took several days to heal, and in which we shouted and cried such words as "betrayed" and "adrift," we agreed to share our past experiences of all major holidays. The fierceness of our scene had sprung from the intensity of our connection and from a dangerous assumption that because we shared basic values and politics, we would of course agree on how to observe some relatively inconsequential holiday.

Being with Susan has contributed to my finding my voice as a writer as well as my happiness as a woman. During our early courtship days, on a walk around one of Minneapolis's many lakes, I found myself talking about my writing block. Susan tightened her arm around my waist while instant tears welled up in me. As I tried to pull away, Susan pinned me to her side and asked particular questions about what prevented me from writing. I answered with sentences previously imprisoned in my own head: "I'm afraid to write because I may be good at it and then I'll have to be responsible for that gift." "If I write, it takes time alone and when I'm alone too long, I revert to compulsive behavior." "How can I have a life with someone else and still find energy for intense writing?" "No one ever asks me about my writing, so I stay stuck where I am." Having blurted out these taboo words amid still-falling tears, I felt terrified.

Susan said little to cheer me up or change my mind, but what she did say seared into me: "I'll support your writing and ask you about it if you want. I'll listen to you read or read your stuff myself if that will help. I understand because I too want to write." In our twelve years together, she has remembered and kept her promise made in the rush of courtship. Of all my critics, Susan remains the one who will challenge me the hardest and drive me the longest to make my work less wordy, and truer.

In 1979, we decided to make a home together and began looking for a suitable house. We knew that we had to have a space in which to write. One of the most attractive features of the place we bought was a finished third floor, complete with the original 1911 skylight and a bathtub with clawed feet. As we discussed use of space, we returned often to an idea of using the third floor as a common writing area. My decision to risk such closeness brought me up against classic messages about the writer's postures, full of secrecy, self-protection, and isolation. It was fine to have an attic—there was a lot of romantic precedent for that—but letting someone else share it as an equal rather than for purposes of serving the artist's domestic needs was unheard of in my imagination.

The effect of our decision has been quite the opposite of what I feared. With Susan working at her desk while I write, I stay put when all my impulses are to turn off the typewriter or computer and do safe household chores. When both of us are trying to write, I feel an aura of love and creativity sustaining me when the blank page stares back unyielding. Toni at work in her fifties is different from the little girl of four hiding between her bed and the wall, hurriedly shaping animal forms or the older child inventing another girl to accompany her on her most precious adventures.

At the same time that Susan was offering tangible encouragement for my writing, Shirley and Mimi, two friends at work, were struggling toward their own best voices. We decided to support each other by devoting one lunch meeting every week either to reading aloud our latest efforts or to talking about our difficulties. Over the past ten years, we have shared specific pieces of writing, long-range dreams, and deep-seated problems. I have given them drafts, trusting that they will read carefully and critically. Such mutuality is precious and rarely available in an academic world devoted to national visibility and educational upward mobility.

Once a chairman tried to exploit our connection. As usual, he had failed to award us our deserved merit points for the year and we had written letters of protest. One day, I received a note asking me to stop by his office. He was prepared to grant me additional points, but when I asked about Shirley and Mimi, he said that his original calculations stood. Without missing a beat, I looked him squarely in the eye and said, "Well, then, don't give me any more, since it would be unfair; they had even better years than I." His expression was of someone hearing a language totally foreign to his ear. Unable to believe me, he offered again, only to hear me refuse again. I walked out feeling like the winner; I had spoken from a position of unity and love in response to his meager ground of money and competition.

The most dramatic support we give each other turns around what and how we write. All three trained in the English Renaissance, we each began careers assuming that we would write standard essays about works from that illustrious period. While we have written on such matters, the essays have hardly been "standard," and in recent years we have steadily inclined toward quite different fare. Each of us has encouraged the others to write poetry and essays about women writers or feminist topics. Most importantly, we have been unflinching in our support of each other's autobiographical writing.

As three articulate full professors in a department like most others, we are feared by some and listened to by all. In our lighter moods, we joke about being the Three Furies to some of our colleagues. At all times, we are sure we are the Three Graces to one another.

One other woman has contributed in ways she probably does not realize to my recovery of confidence as a writer. While working on *So's Your Old Lady* in the seventies, I met Yarrow Morgan and liked her immediately. Being shy and reluctant to let myself have friends, I kept my distance, preferring to talk shop rather than share anything personal. Over the years, we went for the occasional walk or breakfast, until we wound up in the same writing group. There we heard our first poem about father–daughter incest. Within the next few months, two other group members brought pieces dealing with incest or child abuse. One night Yarrow called and said: "I think we ought to edit an incest book so poems like the ones we are hearing have a place to be published—want to?" I answered yes impulsively, and we never backed away from that moment.

Putting together an anthology of women's creative writings about incest (*Voices in the Night: Women Speaking about Incest*, Cleis Press) took three years of steady and unpaid work. For much of that time, we met weekly to read copy and decide whether to accept a piece. Once that process was completed, we began the terrifying task of writing an introduction. Deciding to do it as a joint venture, we floundered for a few meetings before agreeing on a method: we would go outside unless it was raining, sit apart for ten minutes writing independently about whatever the topic was. Then we would read our words aloud before stopping until the next week. After writing on all our chosen topics, we typed our pages and began arranging them, a process that reminded me of shuffling the Tarot deck until the cards are as you intend them. I was amazed at how unrepetitive we were and at how smoothly sections flowed into one another. Our printed introduction includes virtually everything either of us scribbled in backyards or on porches; from a reading of the prose, it is impossible to identify who authored which sections. At first, I kept our typescript so we could check whose sections were whose, but along the way that has vanished and I am no longer certain which are mine and which are Yarrow's unless we are speaking by name about personal experience.

Given my long history of not finishing things, I am immensely grateful. When I felt discouraged, Yarrow kept us at it. When I saw a title page carrying my name, I cried for a long time. I had thought that could never happen, but with Yarrow's parallel vision and labor, one of my oldest fantasies was realized.

A miracle occurred during the first few years of Susan's and my partnership: I wrote poetry easily for the only time in my life. In one of many love poems, I caught something I firmly believe in—the ineluctable connection between sexuality and spirituality. On our second visit to England, we drove from London to Cornwall, through the heart of ancient Celtic country. In addition to stopping often to visit roadside stone circles, we went purposefully to a little town called Avebury to see the wondrous stones erected there centuries ago. This is the resulting poem:

through mists I watch you   priestess
touch the goddess stones
mammoth and friendly
so thick I cannot hear you through them
so tall I crane to find their tops
slate gray like this rainy autumn morning
except for threadings of pink or mauve
or muted sea-green lichens

your fingers trace the ancient markings
searching recesses of rock and memory
for special meaning in the tiny holes
that house bug-like creatures sleeping upside down
with caterpillar feet and armadillo backs;
eons ago we women walked these circles
touching each stone   touching each other
pilgrims at our sacred stations
carving witches' crosses on the rock face:
cuts with equal arms in four directions
cuts you find today and show me   questioning

slowly yet with knowing steps
you weave your way from outer bounds
through inner ovals to the core of worship
where you stop and let your weight
sink down into the mystic dirt

outside the circle, at the entrance stone,
I wait, transfixed before the scene:
your back resembles all the other stones
mute and misted over
you add yourself to this place
alive with echoes from women
come from barrows near and far
to claim the goddess in these stones
to offer smaller gifts of gentle hands
caressing every surface
healing wind and snow scars,
crystal voices singing in moonlight
lulling this female heart of Avebury
season after season   century after century

finished with your solitary rite
you move away
brushing past me   luminescent
as if you'd caught a whisper from another plane
saying things you've always known

so we came, lovers of each other,
lovers of these mythic stones
standing rooted in their meadows
filled with sheep who munch the grass
beneath the monoliths   unperturbed
they watch us as we find the magic
among their leavings
through the Wiltshire drizzle.

A paradox surrounding me and poetry persists: I know how to criticize a poem far more deeply than I do prose; I go to poetry for my lessons rather than reading the additional words required in prose. Yet I feel more secure writing prose than poetry, at least when I want to speak about my own life and perceptions. When I read drafts of poems nestled into journal pages, I feel a warm affection for the Toni of that time, struggling to like herself enough to risk letting anything out of her storehouse. My first attempts at love poetry sound like most beginners' efforts: lots of passionate clichés and prosaic declarations of fidelity or longing or pain, depending on when the poem was written.

My first nonlove poem centered on a woman who had lived with a member of the Symbionese Liberation Army during the sixties. She was convicted of a crime of passion when she killed him, and my poem is full of anger and protofeminist awareness. Reading it now, I understand that I felt some inner connection but was unwilling or unable to invest emotional energy in the writing.

The third volume of my journal includes a torn-out sheet on which I have scribbled some lines with a green felt-tipped pen about brown-skinned women reclining somewhere. Though very poor, this early effort shows a glimmer of promise in lines like, "a breeze that comes from nowhere," and "as small thin rainfall / caressing backs and fields at once."

Though undated, this poem marks a turning point. Touches of eroticism, a woman-identified point of view, and a sharp eye for what's in front of me: these qualities mark the best things I have written and are what I always strive for. Significantly, this poem is not "to" anyone; in fact, I can no longer recall the occasion for writing it. The lines may be a response to some painting I had recently seen, strong enough to evoke not only emotion but a willingness to shape it. While any artist can say this is the force behind inclusion of details or events, regaining sharp responses and the ability to record them is particularly precious to me as I continue moving steadily from fog into sunlight.

That was 1976 and I clearly was in touch with how art could help me in my process of assembling the pieces of me and my life back into a whole picture. In the next three or four years, almost a score of poems poured out of me about leaving my psychiatrist, teaching my first course in lesbian literature, loving Susan, coming upon some natural phenomenon that will not let me go. Here are two examples:

Love Song for Susan

when wind blows your face
your forehead veins show blue
like impressionist paintings
or antique lanterns,
your light source is within

I see dark shadows move behind your skin,
I want to part the curtain   enter the scene
act with you in a hundred stories

I sense you through my pores

I want to put my fingers on your veins
and feel you
coursing beneath my whorls
I want to touch your forehead
as the wind does,
as the wind

A Fall

driving the New York Thruway
later than I mean to
I feel the sky quite near
with little force, my left hand
could reach the dipper
just outside my moving window,
could tip that dipper,
drink water before it makes itself rain

a giant moon perches on a treetop,
still orange from her rising,
lopsided   on her wane to newness,
playful as she floats up the sky
    "twinkle, twinkle, little star . . .
    like a diamond . . . "
            you fall
before my eyes a long, two-second descent,
burning out in slowed motion

watching you and not the highway
I know an answer to the nursery riddle
            "how I wonder. . ."
    you are splendid
    in your final journey
    then lost to blackness
    without violence
    without alarm,
    you leave a space
    without successor

they used to say the stars
were held in place
by hidden pins, behind the ceiling
of the sky,
like sets of dress shirt studs
or a vast array of jeweled rings
piercing all the ears of heaven

did someone pull your pin,
release you from your constellation?
          in any case,
you've gone to where all fallen stars
sleep away the ages,
while I wonder how I hang and shine
and if I ever fall so slowly
with so much ease and so much grace.

One of my happy anticipations turns around a sense I have that I
will write more poems as I get older, as I give myself permission to be
fully eccentric. This vision of myself also includes a sterling-silver-
headed walking cane and outrageous hats for all seasons. When I
consider why I connect eccentricity and poetry, I meet my deep
conviction that prose is the respectable, grown-up form of written
communication. Poetry is reserved for children and others brave or
foolish enough to refuse the mainstream's ability to stipulate what
color cows must be, which notes girls may sing, who can make love
with whom.

Part IV

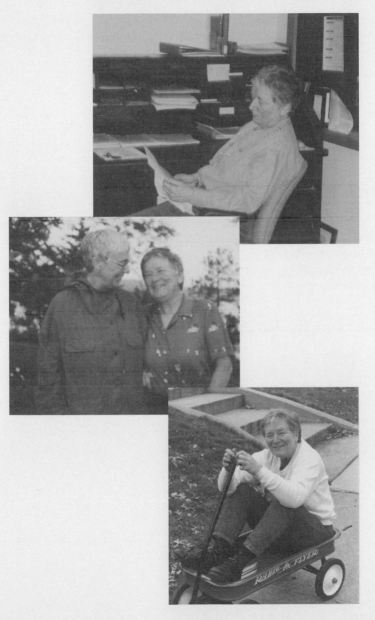

Top right: the author at the University of Minnesota, 2001; *center left:* the author and Susan Cygnet, 1995; *bottom right:* the author, 2000. Courtesy of Toni McNaron.

Memory Bridges

bridge: (n) **1.** A structure, usually of wood, stone, brick, or iron, erected over a river or other water course, or over a chasm, railroad etc. to make a passageway from one bank to the other. **2.** (Music) The transition from the first to the second subject in sonata form (containing both subjects for a time). **3.** (Electricity) A device to measure the resistance of a wire or other conductor forming part of an electric circuit. **4.** A low wall or vertical partition in the fire chamber of a furnace for deflecting flame.
—*Webster's International Dictionary* and *The Shorter Oxford Universal Dictionary on Historical Principles*, 3d ed.

Toni Morrison speaks of memory, or "the deliberate act of remembering," as "always fresh, in spite of the fact that the object being remembered is done and past." She sees it as "a form of willed creation." It is not an effort to find out the way it really was—that is research. The point is to dwell on the way it appeared and why it appeared in that particular way. At this point in my life, the "object" from my past upon which I find myself dwelling is my tenure in the academy. Here I linger in order to figure out why my work experience as a professor of English and women's studies at a mega-university has had the profound effect on me that it has. I want and need to name its impact on my literary, political, and sexual development, even as I conjugate my institution's ability (or lack thereof) to treat me in a respectful way. In the larger mosaic that is my story, the chapters that follow may provide me with an organizing lens as I sever my formal relationship with the University of Minnesota and await with anticipation whatever lies ahead. I know I will write and travel more, that I will discover new facets of my relationship with my beloved; beyond that, however, lie mystery and the unknown. In order to embrace the future, I feel it necessary to put my professional house in more order than it currently possesses.

At this moment, I feel myself standing on a bridge-in-process (which feels more like a catwalk), looking back and all around. From this vantage point, the "object" of memory—my years at the university—seems intricately threaded with ambiguity, that is, capable of being understood in more than one way, and paradox, both contrary to common sense and yet perhaps true. My tenure can only be understood in more than one way, since it simultaneously has nourished and assaulted me, gratified and punished me. For this reason, I have tried not to slant my reflections either too much toward the positive and satisfying, or too much toward the discriminatory and painful. Furthermore, my dual sense of loving my work and being a misfit within its provenance surely flies in the face of common sense but, nonetheless, remains profoundly true to my experience. Such ambiguity and paradox are not particularly valued in the United States, which has tended to prefer either/or constructs and oversimplified truths.

In fact, from its inception this country has exacted a certain conformity in exchange for belonging. Roger Williams was expelled from the Massachusetts Bay Colony because he advocated a distinct separation of church and state, and because he proposed intermarriage as the "simplest solution" to the growing antagonisms of white colonists toward indigenous Americans. Such a response to a maverick member of a freedom-seeking community reveals a fundamental hypocrisy; a dangerous incongruence between ideals and practices. Indeed, the young nation —committed to the pursuit of freedom but built on economic and social foundations of chattel slavery and colonization—exacted a conformity to egalitarian goals while enacting a rigid and oppressive racial classification system. Today's institutions of higher education have not escaped this contradiction between rhetoric and reality. As a maverick member of my profession, I have felt a repulsion to my insistence on both/and constructs and on speaking my truths to those "noble" words carved on Greek revivalist edifices that extol freedom of ideas and openness to all who by birth or circumstance find our ways into these ivy-covered halls.

It was precisely its heavy overlay of ambiguity and paradox that attracted me initially to the English Renaissance as a graduate student in the early 1960s. I still remember how excited and confirmed I felt when I stumbled upon an important work by Rosalie Colie in which she articulates the frequency and cultural significance of this rhetorical strategy in the poetry and prose of sixteenth-century England. They felt like comfortable psychological states to me, though it might seem paradoxical in itself that such an unstable disposition would offer any comfort. Of course, it would be years before I comprehended why this was the case, before I grasped and accepted my own gender ambiguities—gas station attendants and telephone personnel frequently mistook me for a man because my hair was short or my voice was low— and paradoxical interests—I equally liked analyzing a Shakespeare play and sawing up pilfered boards for kindling in our fireplace. It is certainly ambiguity and paradox that excite and challenge me today: whether I am choosing reading material, framing discussion questions for a class, deciding if I want to deepen a given friendship, or sorting out where I belong on the various continua that impact and define me.

So, when the Feminist Press first approached me, in late 1999, about writing an additional chapter for a new and expanded edition of *I Dwell in Possibility*, I unthinkingly agreed. I have felt pleasure knowing that people teach my book in classes about memoir as a genre. I have also liked knowing that I managed to get quite a bit of my coming-to-awareness process into print, even as I admitted to close friends and myself just how much I had left out or abridged. Maybe the new writing could allow me to revisit some of the neglected sites while addressing entirely unexplored territory. The idea that few copies were available to readers saddened me, since my story has been of use to people over the years: people who have been kind enough to write me their responses or approach me in the grocery store or at a concert to say they had given a copy to a daughter or mother or good friend to help that person understand her own (or a loved one's) life a little better. What I did not take into account when I uttered my eager "yes" was the ineluctable nature of change, notwithstanding my fondness for telling students how profound a concept mutability was in the imaginations of early modern English writers. I blandly assumed that I would feel nearly ten years later just as I had felt in 1992, when the memoir was first published, about the events, persons, and ideas I had *already* written about in earlier chapters. Such flat-footed assumptions even withstood for a time my recollection of answering questions after readings with comments such as: "I know I would have told a different story of my mother had I written this even ten years ago, when I still needed to place blame entirely outside myself." Adding to the original manuscript, I reckoned, would be a simple matter of bringing my story up into the present. But I have long agreed with Virginia Woolf and others that writing about our present is much more unsettling than looking back at a past we can delude ourselves into thinking we control—or at least manage. Memory, by definition, has less power if we focus on the present and near-past than it can wield when shaping events, feelings, and motives "safely" shrouded in time. Though my initial enthusiasm gave way to a distinct reticence about the complexities of the project, the challenge of it all won out. I promised to undertake the venture.

As I considered various organizing structures, I rejected a strict chronological approach, choosing instead to intertwine depiction and self-reflection into a single picture. Though the content follows a loose linearity—early on I discuss how I came to accept the job I have held for nearly four decades, and toward the chapters' end I anatomize what it means to walk out of my long-standing academic home—the body of this enlargement diverges from linearity and the straightforward, mirroring that very ambiguity and paradox I find at the core of my mature self. In the early days of feminist theorizing, a Canadian male scholar (whose name I have lost) used the following metaphor to distinguish between such radical new thinking and traditional, masculinist theory: masculinist thinking, he argued, is like a straight line; good for connecting two points and for making rapid surface progress, but incapable of looking back at itself. Feminist thinking resembles a circularly curved line—able to reflect upon itself and alter its final course accordingly, achieving thereby less and slower, but lasting and deeper, progress. Despite the problems of any binary thinking, I embrace this metaphor because I conceive of what follows as a curved-line understanding of my professional life as it moves in, out, and around other aspects of my existence.

In the original memoir, little or no present-day reflection was allowed. My editor at that time, Florence Howe, believed such rumi-

nations would blunt the story that was unfolding of a white southern girl-child who did not fit any of the categories into which she
was being corralled by parents, teachers, peers, and the broader
culture, with its rigidly narrow ideas of the "acceptable." At readings and when visiting classes in which my work is being studied,
I have made it eminently clear to audiences that the *I* in their
midst did not approve of certain behaviors I presented without
much comment in the narrative. But, in spite of such dissonance,
I believe that the narrative is the more powerful for not having my
retroactive consciousness interrupting. And now, ten years later,
my new editors have welcomed, indeed demanded, such backward glancing because they see the expanded edition of my memoir as a synthesis rather than an unfolding. The ambience of the
two versions may well seem at variance to some readers, but I
agree that it would be of little value simply to chart my course as
a professor from 1964 to 2001. Unlike my coming-of-age story,
those thirty-seven years represent a period of intense, retrospec-
tive self-analysis and a growing sense of the unavoidable connections between public and private life. So, instead I will use my
years at the university as a kind of centerfold around which I
build a more complex and interrelated story.

Memoir writing is a tricky business. Life goes on after one's
book has been published, and, more confusing still, our reading of
our own and other people's lives is amended—or even trans-
formed—as the horizon of our lives insists on remaining just
beyond reach. To return to one's published memoir is surely to
invite internal arguments at every juncture, as I discovered when I
reread the original version of my life from 1937 through the 1980s.
Questions rained down upon me faster than I could turn the pages:
Why didn't I say more about this incident, as it was much more
important than I have made it seem here? What was in my mind to
include this scene when my editor forbade me from telling readers
just how much I do not condone what is going on in it? What did
I gain from leaving out some of the most painful parts of my adolescence or from playing down damaging familial patterns and
dictates? Why didn't I include my encounters with this or that person, considering the major impact they had on later feelings or
choices? Why are most chapters so relatively short? And, perhaps
the most critical question: *What was I avoiding in the writing process?*

These and similar questions propelled me to consider some of the differences between truths and half-truths, and to delve more deeply into the very nature of self-discovery. When I ask students engaged in what is now called "independent and distance learning" (formerly known as "correspondence courses") to assess whether curiosity played any significant role in the responses of Spanish and Portuguese explorers when they first landed on North America's eastern shores, I do hope they will conclude that most of those making such voyages were not curious at all. Not only did they refuse to take in anything about the peoples they encountered, but they judged and named them according to pre-conceived ideas that carelessly—or carefully—ignored what was right in front of them. Similarly, if I were truly curious, I would have to interrogate my entire life since the first publication of *I Dwell in Possibility*. Unlike those early conquerors-posing-as-explorers, I would have to assume nothing as I revisited familiar territory from my current vantage point and examined for the first time aspects of my life I might prefer to ignore. The landscape in my case was only personal, but the desire to hang on to the official story of my last twenty or more years as an academic might well lead me to use the same tactics as those employed by Columbus or Cabeza de Vaca, Champlain or Verrazzano. I might force phenomena into preconceived boxes so as to come away with a coherent and "logical" interpretation of events, people, and behaviors quite outside any genuine notions of reality. Once again, then, ambiguity ruled as I began writing, and paradox became the border that would surround whatever I produced. When I made this connection between my tiny voyage and the early discoverers' mammoth undertaking, fear and a certain silence descended upon me, lending to this "simple" process of adding to what already existed a note of caution—and, also, a challenge to write through these difficult feelings.

Sensing my reticence for this reengagement, since it would of necessity call up painful (though also pleasant) memories, Florence tried to ease my mind by suggesting I focus on my career at the University of Minnesota, a subject that figures only slightly in the original memoir but which has nevertheless shaped my life to a surprisingly large extent. I resumed writing, then, "at the beginning"—probing why I decided to take the job offer at Minnesota in 1964 rather than one of the three others I was fortunate enough to receive. After a few weeks of work, slogging through the good, the bad, and finding no indifferent, I inquired about length. "Send more rather than less; we like your prose style, so don't worry about there being too much." So onward I went, discovering surprising themes such as the complex importance to me of several older men and the centrality of the Vietnam War—specifically, student protest to U.S. involvement in that war—to my own political and pedagogical development.

The role of the war is easily explained—it occurred just as I was coming to grasp the connections between institutionalized racism in the United States and what was going on in those jungles and villages halfway around the globe. Furthermore, my growing disaffection with some of my own institution's investment policies in South Africa and certain weapons-producing corporations in this country primed me for the student and citizen outrage that spilled onto the streets of most towns and cities as our government kept sending more young men and women to almost certain death, dismemberment, or mental torture.

But the role of older men in my life is far from well-charted territory. Given my less than thrilling forays into heterosexuality as a young woman, I have tended to gloss over or evade any serious leanings I might have toward men. None of the boys who said they wanted to be sexual with me had the slightest idea about what might give me pleasure, and they seemed oddly ashamed of their own libidinous feelings. Never having arrived at any clear sense of bisexuality and having come out during the heyday of lesbian-feminism (when we wanted very little to do with men), I usually have formed platonic friendships with the men who appealed to me and to whom I seemed to appeal. Often I am a woman with whom they find it possible, even comfortable, to spend time; my avowed lesbianism "removes" the possibility of sexual attraction for them and, on occasion, for their wives. Furthermore, I believe I am someone who could have "played out" a butch identity if she had not wanted in the mid-1960s to be a professor of English in the Midwest. Perhaps most significantly, I have yet to write at length or in depth about my relationship with my own father, who was a shadowy presence throughout my childhood and early adolescence before departing the world entirely while I was a senior in high school. This confluence of emotional vectors, I believe, leaves me strangely vulnerable to a certain kind of attention from a certain kind of man, something I begin to explore in the pages that follow.

The Vietnam War (known as the "U.S. War" in Viet Nam), or more accurately, my reactions to it, may be a primary defining "moment" for me both as a political being and as a teacher. My research about that tiny, besieged country underscored just how important it was for me to become and remain actively opposed to my government's sometimes brutal foreign policies. My engagement in antiwar protests, first with students at the university and later with radical citizens of Minneapolis and St. Paul, toughened my understanding not only of colonial aggression abroad but of racial injustice within this country. My southern roots took on new significance as I struggled to articulate what aggression and injustice can do to everyone involved. White southerners continue to live with the awful legacy of chattel slavery William Faulkner identified in his Nobel Prize acceptance speech, even if many refuse to take responsibility for the atrocities committed by some of their ancestors against African slaves and their descendants, and for the racial privileges enjoyed by all white people. Those determined to perpetuate oppression—or enjoy by accident of birth its privileges—are accountable for the suffering inflicted on the oppressed, often for no other reason than *being able to do precisely that.* Surely most of us came to realize that the tons of bombs dropped on tiny Viet Nam and even tinier Laos and Cambodia were uncustomary in battle, just as lashing a slave with a bullwhip exceeded any "useful punishment requirements." Nearer to home, callously telling students to notice the persons to their left and right and figure that one of each triad would not be in classes the next term "because I will have flunked one of you" goes beyond any desire to instill academic rigor or even to frighten one's students into studying harder. Slowly, I came to recognize the sustaining interrelatedness of a damaged (and damaging) system's institutions, including higher education and the military, and made life-changing connections between what soldiers were doing in Viet Nam and what I was doing as a teacher in traditional classroom settings. My pedagogy began to become an explicit part of the same landscape that included my protests against the war, my growing discomfort with the sexual closet in which I cowered, and my determination to name my whiteness as a clearly defined racial category, breaking with the false notion that racism is a problem solely for people of color to solve.

Contemplating the shape of the new sections of my memoir, then, threw me back into situations and emotions I had assumed were, if not resolved, at least comfortably shelved. The new writing went slowly and, for the first draft, remained as close to the surface as possible. I experienced considerable restlessness, fixing on any household chore that might distract me from my project. Even on good days, as I sat—usually agitatedly—at my computer screen, I often clicked on "Word Count" to see how I was progressing. Amazingly enough, the pages mounted up, one after the other. I had a lot more to say, it seemed, about working at the University of Minnesota.

In "Everyday Magic" I had declared triumphantly that I had resolved in my life both love and work, thereby meeting Freud's standards for maturity and happiness. The person who needed that sentence is the same one who was convinced, when she finally got herself into an Alcoholics Anonymous group, that she could "master" the famous Twelve Steps certainly within one year and then go on her way. Both of those predictions turned out to have been naïve and untrue. Indeed, they may not be possible or even desirable. Love does persist: my beloved partner and I celebrate anniversaries in the twenty-year range, enlarge our gardens each year, return to Paris as a kind of second home as often as time and money allow, and enjoy each other's company doing totally mundane and often silly things together—looking for the right glue to repair a Florentine leather coin purse; taking advantage of our favorite department store's white sale to replace bath towels so worn as to have no nap left to absorb dampness; reading at breakfast about whichever saint has been designated for a given day; reviewing French grammar so we can converse in other than the present tense; walking familiar blocks in our neighborhood beneath the growing evening light.

But work continued to elude me in the years following the publication of my memoir, even though I had learned (as much as possible) not to accept blame and shame sent my way by non-self-reflexive (white male) colleagues and administrators. I accomplished this feat by detaching myself from most academic gossip and infighting and by focusing on people at work who could validate and even like me. In the mid-1980s, I completed several therapy sessions with an eccentric woman whose home was filled with knickknacks that set my aesthetic teeth on edge. But Doris knew how to help me slough off decades of shame dating back to my mother not letting me wipe up the milk I spilt, thereby making an incident where I was simply clumsy into one in which I felt ashamed of my behavior because of what it meant she had to do. Doris's mantra, which I silently mouthed repeatedly at work, was: "I feel you sending blame and shame my way; I don't want it. I'm returning it to you. Do with it as you choose, but don't try to pawn it off on me."

Once I stopped taking their bait, those mean-spirited white male colleagues no longer could displace their own shameful feelings onto me. More importantly, they could not completely demolish or silence me by directing anger and spitefulness my way. But they still could batter and bruise my psyche, which in turn cost me creative energy for the repairs made necessary by their individual abuses—and by the violence inflicted by a larger patriarchal system that encourages and rewards such damaging behavior. Paradoxically, then, I continued to struggle with wanting more time at home and not being able to say "no" when called upon to perform increasingly complex functions at work. Obviously I still needed professional validation from some quarter, even if I had stopped looking for it in my own building. More importantly from the standpoint of memoir writing, I kept being propelled back into earlier moments in my career, feeling anew what I thought were finished resentments, losing an evening with Susan or a weekend in the garden to inflamed old wounds whose scabs I would have sworn were thick enough to stay in place, lashing out privately or to special friends at individuals I thought I had forgiven or at least forgotten. Perhaps having generated new words for this expanded memoir will let me walk old paths with new insights, allowing me, I hope, to finally lay to rest some of my oldest and most haunting academic ghosts.

I offer what follows, then, as a fitting companion piece to what goes before it. The chapter title "On the Cusp" reflects the Janus-like positionality of its content and author. To be on a cusp is to occupy an edge or circumference point. Though the term has valence in architecture, astronomy, and mathematics, I want to accent its significance to the older science of astrology. In that body of knowledge, a cusp is "the beginning or first entrance of any house in the calculations of nativities, etc." Though my literal tenure as a professor is quite long, my comprehension of its true meaning has a distinct "beginning" to it. Virginia Woolf used to upbraid Vita Sackville-West, her sometimes lover and long-time friend, each time she read one of Vita's manuscripts: she urged Vita to pause long enough or back up far enough from her intensely lived life to be able to write reflectively or at least more coherently. The fact that Vita did not follow this admonition in no way diminishes the wisdom contained within it, so I will take to heart this counsel from one of my favorite models. I feel about whole segments of my professional career as if I have experienced them but have not had or taken time to make sense out of them, to shape them into the kind of "willed creation" Morrison finds necessary to the success of her own writing. That said, I ask that you consider this addition to my memoir an entranceway into a process that may take on other manifestations in future years. Poetry may serve some of my purposes, or perhaps a series of speculative essays about academic life using my own story as an exemplar. For now, I am relying almost entirely on memory to help me "dwell on the way [my academic life] appeared and why it appeared in that particular way." Certainly this writing feels like a "deliberate act."

Some aspects of my time at the University of Minnesota have not found their way into these new chapters, just as much about the periods of my life explored in the original text was omitted. All writing is a matter of selection, no matter how "truthful" it may attempt or pretend to be. As I continue to read the seemingly endless string of excellent memoirs coming out these days and to write reflexively about my own experiences, the relationship between memory and fact becomes simultaneously clearer and more elusive. Clearer because I no longer place primary value on ferreting out factual data, since I now believe deeply that *what is remembered* about those data carries more compelling weight. More elusive because I recognize and admit from the vantage point of this psychological and emotional cusp that my version of what has happened in my life is only that, *my version*. Its value may well lie in its very relativity, which prevents all of us from freezing our readings of the present, or even of the past.

Such relativity is a bonus as long as someone's version is not allowed to take on compulsory overtones or to become "the" version of any given reality. Since history has often pined after—and, too often, falsely assumed—such "objective" or "final" statuses, I prefer memoir because its readers can be more easily persuaded to resist codification than can most students of history. Memoir also has no demands upon it to "cover" its territory. And so, the following new chapters make no claims at inclusivity. Some of what is not written would be boring to anyone but me, my partner, and a few utterly devoted friends. Some of it remains too raw or unexamined to be translatable at present into a shaped and reflective format. And some of it is simply too personal to express on paper. The memoirist, as the autobiographer, constantly faces the question of balance between a responsibility to what constitutes the truth of experience and the freedom to omit, a freedom without which many of us never would attempt to unlock the memory hoards that comprise our lives. Given certain omissions, then, I can say unequivocally that everything that has found its way into this addendum, just as was the case in the original text, is true to my understanding of it in the moment of writing. That is most likely all we can expect—or exact—of ourselves or of anyone else.

On the Cusp

*F*or the past thirty-six years, at least four days a week I have gone to my office in the English department at the University of Minnesota. Now, I am packing up the most recent incarnation of that space, having decided to retire sooner than later. Ten years have passed since I finished the original version of this memoir, and for at least that long I have yearned for vast stretches of time to do the things work now short-circuits or prevents altogether—spend time with my partner when both of us are fully awake; write because I feel moved to do so rather than to meet some deadline; garden properly rather than frantically on weekends; travel to places at home and abroad that have beckoned me for decades. I will be sixty-four when I complete my two-year phased retirement program in 2001.

My decision to take this radical professional step was prompted, in part, by an assortment of catastrophic diagnoses visited upon family members, friends, and neighbors, as well as health alerts of my own. For my part, I suffered a bout with shingles in 1998 and a glaucoma scare the next year. My body was trying to tell me something about stress, reminding me of the gulf between *the urgent*—tasks imposed upon me by others, always with ridiculous deadlines attached—and *the important*—activities that give back at least as much as they require, in which I can immerse myself without losing my center. The professional world where I dwell was also delivering messages of its own, specifically about my academic shelf life: I am not enamored with "high theory" or abstruse prose, continuing to believe that language in texts remains the most difficult and rewarding level of engagement within literary studies.

I was ready to listen to these messages because they echoed a voice within me that wished me to deepen relationships and write more regularly, more probingly, and because I was becoming increasingly irritated with younger colleagues who thought me irrelevant, redundant, or just plain boring. All this also dovetailed with a series of heart-stopping cues from my immediate environment that it might not be wise to keep putting off doing the things I truly wanted to do. Certainly I knew of other people's brushes with mortality and had survived the premature deaths of both my parents. But their departures were blunted by all the whiskey I drank, and other people did not matter much to me, not until I had been sober long enough to realize that friends could fill some of the abysses I had depended upon alcohol to erase or bury. Aware of my own mortality and open to friendship and intimacy, I became a willing pupil; "teachers" appeared from several corners.

First, our next-door neighbor was unexpectedly seized in the night by a brain tumor that proved malignant. Though she had it removed, she never again was herself because the medication changed her personality as well as her physical appearance, and the tumor kept returning until it killed her. Marge's light green eyes, one of her best features, were almost entirely lost in the bloat caused by whatever drugs she was taking to ward off another attack. They failed her, the tumor grew back bigger than before, and her husband put her into a nearby nursing home. There she eked out her last months, recognizing no one, fearful that staff members were trying to poison or attack her. Because Marge was only two years younger than I, her death focused my attention on my own overworked brain and how often it was diverted from what it wanted to pursue by what it felt it must.

Closer to home, my older sister Betty's multiple sclerosis, which had been gradually limiting her ability to walk, denied her the use of one leg entirely and made any ambulatory motion excruciatingly painful if not impossible. When her husband died in 1998 after a long struggle with both recurring prostate cancer and a deteriorating heart condition, I made three harrowing visits to North Carolina. Once there, friends and I helped my sister disperse a house full of Mamie's gorgeous antiques and move herself, her wheelchair, and a few personal items from home into an assisted-living facility in Raleigh. A woman who had spent her life actively entertaining hundreds of people, walking for miles at a time, and conversing more fluently than anyone I have ever known was suddenly confined to a cellular space where her main entertainment is watching celluloid images on the Classic Movie Channel—unless someone from the outside world thinks and chooses to pay her a welcome visit. I do that once a year for three or four days, though we speak by telephone weekly for about an hour, talking of everything except her health and her loneliness. I swing between pity for her and fury at her: pity because no one should be reduced as she has been; fury because she acts out "the victim" role, refusing to fight against her disease as she lets it entirely consume her strength and determine her future; all while holding on to damaging maxims like "old people are boring" and "people in wheelchairs should not be inflicted on the public."

Shortly after I settled my sister into her single room, a neighbor's husband died unexpectedly one Sunday morning of a sudden and severe heart attack. Dick died in bed, alone; his wife, Pat, had left their bed early that morning for the garden, sleepless with grief over the recent accidental death of her brother-in-law in Maryland. Now a devastated widow, Pat could not bring herself to use the airplane tickets they had purchased to attend the funeral of her sister's husband; she had to bury her own. I later discovered that, though he was thin and an inveterate walker who no longer worked outside the home and so seemed under relatively little stress, Dick was a longtime smoker. It seems one's chances of surviving a first heart attack as a smoker are quite slim, no matter what else is the case.

Finally, a devastating medical diagnosis descended like an avalanche onto one member of a couple living just half a block from us. Susan was told she most likely had Parkinson's disease, only to discover a few months later that she was under the heavier cloud of Lou Gehrig's disease, or amyotrophic lateral sclerosis (ALS). A marathon runner, along with her partner, Lee, and a group of women friends, Susan went from moving her body easily through twenty-six miles of fresh air to not being able to walk their dog, all within the space of thirteen months. At this point, doctors have removed her voice box so she will not choke on uncontrollable saliva, she can no longer eat solid food but rather pours liquid nourishment into a tube in her abdomen, she falls ever more frequently, and cannot close her mouth or support her head because those muscles have succumbed already to this relentless disease. Her amazing partner has taken early retirement so as to have precious time with her loved one, but has aged ten years since the diagnosis.

My morning constitutional, which I complete in virtually all sorts of weather, takes me daily by their home. Everyday now I slow down and let myself feel how miraculous it is that I will return home, wake my beloved Susan with a few sweet words, and then eat my bowl of shredded wheat. I do not feel frightened or morbid, just grateful that I am being given such a potent context within which to stop taking any aspect of my existence for granted. Bearing witness to these women's slow and painful coming to terms with death has planted firmly my abstract notion of "everyday magic" into the sphere of literal breath and language.

As these events swirled around me, I began to feel it arrogant of me to continue hustling to keep up with work commitments that seemed never to abate but rather, as I became more and more senior in my department and institution, to take on ever more serious, long-term, and time-devouring qualities. So I talked to my partner, to friends, to someone in employee benefits who laid out the various options provided by the university, and finally to our financial planner. The planner ran a highly sophisticated program that included an iridescent blue line representing my liquidity as the years of retirement unfolded. Given the far-too-early deaths of my parents, I was amazed to learn that, barring some unbroken decline in the stock market, there would still be money for me to spend in 2035. I would be ninety-eight years old if I were alive in 2035—not anything I desire for myself since I value quality, not quantity. I told my financial adviser that someone else would get however many dollars might exist inside that still extant, if needle-thin, blue line with its palely shining light on her computer screen.

Poised on the brink of something vaguely unknown but thoroughly exciting, I seek to comprehend the larger meaning(s) to be gleaned from spending more than half my life as a professor of English and women's studies at a huge, mid-western research university. What was it about the white male writers of the English Renaissance or early modern period that initially won my heart and opened my mind? Has my taste in literature changed because of my commitment to feminist writers and writers of color, at home and abroad? How has being an open lesbian in my work-place altered my colleagues' and students'—and my own—behaviors? What "difference" has it made in my life to teach the thousands of undergraduates and hundreds of graduate students I have eagerly and happily encountered over the years? Is the academy a leader in shaping public opinion, or does it inevitably mirror the leading economic and social indicators of a given historical period? How have I infused other facets of my life outside the academy with the things I love about the literature I read and teach and write about? What or who has nurtured my writer's voice since its emergence from my alcoholic haze almost twenty-seven years ago? Is there any other work I could have pursued that might have given me more or different rewards? These questions buzz around my head as I look back to my beginnings as a young and impatient assistant professor.

In 1964, the world of employment for new Ph.D.'s in English was altogether brighter than it is at present. Everyone around me was hired immediately after she or he finished; these days, able young scholars with degrees in hand are lucky if they find academic work at all, much less at an institution like the University of Minnesota, where one's light teaching load reflects the higher priority put on research and where one's students come from virtually every corner of the globe. For my part, I had eight interviews, all at solid institutions, and four offers. In addition to Minnesota, Indiana University and the Universities of Michigan and Rochester sought my services. Michigan and Indiana were easy to reject: Ann Arbor and Bloomington felt too much like Vicksburg, Mississippi, had five years earlier when virtually everyone in town knew where I was because I drove one of the two Volkswagens in town. Furthermore, their English departments had reputations for hiring large groups of junior faculty only to weed out more than half within the first two years. I wrote polite letters declining such insular and revolving-door situations.

The University of Rochester was a much more complicated matter. They made me a very favorable offer and, more importantly, I was promised a mentor should I accept. There the senior scholar in my field was a woman who taught seventeenth-century metaphysical poetry. Present at the interview, she had been extremely warm as she ushered me out of the room. Once back in

Madison, I received her handwritten letter on small pieces of linen stationery, assuring me that I could move into her seminars on John Donne and George Herbert in my second year, which was to be her last. With extreme generosity, she was frank with me about attitudes toward women in her department. About half the faculty was quite ready to welcome female colleagues, but the other half chafed at having to change certain behaviors, whether it be not making decisions in the men's room or off-color, sexist jokes in the faculty lounge. In order to ensure some kind of immediate community, she and others had convinced the department to hire two young women at the same time so neither of us would feel like a token.

But I was reeling from the sudden death of my mother and so not thinking very clearly about my career. Furthermore, a faculty member at the University of Rochester was an old friend of my sister's. I knew that he had spoken on my behalf, urging the search committee to grant me an interview. Though I came to understand that making that request was all he could possibly have done to help me, at the time I naïvely assumed that the offer had resulted only because of his nepotistic gesture. Seeing myself as finally out from under the protective wings of my just-dead mother, fearful of being discovered as the budding alcoholic I was, and wanting to move with some degree of anonymity, I was loath to accept either the official offer I presumed to be tainted by my sister's association or the hand of professional friendship proffered by the kind and forthcoming older woman.

Without consulting anyone, I turned Rochester down and accepted Minnesota. At the time, I was deeply closeted and about to begin living with an older woman even more terrified of being "found out" than I. The fact that Minneapolis was a large city, one in which I could more easily remain anonymous outside the immediate confines of my work, certainly influenced my decision. Though invisibility, at first, seemed both natural and salutary, the (homosexual) closet eventually became a space too small and unhealthy for my habitation. Yet, even today, I still prefer to live someplace where I can attend a cultural event or shop in department stores without recognizing a single person. The little girl who learned to lie in order to survive still enjoys moving through an environment without the threat of being seen—or, more precisely, recognized. So strong is this desire that my beloved Susan has, on occasion, chided me for being ungracious when some enthusiastic former student has intruded into our dining space to tell me how much my class meant to her or him.

Soon after entering the English department at the University of Minnesota, I learned how little I really knew about my new world. In 1964 there were no faculty "home pages" outlining research and teaching perspectives. Since I was ignorant of individual faculty interests, I could not possibly know what kind of literary environment I was entering. But I could assume the same "dis-ease" that my Rochester ally had warned me against, around opening the academy (and, for that matter, the larger professional workforce) to (white) women, existed at the University of Minnesota. For someone like me, taking a job in academe at that time was pretty much buying a pig in a poke. The only woman on staff had been part of the interview team; she had been distinctly cold to me, asking questions far outside my field and indicating no interest in making the occasion less traumatic. I would come to explain her behavior as an overreaction on the part of one closeted lesbian faced with someone she suspected to be a fellow traveler; not personal animosity so much as categorical uneasiness and a deep, troubled need to be the "only one." The men in that stuffy hotel room were all at least thirty years older than I and seemed incredibly remote from my own experiences and concerns. Since I knew no one at the school or in the city, I would be overly dependent upon my lover, a woman who was leaving husband, son, a gorgeous garden, and an active political life behind to be with me. She did not call herself a "lesbian," however, until just a few years ago when, in her late seventies, she finally came out. This refusal to name our relationship scarred both it and me; her silent but powerful denial of our daily reality pushed me even further into the closet and reinforced my own fears about losing my job if anyone "knew."

In August of 1964, at the age of twenty-seven, I packed up my few belongings and drove with my secret lover, in her black Volkswagen Beetle, to the big city just west of the Mississippi River, on whose banks lies its mega-university. While I discovered where to park and how to use the mimeograph machine, the country was plunging ever more deeply into the morass that would come to be known in the United States as our very own "Vietnam War." The Stonewall riots were still a few years away in the lesbian and gay world, so most professionals were still entirely closeted. Both these broader concerns were pushed to some back burner, however, as I convinced myself that I needed to spend countless hours in my library carrel, furiously absorbing Shakespeare criticism before my two courses began in late September. This myopic perspective was convenient, since it sanctioned my inherent shyness in and dislike of such expected social scenes as cocktail parties, chats in the coffee room, and Saturday night dinners. I also was trying to make my half of an office somewhat attractive. When I picture that first professional space on the third and top floor of our building (a building from which English would soon be evicted to make way for the school of mathematics), I flash to a scene that occurred about four years after my arrival. Shortly after the fall quarter began, Little Mr. Humphries —a student who had taken several courses with me over the period of my various office moves—appeared in my office holding something behind his back, and grinning broadly. He was "Mr." Humphries because I called all my students "Mister" or "Miss"; he was "Little" because I had taught his older brother a few years before and felt it necessary to distinguish between them.

Behind his back he carried a white metal sign with large black letters that read *REMEMBER YOUR LEVEL.* He and some chums had stolen it, probably after a few beers, from a brand new downtown hotel parking ramp. He wondered if my downward progress—in terms of office space—had any larger significance, telling me that the theory of the Great Chain of Being, which I had explained in one of the classes he took, entirely appealed to his own sense of order. Little Mr. Humphries could not have known how prescient his pilfered gift would become; nor could I when I laughingly accepted it, admonishing him weakly for stealing property. That sign has gone with me through several office shuffles, a visible if rueful sign of my often painful awareness of how poorly I "fit" into the academy. Recently a colleague asked if I was going to leave it behind for the office's next occupant. My reply, instant and adamant, was: "Absolutely not. It goes home with me to remind me of my outsider status, upon which I count heavily and of which I am finally rather proud."

After a year or so in my first office, which looked out on a majestic oak tree, I was "asked" to move to the second floor to share space with a tall, dark man who loved Victorian literature. We did not socialize: Gerhard was shy when not talking about

Tennyson or Cardinal Newman; or maybe I was drinking more by then and so was not available; or perhaps I felt there was no point in beginning some human exchange since my lover had become unwilling to entertain people from the university, fearing one of them might know someone who might know one of her psychology professors and so "give her away"; or maybe he and I both fancied we needed camaraderie less in our third year as we struggled independently to keep up with classes and publishing efforts. My fourth year saw my office moved yet again, this time into the basement.

No matter which floor I occupied, however, students found me, and in ever-increasing numbers. And they wanted to talk about a range of topics, only some of which were text-based. Because I found the classroom to be a place of excitement and solace, I must have seemed especially accessible to those young people. While I wanted to be seen this way, I also recognized that all the hours spent talking with and listening to students kept me from figuring out how to make connections with more of my peers, something at which I was not at all adept. But, once the door closed on me and a roomful of expectant and teachable mid-westerners, I relaxed my guard and threw myself into whatever (white male) writer was on the docket for that day. I also refused to obey the stated injunction to steer clear of "values education," since it seemed to me impossible to do that while teaching literature and cowardly while teaching anything. Teaching became my safe landscape, and I lavished time and energy upon the preparation of lectures and my evaluations of student work.

Whenever my office hours failed to accommodate the line of intellectually hungry young people who began their visits with a specific query about Spenser's poetry or Dr. Johnson's ethics or Matthew Arnold's depression, I simply worked overtime. I was reluctant to send the students away unheard, despite my growing need to pursue my research. Quite often, it became clear that they really wanted and needed to talk about other things: Should he go to medical school as his doctor father expected or switch to drama because he came alive in theater classes? Did I think she could have it all—marriage and children and law school? What could he do about teachers who seemed to want one thing on an assignment but then graded down when they got it? Did I know anyone she could see (for free) about what she was beginning to think was abusive behavior from her boyfriend? And, once the United States was fully embroiled in Viet Nam: Should he flee to Canada or try to swallow his fear and moral repugnance at the war?

This last question was asked directly or indirectly several times by earnest young men torn between old-fashioned patriotism and strong disdain for killing—or being killed. But when students asked me what they should do, I dodged. I knew enough about my own annoyance at being given "advice" to refrain from offering specifics to the young people who appeared at my office door. Rather, I listened intently and asked the questions I hoped would let them find their own way.

One such instance stands out in my memory. "Big" Mr. Humphries, the older brother of the young man who brought me the prescient sign, sat facing me in my office for at least an hour, vacillating between cynical rage and youthful tears. His number had been called by the local draft board; he was to report for induction in three weeks. He was twenty-one and I was twenty-eight, but we occupied entirely different positions within the academy—and the world. I was supposed to have some cooler "take" on the whole matter, but my own emotional reactions to U.S. involvement in Viet Nam felt and sounded just like his. The nightly news reports, complete with on-site pictures of soldiers shooting into a jungle, or the flaming aftermath of one more massive bombing raid, at first made my stomach turn, but then less and less—until I noticed that I was no longer having any visceral reactions at all. Like many Americans "experiencing" this war via television broadcasts alone, I was becoming inured to the violence and carnage. Soon I stopped watching or reading about our latest atrocity, directed at what seemed a very small and vulnerable country.

In addition to asking Mr. Humphries the same questions I had put to his predecessors, I broke my own rules about avoiding personal territory: "Are you afraid?" "What do your parents think?" "Are you worried about what Little Mr. Humphries might think if you went to Canada?" "Does going there seem like 'fleeing' or 'cowardice' to you?" I now believe I was identifying with this young man, seeing my decision to leave the South because it was just too hard to combat racism every minute of my waking day as somehow parallel to his own dilemma (though for me, in my skin, less physically risky). He seemed to welcome the more intrusive questions, words spilling out faster than he could frame them or I could absorb them. By the time he left the office, the sun had set, the janitor had agreed to return to empty my wastebasket at a later moment, and Mr. Humphries was considerably quieter and more centered.

A few days later, he returned to tell me he had decided to go to Canada to avoid being drafted. We both burst into tears—mine were of relief that someone I felt far too sensitive and vulnerable to handle combat had made a difficult decision that would probably be better for him in the long run; his may have been much the same. No longer thrashing his way through what seemed a hopeless maze, this young man seemed instantly older: I thought of Coleridge's phrase about being "a sadder and a wiser man." I may have repeated those words to Mr. Humphries or I may just have thought them inside my head. But when he rose to go, I held his hand in both of mine longer than required for an official well-wishing gesture. Later I would wish I had broken another of my own rules by asking him if he would like a hug. Down through the years, there have been other moments with both female and male students when I have regretted not being able to establish physical contact in moments of intense emotional significance.

I never dared ask Little Mr. Humphries about his relative in exile for fear of compromising them both. Once, about ten years after the United States finally withdrew from Viet Nam—betraying them at the last just as surely as we had obliterated them from the beginning—I ran into Mrs. Humphries, mother of both boys who figured so prominently in my early years at the university. Since it was shortly after some president had declared temporary amnesty to "draft-dodgers" (the opprobrious term never changed), I braved the occasion and asked how her older son John was. She smiled wanly as pain broke across her face and tears came unbidden to her eyes: "He decided at one point to come back to the States with his lovely wife and little boy, but they don't live here. They live a very quiet life elsewhere. His father and I have visited a few times. He'll never be the same carefree boy I remember, but I'm so relieved he's alive. I think he is as happy as could be expected under such circumstances." No words came to me in reply. I just looked caringly at her and held out my hand, once again finding physical connection more meaningful than language.

•

If I were a duck in water in the classroom, other sites saw me floundering from a lack of requisite skills. My writing suffered, at first because no support came to me from the senior men in my field and later from my slow but steady slide into alcoholism. But I never missed a day of class, not even when I was nursing severe colds or severe hangovers. My students gave me large doses of positive reinforcement, and I came to enjoy a reputation as a fine teacher. But none of this would move in my favor the full professor who taught metaphysical poetry; he refused to let me offer any version of such courses, even during his sabbatical years. The first time I asked him if I might offer the undergraduate course during his absence (assistant professors knew seminars were reserved for their elders), he looked me straight in the eyes and replied: "Over my dead body."

I went home that Friday, got drunk quickly, and stayed that way until late Sunday night.

Though expected to teach the beginning Shakespeare classes several times a year, I was denied access to courses focusing on sixteenth-century English-language poetry and prose. During my initial ten years at the University of Minnesota, all my teaching went to undergraduates or, in the case of a Milton course I inherited and loved, brand new graduate students. This system of ownership, buttressed by sexism and ageism against younger faculty, kept my own thinking about my own period from being refurbished as it would have been had I been offering graduate seminars. Gradually, I internalized my senior colleagues' attitude toward me; I began to think I probably did not know enough about the Renaissance to be entrusted with such a course. I began to doubt myself. It was true, after all: I could neither decipher nor respond "appropriately" to notes from my chairman—which were, incidentally, written in Latin. That students gave me high rankings on evaluations surely signaled my lax approach to classroom teaching—never mind the awards from outside the English department or comments from students swearing that my class had been the most demanding of any they had taken while at the university.

During that first decade, I occasionally let myself fantasize about what I might be teaching and writing had I gone to the University of Rochester and inherited the courses of the older woman who had so wanted me as her successor. These musings seriously depressed me. My relationship with the woman who left Madison to live with

me had come to a skidding and ugly halt when we tried to inhabit
a triangle that included a new Ph.D. candidate whom I had met
through a mutual interest in Emily Dickinson. After months of
friendship, the young woman proposed a ménage à trois. It lasted
too long and was singularly painful for me. In the end, my lover
went off with the third woman, leaving me to knock around our
large apartment, passing out every night from too much bourbon,
feeling distinctly sorry for myself. To take control of my life at this
very low point in the mid–1970s, I bought a little maroon Datsun
pickup truck on a whim; I also convinced a doctor to put me on a
protein diet so I would lose the pounds I had gained during my
personal breakup and professional lockout.

The picture was not entirely bleak, however. Four years after
my arrival, in 1968, I had tenure as an associate professor and an
award for outstanding teaching. One more year brought a second
teaching award, this time at the all-university level. Because most
of my immediate colleagues seemed unable or unwilling to
acknowledge my talents, I began what would be a decade of frantic participation on college- and university-level committees. It
began innocently enough: I was asked to serve on the College of
Liberal Arts Instruction Committee—a new creature formed in
response to a growing number of student complaints about idio-
syncratic and/or poor classroom instruction. I loved the métier of
ten to twelve faculty members from various departments sitting
around a table to discuss what we might do to make students'
learning more effective and less stressful. We began on a small
scale—after all, we considered each professor's classroom a world
unto itself, almost as sacrosanct as the nuclear family, in which
patriarchal teachers could inflict serious emotional pain and intellectual damage to individuals with virtually no recourse against
such abuses. Protections provided to both entities seemed to favor
the wrong people and to foster destructive secrets that under-
mined real growth and creativity. But my first move was timid,
since I understood that if I let faculty know some of my broader
ideas about open classrooms, coteaching, and the enabling of students as teachers as well as learners, the committee's ideas would
be hastily consigned to some forgotten file.

We designed three courses—Directed Study, Directed Research,
and Directed Instruction—to allow students to work independently
for credit with individual faculty members. Directed Instruction

was entirely my idea and caused considerable disagreement, even among committee members. I felt sure that our best undergraduates could help their less-prepared classmates improve even as they themselves deepened their comprehension of the material under study. After all, I was learning far more about literature by teaching it than I ever had as a student. Though some of my colleagues were unable to cede that much power, I was able to convince the committee and, later, an equally reluctant college assembly to adopt the course on an experimental basis. The rubric still exists not only in my college but throughout the university. In the early 1970s, when I converted my hunch into practice, the concept of active learning was not current within the academy.

During the next three years, while I served as chair of the Instruction Committee, we pushed through such then-radical ideas as requiring the faculty to provide students with a syllabus for their courses, outlawing the practice of adding projects or papers during the last few weeks of classes, and supporting a student service to hear informal but nonetheless upsetting complaints about the faculty's whimsical-to-cruel behavior, e.g., asking graduate students to collect dry cleaning or fetch books from the library, assigning a last-minute report or paper just as students were trying to study for final exams, or insinuating to certain students that they could cinch an A by engaging in "a little sexual byplay." We were challenging a system that assumed passivity as the best learning stance; that rewarded rote learning rather than less-polished but more substantive cognition about principles, issues, and motivations; and that depended upon having a captive population who agreed to relinquish all agency in hopes of securing the golden ring. My committee, in dangerous contrast, sought to graduate people who knew how to fish, not people with a sack full of walleyes or rainbow trout.

My primary impetus was not inspiration, but displacement. Displacement—the act of moving something from its proper position or of crowding out one thing with another—is a convenient defense mechanism, and I used it vigorously during this period of my life. It was altogether easier to question and work to change current pedagogical theory than it would have been to anatomize the personal impact of such destructive and entrenched traditions as racism, sexism, and homophobia within and without the academy, and, importantly, within my own psyche. Displacement also allowed me to continue drinking in order to numb all feelings and avoid the slow, hard work of refusing cultural messages about who I was and what I really wanted.

My reputation as a hard worker and clear report writer spread quickly over the somewhat arid and vacuous surface of the academy, and I was soon being tapped for all-university level work on committees and within the faculty senate. Starved for recognition from my immediate colleagues, I kept saying "yes," filling my late afternoons, evenings, and occasionally weekends and quarter breaks with work that always seemed urgent and occasionally was important. Meanwhile, I wrote less and less and drank more and more, hoping vainly to escape the isolation and hostility around me. I continued this self-destructive behavior until 1974, when I finally admitted that I could not without help stop drinking and that I was a lesbian who needed to incorporate that fact into her teaching and research. Only then could I begin the arduous and steep climb out of the excessive approach to work that I embraced to fill my lonely hours.

Because the men in my field who rightfully should have served as mentors could not (or would not) fill that role, I threw myself into teaching and service. The classroom seemed a magical place where, for a brief period of time, students and I could forget everything else but the words before us, their sounds and significance, their narrative and emotional power over us. Of course, the study of literature draws one ever deeper into self and the larger world, so even in those classrooms, I might suddenly be thrust into thoughts and feelings from which I was consciously trying to escape. But my classes went uncommonly well: students worked hard at analyses of poetry and drama, while I delivered rich and highly organized lectures day after day in three different subject areas during each of three different quarters. When I try now to articulate what let me continue believing in my talents as a teacher, even as I slid further into silence as a scholar-critic, I see a photograph of my mother taken in 1954, eleven months after the sudden death of her husband, my father. She is standing in front of our whitewashed brick fireplace in Fairfield, Alabama. Above that fireplace is a huge pier mirror; a single gilded branch is suspended from the top and laden with Christmas balls of all sizes. For many years, my mother had decorated the mirror in this way, but I had assumed she would not do so that particular year because she had been in deep mourning since early January. But she did it all again, as I have recounted in an earlier chapter, and I believe I have drawn tremendous courage from that simple act of hers.

Nine preparations a year are exhausting, but, in my case, they were the more so because I was so entirely present in each of them and because I believed that students would learn best by witnessing passionate engagement with the material at hand. And learn they did, especially those who took a year-long survey of English literature from Beowulf through the Victorians. That class met five days a week for nine months, and credit could not be received for any one of its quarters until all three were completed. Most students who were sitting in my classroom in mid-June had been there since late September—an unheard-of phenomenon even in those slower days of academic life. Though undeniably rigid and grueling, the unconventional structure meant that the students and I formed genuine relationships, in some cases lasting more than three decades.

Joyce, a student during my second year of teaching that British literature survey, currently takes, along with her partner, Betsy, Saturday community classes taught by Susan and me for the past twenty years. Her gray hair and distinctive wrinkles remind me just how close I was in age to those students—they were nearly twenty and I was nearly thirty, so they are now in their mid-fifties. Some will be successful at whatever they have chosen as vocations. Many will have reared children and now be enjoying grandchildren. One such pair met in my survey course. "Miss" Behr and "Mister" Emmings sat side by side for a year and, though an unlikely pair, they went on from my classroom to marry and live a long, mutually productive life together. Unlikely because she was delicate and passionately caught up in virtually every writer we studied, while he was laid back and on his way to law school. They recently honored me by attending my retirement gathering. Pride and satisfaction flooded my heart when I saw them standing in line to greet me. Judy has beautiful wisps of gray in her otherwise dark brown hair while Steve is mostly bald but still in possession of an uncommonly kind smile and a piercing gaze. A snapshot of our reunion shows me in happy tears as I look fixedly at them both; they return that penetrating look as we reminisce about our time together.

My second year, one of my favorite students was a young man who was jailed for his active and militant participation in Minneapolis's antiwar protests. He also was a writer, not of work for public consumption but for his own clarity and sanity. His journal, which I saw but never read, was laden with pages of angry script. I know this because, one snowy afternoon, he perched on the student chair in my office and read me an entry in which he expressed considerable knowledge of the workings of multinational corporations such as Honeywell—producers of the loathsome antipersonnel bombs that killed and mangled thousands of peasants in Viet Nam, Cambodia, and Laos, and the object of intense activism in which I participated. Hidden within Fran's fiery language, not surprisingly, was an idealist deeply disappointed in his country and its leaders, trying the only way he knew how to register loyal opposition. I had tremendous admiration for him, but there was more to it than that. He was like secondary smoke for someone trying to quit: I would have liked to be as visibly outraged as he, but timidity or prudence held me at bay. So, instead of getting arrested for shouting my rage at what was happening in Southeast Asia, I spent many (safe) hours listening to my student's melancholy and righteous renderings of current affairs.

Sometimes he arrived at my office with his seat mate, another Judy, angular, with dark, haunting eyes, and intensity exuding from every pore. Perhaps because her father was on the faculty at the university, perhaps because she was a young woman, her voice was almost inaudible and her rhetoric distinctly muted. Someone, most likely her mother, had taught her the same values around women's voices that King Lear propounds about his favorite daughter, Cordelia: "Her voice was soft, / Gentle and low, an excellent thing in woman" (*King Lear* 5.3.274–75). Though profoundly quiet, especially when visiting me with the melancholy protester who often reduced me to a similar muted state, her literary analyses were stunningly accurate and fresh. Why did both of us, highly intelligent women who were already experimenting with ideas that would soon become known as "feminist," let one raging young man cow us in this way? Had social conditioning been permanently successful? Were we both feeling guilty because, as women, we were forbidden from engaging in life-threatening combat and so were "outside" the turmoil that wracked Fran and many other young men of the day?

Whatever the answers to these troubling questions, I still remember Judy's excitement over Edmund Spenser's *The Faerie Queene*, not a work immediately accessible to nineteen-year-olds but one that moved her by its sheer exuberance of language and by the depth of its exploration of subjects like friendship, fidelity, and sexual anxiety. She also astounded me by seeing in Tennyson's dramatic monologues a profound sadness over the human condition, the same sadness that brought me to tears at Tithonus's having wished for immortality without remembering to ask for youth. She would go on to marry and divorce the idealistic protester, become a midwife, and then take on the medical school at the University of Minnesota as a student who insisted that the school offer courses (which eventually became an entire program) in midwifery.

Perhaps the most illustrious alumni of those early classes are Garrison Keillor and Patricia (Trish) Hampl. "Miss Hampl," as I knew her initially, impressed me with her keen ear for poetry and her fascination with narrative strategies. She would go on to write several memoirs, *A Romantic Education* being the best known, and later to be awarded a MacArthur "Genius" award. Years after being my student, Trish was a finalist for a position in our creative writing program. At her interview, she read a marvelous description of her piano teacher, only to tell us at the end that she had made most of it up. While this announcement shocked and irritated some of my more conservative colleagues, it opened my mind to memoir as a form perhaps more rewarding than fiction or fact because it insists that what we remember to be true is far more important than what may or may not have "happened."

Garrison Keillor, currently a household word in much of North America, enrolled in my Milton class and quickly came to my attention as someone with a gift for interpreting the language of others and a flair for using it. I still recall his paper on *Paradise Lost* because it had a wry humor about Adam and Eve's predicament in the Garden of Eden and a stiletto-like clarity about Milton's insoluble and ludicrous dilemma in attempting to represent God through dialogue. The problem with Garrison, however, was his attendance and consistency of performance. He cut class more often than I could sanction—always in order to meet some deadline for the campus literary magazine that he edited—and failed to hand in about half of my many assignments. So, while the work he did was superior, even original at times, I felt I simply could not give him an A. I gave Garrison a B+, the only such mark he received while an undergraduate at the University of Minnesota. When I listen to him on my car radio as he displays his extraordinary skills as a raconteur, I think back to a tall young man loping into Milton class, often late, settling his lanky frame uncomfortably into the stiff desks that were standard fare in the late 1960s, looking intently but wryly at me from behind thick, horn-rimmed glasses, much like those he wears today. I gave him the B+ because I wanted him to take more responsibility for his talents. He obviously has done precisely that, to his own and the country's delight.

Most of my students have not been on their way to fame or fortune. They have been young people eager to learn and to become more articulate about what they find within literature. So our work together has been mutually gratifying. In the last twenty years, anyone finding her or his way into one of my classes has known exactly what to expect. In my courses on women writers or feminist theory or lesbian culture, this has been particularly noticeable. The women who enroll are usually motivated to stretch their minds by tackling difficult prose or poetry written by women of all sorts and conditions. Silences persist, however, most often about childhood sexual abuse; battery within relationships, especially lesbian ones; experiences of having or agonizing over having an abortion—sexual silences, in other words, reflecting the profound depth of embarrassment and guilt women in our culture are still made to feel about our bodies. The (relatively few) men who show up are unusually adept at literary work and sensitive about not monopolizing classroom air space. Often gay or transgendered, these young men seem genuinely eager to read about and listen to what women are saying; they seem especially drawn to me as an alternative model for how someone old enough to be their parent can live her life.

From the time I first came out as a lesbian in my classes and curricula, many students across various sexualities have seen that openness as an invitation or opportunity for them to explore and speak about their sense of themselves as erotic beings. I think of a heterosexual graduate student in an Emily Dickinson seminar (enrolled entirely with women graduate students) who spoke eloquently and tearfully at our last session. We were going around the table, each sharing some important realization she had come to during our study of the Amherst wonder. People said predictable things about how reading all 1,775 of Dickinson's poems in ten weeks had immersed them in her language, or how working in cooperative research teams had helped them move beyond the isolated protection of "their" ideas. Then the student I remember said: "I've never been in a class that forced me to examine my sexuality before. This one has. When you told us, Toni, that being a lesbian had tremendous impact on how you read and theorized Dickinson's poetry, I felt obliged to ask myself if being heterosexual was in any way pertinent to how I read and theorized her work. What has resulted is far wider than this set of poems; I've tried to figure out when and how I have wound up with a John rather than a Mary, and that has changed my marriage for all time." With responses like this to buttress my nervousness before each announcement of my sexual orientation, how could I ever become jaded or blasé in the classroom?

The other thing that has kept me fresh is a promise I made to myself sometime in the mid-1970s, about a decade after I began work at the university: I would not keep saying the same things about the same works year after year. I remember seeing yellowed edges on the pages of some of my undergraduate school lecturers' notes, wondering even then how the professors could maintain their enthusiasm when speaking the same words used so far in the past. Yet, every time I read a given great work—*Hamlet* or Keats's odes, say—I found it to be about new things. Sometimes this fact depressed me: surely a more sophisticated reader would find the same points of content and form gratifying or challenging. But, at other moments, I liked my mutable responses, which seemed to prove that I was still engaged with the texts and that my own life was deepening. Gradually, I came to pride myself on this ability to find new things in old works. It let me respond more genuinely to students as they discovered their own initial windows into these texts; to hold back from saying what I heard from colleagues in the coffee room: "Well, that's a fundamental level of comprehension; can't they muster up something more original?" or "We've known that for years; they'll have to do better than that in *my* class."

As life would have it, events overtook my promise, making it unnecessary for me to force myself to discard old notes in favor of new ones. During the 1970s, the Vietnam War and feminism crashed onto campus and compelled me to alter my pedagogy, my curriculum, and even my basic ideas about my position vis-à-vis students. I viewed our presence in Viet Nam as one more example of a war fostered by older white men het up about abstract issues; a war fought by increasingly larger numbers of men of color and against/within a nation populated by people of color. As Dr. Martin Luther King, Jr. spoke more and more eloquently about the U.S. military's drafting disproportionate numbers of African American males for combat, I became firmer in my resistance to the rapid buildup and escalation of fighting ordered by jingoistic leaders from behind the protection of their mahogany desks in corporate boardrooms or at the Pentagon. I believed King and others who argued that our presence in Southeast Asia had both racist and capitalist overtones, that we might be "fighting communism" but not in the same ways there as we did, say, in countries behind the Iron Curtain and populated predominantly by (white) Europeans. In fact, my "take" on all the wars—or "conflicts" as the spin doctors prefer to call them these days—in which we have engaged since the Vietnam War has been profoundly influenced by the educational process I went through as we sent thousands and thousands of our younger generation to their deaths or, perhaps worse, to a despair and cynicism from which many never recovered.

When an activist student presented me with a little white card, asking me to carry it as a sign that I had pledged to act against the massive silence about the war from groups like college professors, I agreed easily. Of my immediate faculty associates, only two or three others participated in this seemingly tame but actually quite soul-shattering activity. Shortly thereafter campuses began to erupt across the country. First, students (and a few faculty) from the University of Minnesota attended rallies in downtown Minneapolis and joined community marches protesting our country's presence in Southeast Asia. Standing in cold pre-dawn huddles in front of the federal building in support of young men who were refusing the draft, I did not think to ask myself why I was there. It may have been from residual guilt over my failure to be part of the civil rights struggles in my own state of Alabama, or it may just have been an unconscious need to stand in solidarity with some group of human beings, since my gender or my sexuality or both so often cast me outside the circle of acceptability.

Also I noticed that I refrained from drinking myself into a stupor on nights before I was to report to a demonstration hub at dawn, so my political activism also granted me brief respites from the depressed fog that usually began my days. From this experience, I learned that I could "live dangerously" by heightening rather than losing consciousness. Working for a cause greater than myself would eventually be a source of sufficient strength to allow me to stop drinking and begin writing.

After the violent police shootings and deaths at Kent and Jackson State Universities, students at Minnesota called for a campus-wide strike and set up picket lines in front of all major classroom buildings. I was teaching Milton to about fifty advanced undergraduates and a smattering of first-year graduate students and was not inclined to cancel classes. As a young girl, however, I had listened to my father rail against men at his company who crossed the picket line when fellow workers were on strike, trying to wrest from management halfway decent wages or minimal job security. My father had told me never to do that because it weakened the chances of success for people who desperately needed more money, a decent retirement package, or safer workplaces. I was not at all sure he would have recognized the students carrying antigovernment signs as "legitimate" strikers, but I knew it would be physically—and psychically—impossible for me to break through their silent marching in order to enter my building.

Some of my lazier colleagues jumped at the chance to call off classes while seeming to support the striking students; some unfocused students jumped at the chance not to have to study or produce work while seeming to be "radicals." One splendid role model in the political science department, who wore red ties to work every day, fought against considerable odds to be able to teach a course on political systems that included material on communism. He also wrote a searing editorial for the school newspaper, calling all faculty to move their classes off campus as a way of incorporating intellectual study with direct allegiance to practices and ideals that flew in the face of much that any institution of higher learning stood for. I decided to follow his advice.

I wanted my students to read Milton closely at a moment when police and university officials alike were attempting to muzzle speech that accused governments and administrations of colluding with (if not actively contributing to) the horrors we were, by then, viewing nightly on our television screens. After all, works like *Areopagitica* could give them historical backing for their position. Milton extolled the individual's freedom to argue any position on any issue, no matter how outlandish, threatening, or even foolish it might seem to those wielding power. So I found out which students lived near campus, organized pickup schedules using the little red truck I was driving at the time, and proceeded to transport class to various apartments. Looking back, I perceive a deeper significance to what seemed at the time like a combination of political action and sheer fun; I now believe I was beginning to stumble then on to an alternative, subversive pedagogy about which I would theorize all through the 1990s.

Discussions in those cramped spaces were more urgent and pointed than any had been in our dingy classroom. Students and I felt charged by the knowledge that we were studying under (relative) duress, that Milton somehow mattered enough to justify the minor inconvenience involved in continuing class. We finally understood the intimate and profound impact literature can have on the larger social order; I no longer had to convince them that reading someone who had lived and written in a time remote from their own could nonetheless be of immediate use to their own political and personal struggles. Some students even spoke in class—and during the truck ride to and fro—about their interest in learning more about radical Minnesota political action during the early decades of the twentieth century: actions involving farmers who spilled thousands of gallons of milk to protest devastatingly low prices for their product; or white women garment workers in St. Paul who walked off jobs they desperately needed to feed themselves and their children in an attempt to force management to install safer machines and better lighting. I talked about French students, with their long history of moving beyond their libraries and textbooks to march with workers because they understand the relationship between better working conditions, a greater voice in the running of a country, and the life of the mind. Most of the undergraduates in my class had no history with unions or strikes or picket lines. They probably did not grasp the degree of their own privilege, to be able to pick and choose their "causes" rather than being unable to avoid them because of the material impact of various issues on people's daily lives. But they came to feel the validity and empowerment of standing with people they might not know personally but whose "cause" they could support in a small but tangible way.

When I was not shuttling students in order to analyze Milton's poetry and prose, I often found myself smuggling food inside our student union, which was taken over for several weeks by ardent student antiwar protesters. Because they feared never being able to reenter should they leave the premises, guarded as they were by campus police, their only source of food was faculty, who could come and go at will since we were presumed too mature or rational to participate in antiadministration protests. Once, loaded down with crackers, cheese, and cold cuts, I found myself sharing an elevator that connected the parking lot to the union with a benign-looking man whose beard was going gray and white. He, too, had several grocery bags, so I took a risk and asked if he were taking those to the protesting students. He smiled with relief and said he was. From that meeting, this history professor and I became close and continuing friends, discovering, as is so often the case, that a single behavior is metonymic. It turned out Clarke Chambers and I also shared views about pedagogical principles, liberal arts reformation, undergraduate student excellence, and the need on occasion to bend all rules in order to salvage a soul in danger of becoming lost.

Reading my earlier account of participation in the antiwar protests on campus, I notice that I spoke at some length about an incident in which a graduate student named Bob and I were brought face-to-face with police brutality. But I omitted any reference to Clarke and me as faculty determined to incorporate our broader ideas of politics into the university environment and to use our intellectual knowledge to deepen students' understanding of politics. High drama must have seemed more appealing to me a decade ago than it does now; or perhaps I currently value long-term connections more than I possibly could have a decade ago.

Our salvage operation occurred in the early 1980s, as the country studiously avoided the facts and people involved in the Vietnam War era. Few parades had welcomed our "gallant boys" home; we had so clearly not "won" the war we had sent them to slog through. At the time, I was teaching a young man who was extremely talented, full of satiric clarity about social injustices and academic charades—and well along the steep descent into drug addiction. Quite often he came to class "stoned," as we said in those relatively romantic days when many of us experimented with marijuana. By the end of the quarter, however, Billy had progressed to harder drugs, heroin or cocaine I presumed. Though I had never tried either, his symptoms were very like my own during years of alcoholic drinking: glazed eyes, sweaty brow, fidgety postures, short attention span. I probably identified closely with Billy because, though I had accumulated by then several years of sobriety, I still wanted to drink almost every day and was hanging on sometimes by the thinnest thread of hope.

By about three-quarters into the Milton course, producing coherent papers was becoming impossible for him, and my standards for making even a C involved writing many papers. Unsure what my final course of action would be, I mentioned my dilemma to Clarke one day when we were at some interminable committee meeting. To my relief, I discovered that he had the same young man in his undergraduate seminar on the Vietnam War as a historical event in U.S. history and culture. We both recognized this student's unique strengths and the disastrous course he was traveling. That afternoon and during many afternoons that followed, we spoke painstakingly about Billy, finally deciding that he was worth saving at any price. We were convinced that if he could remain inside an educational institution where his intellect was challenged, he might come out of his drug use and be able to pursue the talents he clearly possessed. And, if he were forced to leave the university because of what he would most surely view as its rigidity in the name of abstract standards, he might never exit the drug-induced fog in which he was spending more and more of his time.

So Clarke and I decided to give him B's in both our courses, even though he could not in either case fulfill the stated criteria to earn such a grade. We also made a pact to speak to him—without euphemism—about the downward spiral of drug addiction. Billy did stay in the university long enough to graduate and begin a career as a music critic; a career violently interrupted by a terrible motorcycle accident. That split-second accident put him into a coma for weeks and left him permanently crippled. More devastating to what Clarke and I found so compelling about him—his keen perspective on contemporary culture—Billy was left somewhat slowed down mentally and even in his capacity for speech.

The superb ending of Billy's tale is this: by sheer dint of determination, Billy underwent enough physical therapy to regain almost full speech; his mind has returned to him and has served him well over the thirty years since that devastating accident. He has become an accomplished filmmaker focusing on disability issues, winning national awards, and securing major grants to continue with his extraordinary artistic and political work. When Clarke and I see each other these days, we often reminisce about our entirely fortuitous elevator meeting, agreeing repeatedly that one of our very best accomplishments began on the afternoon we decided to "give" our student a grade he had not "earned" in order to help him exit from a self-destructive path. I still receive notes from Billy, now in his fifties with a name recognized in many film circles. As I read them, I often find myself weeping and knowing all over again that I did the right thing, even though at the time my academic conscience accused me of wrongdoing when I was too tired or upset to sleep through the night.

In addition to affecting me in significant personal and political ways, student protests against the Vietnam War brought me into contact with two other remarkable colleagues—Val Woodward, a professor in cell biology, and Roger Jones, a professor in physics. I had heard a bit about Val and his wife, Claire, two white faculty members who ran a faculty/graduate student discussion group to explore ways of combating racism on campuses like Minnesota. As for Roger, who was also white, I knew he had written a book entitled *The Tao of Physics* and that his colleagues viewed him as beyond "the scientific pale." After I decided to attend a late-afternoon discussion of possibilities for forming an alternative "college" within the university, I quickly came to understand that these two men were extraordinary by any standard. I also felt a strong desire to know them better and to align myself with the entirely radical plan they were articulating at this meeting. As scientists, they fell outside my stereotype of who might be at the forefront of educational reform, especially since they proposed courses that invited—or forced—students to relate emotional responses to intellectual analysis.

Roger and Val thought faculty across the country were solemnly obliged to assume some leadership in showing undergraduates how to retain intellectual integrity and study important subject matter while integrating such heady activity into the politics of reality. We were to set some kind of moral example, in other words. This idea appealed to me since I had never been entirely comfortable with the "objective" model of higher education that forbade us to discuss values with students, as if every subject at our university were not intimately and inextricably tied up with some set of values, even when hidden from students. I wanted to foreground such unpopular ideas as acceptance of diverse peoples and systems, and to register protest against the hegemony of one system, e.g., compulsory heterosexuality or capitalist democracy (which certainly did not much resemble democracy as I envisioned it).

They (and I, as it turned out, once I stopped letting male colleagues name for me the oppressions of which I was acutely aware) empathized with the angry students building barricades across the main street that cut through campus. We also were committed to rigorous intellectual study. If these students—some of our brightest undergraduates—could be persuaded not to drop out as so many were doing elsewhere, perhaps their intellectual progress would not be wholly interrupted by their country's ever more futile and inhumane interventions in Southeast Asia.

We proposed an alternative "college," with classes offered in a big brick building just on the edge of campus that sported a stunning art deco skylight dome, the same building in which the initial discussion meeting took place. It was technically off campus though just across a busy thoroughfare from Folwell Hall, a sprawling and architecturally delightful old building that housed all the language departments other than English. The building also is a symbol of power from an earlier era of university education when no one would have dared ask the kind of questions we three alternative educators were raising. But being across that boundary was essential for the kind of student who might avail herself or himself of our program because it meant classes would take place outside the strike zone drawn by the protesters. Not only did Val and Roger propose getting the university administration to approve this unit and its course offerings, but even to grant degrees to students who completed the entirely rigorous if unconventional requirements we would devise. I say "we" again because I quickly had made it known to Val and Roger that I was ready to join with them if they wanted me. It seems my reputation as a passionate and iconoclastic teacher had preceded me; Val and Roger were thrilled to include me.

For several evenings, we met to draw up the design for our college—UWW became its acronym, University Without Walls. UWW would offer seminars that brought students from various disciplinary persuasions together to argue huge cultural issues such as: How can peace be maintained in a capitalist society? Does the military-industrial complex see the Vietnamese as "feminine" and so have no trouble overbearing and raping them and their land? What ethics should govern interactions with people whose politics seem to one totally immoral? Where are the parallels between U.S. policy in Viet Nam and racism within our own states and cities? Of what use is higher education in a world hell-bent on conquest and exploitation? (None of us ever raised questions about homophobia or misogyny: I was still closeted at work, and those issues had not yet registered on Roger's or Val's screens.) Our college would allow students to "count" political engagement outside the university classroom as part of their degree program if they wrote self-reflective essays around such activism, relating this historical moment to others before it. We would sponsor colloquia with faculty who shared our vision for retaining some of our most disaffected students, who were willing to speak openly and honestly about their own deepest views about the war in Viet Nam, venture capitalism, university investment politics in South Africa, and a host of other sensitive topics about which many of our colleagues and administrators preferred we remain silent. In order to graduate, students would submit portfolios containing all their formal work to be evaluated by a committee of three faculty, one fellow UWW student, and someone from the broader community with whom the student had worked. Once that portfolio was accepted, the student would be part of an oral examination at which her or his committee might ask any questions that seemed relevant and fair.

To our amazement, the vice president for academic administration approved our proposal with almost no questions or objections. Perhaps he figured no one would ever present the requisite credentials, since all such potential students were suspect according to his way of defining proper academic life and rigor. Well, we graduated between ten and twenty superb students, many of whom would never have stayed in a traditional, insular discipline where the street was considered entirely irrelevant to the subject matter at hand. Some went on to graduate and professional school once the United States finally withdrew its military from Viet Nam; most put what they had learned with their maverick faculty advisers and sponsors to excellent use in community activism; a few have run for school boards or local political offices. As I read their various portfolios, I became convinced that they were far better prepared, both in subject matter and in the application thereof, than even honors students pursuing regular degree requirements. They knew what they thought, why it mattered, the implications of what they learned for the lives of human beings, and the final limits of purely intellectual knowledge. I was proud to have helped them join their intellectual pursuits with their beliefs and to have forced the system to recognize their paths as legitimate.

Hindsight is not always twenty-twenty. Because memory operates within its territory, we are just as apt to make of some past enterprise or experience what our later philosophies or needs require. But I believe my recollections of those late-afternoon and evening discussions of texts and theories (no classes were scheduled during the day—our students would be busy rallying on the streets or participating in a sit-in at the administration building) actually were as spirited and challenging as I remember them. Furthermore, I have portfolios of some of our graduating seniors as evidence that they had learned tremendous amounts. They were self-selected, entirely motivated to study as they organized politically and to wrest from the offending institution the coin of its realm. I applauded all aspects of their choices and still do.

Feminisms and Friendships

As the vibrant 1970s slid into the more individualistic 1980s, I began to notice a growing divide between students who truly applied themselves to the study of literature and those who enrolled in English courses because they expected an easy ride while they took "hard" courses like mathematics, economics, biology, or mechanical engineering. Given the prevalence of binary thinking within U.S. culture, *hard* also tends to mean masculine, good, and valuable, while *soft* connotes feminine, bad, and worthless. Those disciplines that considered themselves to be in the former configuration tended to dismiss "softer" fields of research and study such as ethnic studies, women's studies, and gay/lesbian/bisexual/transgender (GLBT) studies. In this regard, universities and colleges simply mirrored the broader culture, which under the Reagan administration began a slow but sure retreat from social programs ostensibly designed (and often failing) to assist poor and working families. My students' goals reflected a definite slide toward conservatism, materialism, and the institutional displacement of blame onto individuals and away from the faulty infrastructure itself. It had seemed only a short while since virtually all of my students were eager to read and analyze literature, searching for one more way to understand themselves and the world they would inhabit once out of college. I missed their intensity and willingness to argue with one another and with me; as a teacher I soon felt dragged down by the ever-increasing emphasis students placed on a course's potential to move them closer to gainful employment. Since more of them were the second or even third generation within their families to attend college, I deduced that the shift was not motivated by raw economic need. Rather, they seemed caught up in a general frenzy to acquire more and more objects—i.e., signs of material prosperity—in order to feel successful or even adequate.

The notable exceptions to this drift toward utilitarianism came, in the 1980s, from female students in my English and women's studies classes and, in the 1990s, from an increasingly visible and vocal collection of lesbian and gay students at both the undergraduate and graduate levels. Though I seldom taught a student of color, these white women and men read novels and poetry by writers of color, about whom I persisted in teaching. While most welcomed this multicultural curriculum, many of my white female students rushed to elide racial or class distinctions. For instance, a common student refrain when we read works by African American women writers was: "We are all women after all, so I can really identify with [fill in the character's name]." My comments became cautionary, articulating the dangers of appropriation and of false, oversimplifying unities. Soon I began to introduce students to theories of culture that emphasized the complex and intersecting matrices of race, class, gender, and sexuality—lenses that illuminate one another even as one might challenge the rest as too narrow or privileged for the analysis of history, social systems, or personality. These students soon began to demand courses and research opportunities in which they could explore knowledge; pose new questions; and continue to produce fresh interpretations of texts and social, historical, and cultural issues. In response, I fashioned a series of feminist, lesbian, and, eventually, GLBT courses, that have expanded my own framework for considering both literature and life choices.

While my academic framework and influence may have been expanding, the number of students who seemed interested in what I had to offer seemed to be shrinking. My classes no longer had long waiting lists, and a certain number of students dropped my courses early in the semester either because the workload was too strenuous or the emphasis too unfamiliar. But sharp images remain from this last decade. If I think of faces, I see a white heterosexual middle-class woman back in school after rearing children and divorcing her husband; discovering Adrienne Rich's poems about the difficulty in trying to talk to men; going on to write her own first rough poems; and eventually entering formal classes in creative writing on her way to becoming a published poet. I see the African American gay man trying to make a joke out of the fact that he "stands out" on the streets of Minneapolis in ways that had not been true in his native Chicago. I see a white transgendered undergraduate in my GLBT literature class blurting out, "But it's just a *dress!*" as we discussed the ethics behind the protagonist's refusal in Leslie Feinberg's *Stone Butch Blues* to dress as she was asked on the occasion of an old bull dyke's funeral. I see a heterosexual East Indian undergraduate struggling not to become disaffected or bitter in the face of the blatant and painful marginalization she had suffered, from both student and faculty participants, at a student leadership program in Washington, D.C.

As one of my most recent memories, I see twenty-eight honors students taking my last Shakespeare course before retirement, bonding within the first two weeks of class as they prepared to "present" Rome and Egypt as conflicting worlds behind the love story of an aging Antony and Cleopatra. They worked their hearts out all semester so I might leave with nothing but positive memories of teaching, climaxing that effort by staging in our dreary classroom the closing scene of *The Winter's Tale.* Over the delicious refreshments that followed, served on a desk covered by an elegant cloth and finished with a silver-and-white candle arrangement, my final class told me that in my course they had relived their first thrills from reading literature; that Shakespeare could be helpful to them as they tried to become responsible and caring citizens—all while I sat engulfed in tears of joy and appreciation.

Alongside my passion for teaching has been an extended record of leadership, initially around the anti–Vietnam War demonstrations and formation of ethnic studies programs at the University of Minnesota and, later, as a launching voice in both women's and gay and lesbian studies. The initial phase came as I became clearer about my academic politics. Sometime in the 1970s, I discovered and read Peter Elbow's controversial essays on higher education's abusive treatment of students and the essential fallacy behind an exclusive dependence on lecturing. His argument about the problems inherent to lecturing without having the slightest idea whether or not what we say is of any value or even interest to our students made deep sense to me, in part because I had so wanted to share with my own college teachers what I thought about Shakespeare or Renaissance painting. So, I decided to stop doing it—lecturing, that is—even though the lectures I delivered in my first ten years of teaching were marvels of their genre. I became convinced that I needed to find out what students wanted to know rather than holding forth as if whatever I chose to profess was what they should hear on any given day. That I stumbled upon Elbow's work even as I was joining antiwar protesters—e.g., sitting down in the middle of Washington Avenue, the major street cutting through campus, to block traffic—surely informed my new understanding of "relics" like lectures and grades as a form of (academic) colonialism, which I no longer cared to perpetuate.

One example of Elbow's radical teaching strategies ran much like this: he would open class by saying, "Today we are reading Melville. What do you want to ask me about him?" If students could not tell him, he would walk out of class. I decided to emulate what I thought of initially as his bravery in the face of decades of tradition, not realizing that he was only changing modalities while leaving power entirely in his own hands.

The initial results of my experiment are ludicrous in retrospect and were incredibly awkward at the time. On the first day of class, I would proclaim my newfound perspective on lecturing as a kind of mental prostitution in which teachers "sold" ideas to pacified learners. Aside from shocking many of my fresh-faced undergraduates by this comparison, I made it abundantly clear that I would not appear at the next class meeting with pre-packaged notes. Rather, I would come prepared to work with their questions. It now seems obvious that I overlooked, at the time, a key element in the educational formula: one reason students were enrolling in my course was because they did not know much about the subject. This fact made it extremely difficult for them to raise intelligent or interesting questions at the beginning of class, and so, reluctant to sound foolish, they clammed up entirely.

We often sat in stony silence for ten to twenty minutes before I archly dismissed the students, upbraiding them for their lack of passionate engagement. This pendulum-swing approach confused and frustrated many young people that first term of my non-lecturing career. More seriously, it constituted no transformation of my own position in the classroom, since I was still controlling what we did and did not do; I was still the boss, still the center of attention. Not until those first disastrous days had come and gone, and I had meditated long and hard about some way I might truly share power with my students, did it occur to me to move away from the poles—i.e., my constant talking and my refusal to speak at all—and toward a more central position on the spectrum. Probably this decision was influenced by my reading ground-breaking feminist thinkers like Shulamith Firestone, Kate Millett, and Robin Morgan, all of whom called into question some central tenets—and power asymmetries—of traditional culture. I also was attending early National Women's Studies Association (NWSA) conferences, where I listened to feminist pedagogical theorists speak of arranging classes in circles so everyone was not facing "the teacher"; of structuring discussions by using a "rotating-chairs" system in which the person called upon would recognize the next speaker, and "the teacher" got to raise her hand and be granted permission to speak, like everyone else; of asking students to keep journals in which they responded both intellectually and personally to readings, lectures, classroom discussions, and all research work. These and other strategies encouraged genuine *active learning* before the term became an academic buzzword. They also helped decentralize power in the classroom and facilitated the learning of broad-based ideas rather than a mere accumulation of facts.

Adopting these and other progressive pedagogies has aided tremendously my goal of empowering students. I will not lie: some days I have missed the old sense of having delivered a stunning lecture to a room full of students who recognized just how good I was at it. In all honesty, at the end of *most* classes over the past ten to fifteen years I have suffered a brief moment of disappointment that no one was applauding the way they did in the late 1960s; applause that echoed in my ears all the way down the hall from the lecture room to my office. But then I step out of fantasy land and know anew that learning is more significant than teaching, that opening students to their own ideas and questions is much harder than impressing them with a prepared talk.

Whereas my understanding of U.S. colonialism in Viet Nam and elsewhere invited me to abandon power and to affirm a connection between that colonialism and our own homegrown racism, academic feminist theory and practice compelled me to analyze that connection and to share that power. During the 1970s, academic feminism introduced into the academy such radical concepts as faculty accountability to educators and to our students. I am accountable for my training and learning, just as I am accountable to the people who come into my classroom. I cannot simply decide to stop teaching them because I have an epiphany about the potential abuse and guaranteed boredom inherent in an exclusive use of the lecture format. What I can do instead is tell students that what they feel is as important as what I feel, even if what I know about a given text or topic is considerably greater than what they know about it. Furthermore, I can help them see that having the time, support, opportunity, and resources to accumulate and practice such knowledge is a privilege in itself, closed to many in our culture because of economic and ideological constraints. And with privilege always comes responsibility: to oneself and to the knowledge, of course; but, significantly, to those too often barred from its acquisition and application. Equality between the students and me, however, stems from our responses: if I can allow theirs to figure importantly in my pedagogy, then I am more truly sharing our common space. For example, if I feel elated over a certain poem but a student is unmoved by it, I must allow for that emotional difference. But if one of them thinks the poem is about chickens when it is clearly about pigs, I must show her or him that the poem is not about chickens. Conversely, if a student can show me textual evidence to the contrary, or even raise a substantive doubt, then I must find the grace to admit that my reading may be askew. Such declensions of power do not come without resistance or even fear; but come they must if our classrooms—or our lives for that matter—are ever to change.

During my first six years at the University of Minnesota, I had no one on the faculty with whom I could discuss my emerging ideas about Renaissance literature, or how I felt about the evening news or, most certainly, what was going on in my life outside the university. But just as I was embarking on what would be my wisest pedagogical alterations, women students began clamoring for courses in feminist history and culture, and my department hired two additional women to the faculty. Since my white male colleagues were deaf to such student demands, the hire was an accidental answer, definitely not a conscious response. It would bring me, however, two wonderful, long-term friends and my first genuine colleagues: people who would join me in forcing a reluctant department to assume its rightful place of intellectual leadership in the then-emerging areas of literary study—feminist literature and theory, multicultural literature and theory, and eventually, post-colonial and GLBT literature and theory. In 1970, Shirley Nelson (Garner) was hired and, to my amazement, only one year later Madelon (Mimi) Sprengnether joined us.

Both Shirley and Mimi had degrees in sixteenth-century English literature—Shirley's dissertation was on George Gascoigne, while Mimi's focused on narrative structure in Philip Sidney, Edmund Spenser, and Thomas Nashe. We could talk about authors and texts loved and studied by all of us, thereby enriching each of our perspectives on these standard works. As our association deepened, we remarked on how striking it was that all three of us were white southern women; and that each had chosen to study literature written when England was ruled by a powerful woman and when sexual ambivalence and literary experimentation were in full swing. Shirley, Mimi, and I felt it miraculous that we should all converge on the same department, finding a way to cut against competition in forming friendships that carried us through personal and professional assaults by our white male colleagues who continued to feel threatened by our presence. They were used to women being docile, silent secretaries, unaware of the perhaps small but nonetheless important acts of defiance, agency, and even creative revenge expressed by such staff members. The "lost" telephone message here, the left-out *not* that completely changed a letter's meaning there: acts that paralleled domestic agency work at home where wives served husbands meat just over- or undercooked or burnt toast too many mornings to qualify as an accident instead of as subversive payback. But women like us—who were insistently leaving the private sphere and becoming part of the intellectual currency of "their" professional space—tended to evoke feelings of mistrust, dismay, and downright hostility.

While I had nothing to do with Mimi coming to Minnesota, I was on the hiring team that went the day after Christmas 1969 to the Modern Language Association (MLA) convention in Denver, determined to bring at least four bright new Ph.D.'s into our midst. This meant I took part in Shirley's interview, during which I was impressed by her integrity and commitment to solid teaching, alongside her enthusiasm for things Renaissance. As a lagniappe, she was from Texas and so sounded like home when she talked.

Though our outward styles were quite dissimilar—she gave the impression that she should be at a late-afternoon tea conversing about a play or musical from which she had just come, while I was noticeably stiff in social situations, giving off a distinctly anti-tea-party aura—I sensed the possibility for a friendship from the start. My male colleagues had asked Shirley routine questions about her writing and the courses she might like to teach. But as I ushered her out of the interview space into the hotel hallway, I took a risk by moving the conversation away from school and toward the rest of her life. I asked if she had a family, and she responded directly (and, I imagined, gratefully), saying that she had been married but was currently divorced without children and looking forward to living with herself. Though Shirley and I had made different decisions about how to live our private lives and certainly managed our professional self-presentation in vastly different ways, I believed without tangible evidence that we shared, at some rudimentary level, an outlook on life and a set of values. That hunch was proven correct with each conversation we had, whether it was about academic politics, the world at large, or relations between women and men. As time passed, it became clear that, if anything, some of Shirley's ideas for how to change academe or how to trouble conventional heterosexuality were more radical and far-reaching than my own. At first I admired her "proper lady" performance because it lent her what I would soon realize was much-needed cover for her honest views, providing her space within which to work without the immediate disapproval I suffered from so many of our male colleagues. After I saw how furious those older white men soon became with her, however, I began to imagine that they felt betrayed because of their original impression of her as the "tea-party femme"; with me, at least they had known from the start what they were getting. But even so, my male colleagues experienced persisting discomfort in the presence of my no-nonsense butch.

At the end of a long day of interviewing ten bright young people, we discussed our favorites. My counterparts, all male, were drawing up a list of especially desirable candidates to invite to dinner later that evening; Shirley was not on their list, though they had all agreed that we wanted to make her an offer. When I pointed out this obvious lacuna, they sheepishly admitted that they did not think she, as a woman, would get the same high-pressure treatment as the best of our male candidates, who would be desired by many departments. At my insistence, we took Shirley to dinner, where she enjoyed a delicately prepared *pampano en papier* and expensive wine. Later in that week we made her an offer that she, thankfully, accepted.

Our friendship was immediate and has persisted into the present. I often remark that if Shirley had not come to the university, I doubt I could have stayed through the worst phases. People often think I am exaggerating when I say that, but I mean every word. Several young women hired during the early 1970s left Minnesota abruptly, and not always for employment elsewhere: in at least one case, the person detoured into a mental hospital. Coming to trust that I could tell Shirley anything and get attentive support made it possible for me to stay put. Her presence gradually countered the leftover hurt and anger I felt toward the woman hired when I was; she had flagrantly spurned my attempts at friendship, I suspect, because she felt it might impede her search for Mr. Right. Shirley confirmed for me that it is possible—and desirable—for a woman to form close and loyal attachments to other women and still build a life with a suitable heterosexual partner if she chooses. She also had no projected or unexamined fears about making friends with someone who she knew was a lesbian, though it would be a few years into our relationship before I explicitly came out to her. As I have observed the difficulties many academic women have in resisting the institutional pull toward competitiveness, I have come to cherish my deep and loving friendship with Shirley all the more. Though we certainly have had our arguments—no two people with strong views and verbal acumen could know each other for thirty years without them—we have always known that a piece of good fortune for one of us is a gift to the other.

When Shirley remarried, a few years after she arrived, I worried that this might alter our relationship; certainly life and novels are full of instances where a husband has supplanted a good friend. Nothing changed except I got to know and like her husband. When they had first a boy and then a girl, I made a promise to be present in those children's lives no matter what else was going on in my own. I kept my promise even during Hart and Celia's first years, though I was still drinking. That I was able to meet certain obligations and keep certain commitments while living with my alcoholism—showing Hart and Celia I loved them, never missing a class at school because of a hangover, executing demanding committee assignments—but totally unable to stay sober long enough to write coherently, or consider whether my next lover was someone I liked, or embark upon a therapeutic journey to self-clarity—certainly speaks to some fundamental paradoxes of my makeup. But I am so glad that Shirley's children always occupied the positive column; and that recovery has allowed me to move myself and my own deepest desires into that same space. As they matured and entered high school, I shared my own adolescent rebellion especially with Hart, who needed to test parental boundaries with some frequency. Now he is finishing medical school and living with the first young woman about whom he has seemed to feel serious enough to enter into such labors. It mattered to Hart that I "meet" her and give my approval to their connection. I felt trusted and "special" to Hart, able as he was to be so uninhibited in seeking my approval of his heterosexual relationship; at that very dinner, however, his girlfriend and I spoke animatedly about persistent discrimination against lesbians and gays in her corporate world. I gave him my wholehearted approval, along with a small cedar-lined trunk; in fact, I intend to pass along several other antiques from my own childhood home if the couple settles into more permanent quarters.

As for Celia, named for one of Shirley's oldest and best friends from Texas—she is a genuine young friend. Though we would never have known each other had it not been for my friendship with Shirley, as Celia has become her own person we have worked on and developed a solid connection that stands alone. Just prior to beginning her junior year in high school, Celia traveled to Colorado for a twenty-three-day Outward Bound program; she returned a changed person. In successfully completing the four-day challenge of living in the woods alone and with minimal provisions, this young woman discovered that she is not only physically strong but in possession of vast inner resources. I could hardly avoid remembering my own inner resources and suppressed talents. These strengths, and the activities they suggested to me, were discouraged by girls' guidance counselors and many teachers at school, and by most adults elsewhere. My mother gave me distinctly ambivalent messages in this regard. For instance, she pushed me toward "classic" femininity, ending in marriage and motherhood; but she also used to say with regularity, "You need to be able to earn a living, honey, when I'm gone and in case things don't work out." I assumed then and still do that "things" meant the aforesaid marriage and motherhood, but she never got that specific. Celia clearly has had an open road before her and many rooters along the way, among whom I am certainly one of the staunchest.

On a walk several days after Celia's return to Minneapolis, I noticed not only her tanned and fit body but a change in the timbre of her voice and the nuances of her opinions and questions. Poise does not capture the sureness I heard as she spoke of her time away and of her fresh understanding of several friends as they coped with divorce, sex, and uncertain futures—terribly "adult" realities she seemed fully to comprehend. When I remarked that she seemed to have gained a clarity that I found extraordinary, Celia smiled and said, "Well, it feels like I can handle most things now after managing my last days in the Colorado mountains."

After a highly successful four years at Brown University, she decided to take two years away from academe, reminding me what a different world it is for young women now than when I was twenty-one years old—or how different her mother is from my own. I was not even allowed to consider a summer job after graduating from college because Vanderbilt University, to which I had been admitted for a master's degree program, had mailed out a reading list, and Mamie was determined that I arrive having read every title on it. Even to have fantasized a hiatus in my educational path was unthinkable, and, though I applauded Celia's decision, I felt twinges of an ancient resentment about the lock-step march my family had expected of me. But a freer Celia spent her first year mostly in New York City, absorbing the city while working at an undemanding but, finally, unsatisfying job. Then she went to Quito, Ecuador, where she lived with a host family, sharpened her Spanish, discovered salsa dancing, and became attached to a wonderful young man. Soon she will enter the same excellent medical school from which her brother will shortly graduate.

Shirley's children have come to be the closest to having my own. I love them unconditionally and fiercely, and they love me in return. From the start, Shirley and I have both known that if anything were to happen to her or Frank, I would step in instantly to be sure Celia and Hart had love, care, and protection. Sometimes, when I am having dinner with Hart or walking with Celia, I return to an old and unanswerable question: What kind of mother would I have been? Though I toyed with the idea of adoption sometime during the 1970s when lesbians first began to do that, always hiding their lesbianism because it would scotch any such ventures, I never pursued the matter seriously. What stopped me every time was what I can only term my ultimate "selfishness": I could not picture myself gracefully laying aside travel or writing or my own personal engagements in order to meet the myriad demands of child-rearing. Many years ago, Johnny Carson scheduled an interview with Katharine Hepburn on his late-night show. Since Hepburn almost never gave interviews, I was determined to be in front of my television set to witness the momentous event. As life would have it, the Hepburn interview clashed with an evening lecture I was giving at a liberal arts college about an hour south of Minneapolis. By sheer concentration, I ended the talk with barely an hour to spare, sped up the highway, and turned on the set just as Carson was introducing Hepburn. Totally enthralled by her, he lost his trademark urbanity; at one point, he even stooped to asking, "Well, Miss Hepburn, do you think you missed anything by not marrying and having children?" It was probably 1975 or a little later. Carson would *never* have asked such a question of any "bachelor" he might have brought onto his program. Quite the opposite: being unattached would only heighten such a guest's allure for the audience, suggesting that he had more "serious" or "exciting" fish to fry. Such questions were (and still are) reserved exclusively by our culture for women.

Rather than cuffing him, she sat quietly for a few moments and then said, with one of those enigmatic smiles that used to win us all, "Of course I missed something; but my father told me long ago, 'Kate, for each thing you decide to do, there will be at least one thing you will be deciding by default not to do,' and I've found that to be profoundly true. So, while I have missed having children (the *husband* dropped out of her consideration altogether), I have enjoyed having a career that has let me meet and associate with endlessly fascinating people." I thanked her that night as silent tears rolled down my cheeks and I have remembered her words whenever I have felt twinges about not having borne—I would not have opted for adoption, finally, since I would have wanted the physical experience of pregnancy—and reared a daughter or son of my own.

●

As my friendship with Shirley developed, we were joined by Mimi, fresh from Yale via a short stint teaching at Middlebury College. Mimi is tall and majestic, with mounds of naturally curly hair and a striking presence. If one were to picture her someplace outside the academy, it might be at a museum opening frequented by artists, critics, and arts patrons. She quickly bonded with Shirley and me, and the three of us became quite an "item" in the English department. Though we came to think of ourselves as the "Three Graces," our male colleagues quickly altered that to the "Three Witches" from *Macbeth* or the "Three Furies" of mythology. I know this not to be apocryphal, because we once saw a private communiqué from one of our esteemed colleagues to another in which we were so referenced.

When feminism made itself felt in the academy, we jumped at the chance to develop and refine our inchoate readings of Shakespeare's plays, Spenser's *Faerie Queene*, and even Milton's writings. At the same time, we saw within feminist discourse an opportunity to branch out into women writers from the nineteenth and twentieth centuries, both in England and the United States. Given the serious limits of feminism at this time—with its focus on white middle-class heterosexual women inhabiting the global North—its entry into an even more retrogressive academic climate nonetheless constituted a major rethinking on the part of many of us hungry for an internal systemic shake-up. Feminism, of course, had been flourishing for quite some time outside the academy; we had all taken part in some kind of consciousness-raising (CR) group in the community several years before the university saw fit to let anyone teach a course raising feminist questions. Students were responsible for pressuring already sympathetic faculty to teach such courses, faculty who in turn began to pressure various administrators to acknowledge the exciting new scholarship emerging from feminist thinkers. Fortunately, the dean of our college was not afraid to sanction such research and its concomitant teaching, so we began what would become a paradigmatic shift within higher education. Not only did feminist scholars recover and install into our books, articles, and curricula material by and about women; we also dared to question material by men and about everything else that, until that point, enjoyed an unassailable or "universal" position. This paradigmatic transformation continues to benefit later generations of students and faculty alike.

My response was to offer the first single-author course on Virginia Woolf in the United States. I believed it to be the "first" based on my perusal of catalogues for Big Ten universities, women's colleges, and progressive liberal arts colleges. I chose Virginia Woolf because my own world had been expanded and enriched by reading most of her novels, not for any class or credit but because a former lover had introduced her to me some ten years before. Operating within a perfectionist system, I delayed offering the course until I had read all her novels, her then-extant essays and letters, several biographies, and scads of critical material. The students who enrolled were mostly women, mostly English majors, and extremely motivated to like this tall, angular, and intense British modernist. The students, still overwhelmingly white and middle-class themselves, read Woolf voraciously and came to class eager to explore the accommodations her female characters made in order to win security or social approval or both. Her language challenged them but they came to revel in her dense prose, aware that their own inner feelings deserved similar linguistic complexity. Breaking out from my usual offerings in Shakespeare and Milton, I began to read with pencil in hand writings by other women—women of color and contemporary white women—often passed along to me by friends. Quite by accident or perhaps serendipity, I took as my curricular focus feminist (and then lesbian) literature; I even suspended my disappointment over not being allowed to offer courses in sixteenth- and seventeenth-century poetry as I drank in novels by Morrison, Naylor, French, Marshall, and Piercy.

As Mimi, Shirley, and I talked over long dinners, we began to envision bringing some minimal organization to our random musings about writers as disparate as Emily Dickinson, Toni Morrison, and Kate Chopin. Then fate intervened. Every fall, the department held a faculty meeting at which people ready to be considered for tenure were discussed and voted on. It must have been 1978 and that year's meeting had gone on too long: afterward we decided not to go straight home, needing to clear our minds of the cant we had just endured. Over dinner we conceived a brand new subfield: Feminist Studies in Literature would be its name and its mission would be two-fold. First, we would search out those faculty at the university who were raising in their teaching questions about women as writers and subjects in writing; second, we would organize biweekly bag lunches for graduate students and faculty to talk about primary and critical work by and about women. This would be a feminist mini-college: all courses, colloquia, and debates would swirl around issues of gender and how it was impacted by race, class, and sexuality. The goal would be to form a community within the larger institution focused on the very questions that intrigued us in our so-far private conversations. In those initial heady days, we frankly did not think about what our modest enclave, embedded inside a fairly conservative department and college, might "do" to the larger institution. We felt excited and mischievous—and only a little apprehensive about how this notion would be treated by those in charge of such things as "subfield formation."

I agreed to coordinate our efforts, and within a few weeks I had amassed about ten feminist and proto-feminist courses from colleagues in language departments, women's studies, and speech communications. Because we knew that other faculty were beginning to offer similar clusters of courses at their own institutions, we designed, had printed at our expense, and distributed widely a brochure whose cover included an image of the Virginia Woolf plate from Judy Chicago's Dinner Party art installation, a plate that featured two rows of little "peas" surrounded by lush pottery folds that could not help but suggest labia.

We terrified many male colleagues, who kept asking us if we wanted to prevent students from taking courses in such giants as Shakespeare or Emerson or Thoreau. At first we tried to laugh off such outlandish fantasies, but it became apparent that some deeper anxiety lay just beneath such queries. Perhaps they thought we were coming to find *them*, as well as their "giants," superfluous. My reply to all such questions was simple: we were not interested in taking men's books off library shelves—that kind of exclusivity would only invert the system we were trying to change—but rather in building additional bookcases.

In the fall of 1981, we hosted a regional conference for scholars who were doing similar work at their own institutions. None less than Adrienne Rich agreed to deliver the keynote, a lecture that would become her essay "Toward a More Feminist Criticism." I had met Adrienne shortly before 1981 at a Berkshire women's history conference where she and her lover Michelle Cliff gave talks—Michelle's about the role of the belt in Renaissance women's

fashion design, Adrienne's about the power of poetry in the contemporary women's movement. To my amazement, I wound up
dining with them at an out-of-the-way Italian restaurant. The
restaurant was suggested by one of the local lesbians at the conference; we had spoken at length while drinking soda water at one
of the receptions where wine and spirits flowed. It seems Adrienne
had liked whatever it was I said over lasagna and salad, so that
when she got an invitation from me to be our keynote speaker, she
decided to fly out to continue our conversation.

Because I had done all the organizational and advertising work,
it was my privilege to pick her up at the airport and escort her to
the Curtis Hotel, a vestige from a much slower time in
Minneapolis's history. Wasting no time on small talk, we discovered quickly that we shared a passion for traditional literature and
that we believed in speaking the truth about our lives and about
the broader culture. By the time we reached the hotel, we had
already begun to spin a magical connection that continued after
her lecture and lasted several years after her Minneapolis sojourn.

When I stood up that night in the packed lecture hall on campus, I announced that the evening had special significance to me
because I was marking my seventh anniversary without a drink.
What I did not say, however, was that scarcely a week had gone by
without my wanting to feel bourbon slide down my middle section
on the way to granting me at least momentary relief from feeling
or avoiding feeling. Even today, twenty-seven years since any
liquor has passed through my lips, I still have fantasies and body
memories tied to alcohol. Despite these silences, the audience
burst into spontaneous applause when I shared my anniversary
date. I suspect that lesbians in that lecture hall knew how crucial it
is that we not numb ourselves if we hope to achieve political gain
and personal happiness. I believe they also simply wanted to register support for anyone choosing life over fog and pain.

Rich spent her hour enjoining academic feminists to stay connected with women outside academe, to be sure our theory
smelled of the earth and did not become so rarefied as to be useless to women (and men) trying to construct or reconstruct their
lives. The day before her flight back home, we sat in my living
room talking late into the night as if we had known each other for
years. I decided to tell her something quite personal: "The only
virtue I still pursue is clarity." Immediately she rummaged in

some side pocket of her large purse, pulled out a small chunk of raw amethyst, and told me that in ancient iconography it signified clarity. "In sisterhood," she said as she pressed it into my left palm, gently closing my fingers over it.

After that successful conference, we settled into offering courses and holding our wonderful biweekly discussions; in fact, the Feminist Studies in Literature Research Group lasted until 1994. At that point, however, it became clear to me that no one else was willing to do the legwork needed to produce our yearly brochure or to facilitate the biweekly discussions of feminist writers and critics. But I needed not to be the "mother" of this venture; if my faculty colleagues were not willing to take their turn keeping us afloat, then I had to question the validity of the enterprise. I had to face the dispiriting fact that I was usually the only faculty member present at these important discussions. When I questioned my feminist colleagues about their absence, I heard predictable laments about being overcommitted or stretched too thin, always accompanied by promises to try harder to make the next meeting—promises that fizzled out just before the appointed day and time. I experienced a deep sense of personal and intellectual loss when we folded, accompanied by a gnawing fear that institutions win far more often than they lose. They wait out or wear down the movers and shakers until the new vanishes, leaving a few trace elements from which we can only hope that others will build alternative settings at some later moment in academic history.

Soon after I taught my first Virginia Woolf course, I eagerly joined a few other faculty members in the College of Liberal Arts to form a women's studies program. Our enterprise quickly became a beacon for other mid-western universities and colleges as they launched similar ventures. I believe my university took the lead because of its geographical location in the Twin Cities. Long known as a locus for radical movements of all sorts, Minneapolis and St. Paul spawned an array of feminist enterprises before most other metropolitan areas squeezed between the coastal bookends of New York City and San Francisco. In addition to flourishing CR groups, we had printing presses; bookstores; recovery programs for battered women, incest survivors, and women coming off drugs or alcohol; reading and writing groups; collectives to promote the arts; softball leagues; alternative therapy collectives;

advocacy groups for bias-free curricula and Title IX sports programs in the schools; and caucuses for women in law or business, not to mention many smaller fringe groups. Amidst such a fertile atmosphere, it was only natural that the Twin Cities' major institution of higher education would launch a vigorous women's studies program.

When the program searched for its first chair, I applied and was delighted to be chosen. From 1973 until 1976 I served in that capacity, working with a superb graduate student in the English department who advised students and managed the office, and an active steering committee of dedicated feminist faculty women and a few male allies who never called themselves "feminists" but who fully comprehended the importance of our research and teaching. A supportive male presence also provided our proposals to the dean with ballast and credibility. We were, however, still all white, a flawed reality that did not change for another five or six years. And, unfortunately, a handful of faculty were assigned by the same dean who supported our efforts, to act as "quality" watchdogs. Since this second cohort was not involved in feminist theory, research, or pedagogy, they often asked obtuse questions and threw up false roadblocks that impeded progress for those of us intent on nothing short of transforming the curriculum. But their presence on the committee was part of the deal that let us exist, so we suffered their skepticism and ignorance with as much grace as possible, reminding ourselves of the inevitable compromises exacted by mammoth and conservative institutions.

After much wrangling over space, we secured a tiny corner of an office designed to serve students who were cobbling together their own interdisciplinary and often intercollegiate programs of study. We had two desks—one for me, the other for the adviser—and we shared a secretary with the intercollegiate program. Into this cramped but precious space our first students came for advice and inspiration. Behind on all deadlines for course descriptions, listings, room assignments, and advertising, we depended on what I rapidly came to know as a group of knowledgeable and competent women. Our remarkable allies slipped in our overdue materials while no one was looking, got (or, in emergencies, forged) signatures from associate deans for curriculum, and miraculously found rooms with movable chairs that were not occupied at prime hours of the school day. Without their subversive support, the program would have stumbled through its first year. Instead, we enrolled beyond capacity, turning students away with an urging to speak to their ombudsperson, who could in turn speak to relevant faculty groups to lobby for more and better-supported courses the next term. What I discovered was the latent feminism inside these staff women, waiting only for someone to "call" it into visibility and action. Our male colleagues, accustomed as they were to the grinding pace of academic change, marveled at how we did it. I never told them, but at every opportunity where feminist faculty and students congregated, I sang the praises of our loyal cadre of powers behind all the thrones of the College of Liberal Arts, who gave us the essential help we needed.

As we grew better acquainted, we broached the difficult subject of our differences because of where we fell within the university's hierarchy. Not wanting to pretend to a false sisterhood when crucial divides existed in terms of status, salary, and working conditions (to name the obvious), I urged them to tell me about resentments and how they felt rewarded by their efforts behind yet another scene, barring its immediate and relevant focus on women's lives and work. While tensions occasionally erupted when a feminist faculty colleague failed to treat the civil service women with whom they were working with respect, my encouragement to voice complaints kept our alliances refreshingly free of institutional static.

Perhaps the single most tangible measure of commitment from this group came when one of their numbers retired. Mabel Powers had served the college for decades, first as an adviser to undergraduates who found themselves overwhelmed by the university's sheer size, and eventually as the director of undergraduate advising for all units in the college. A woman of tremendous integrity with a presence that commanded respect, Mabel realized as soon as I spoke to her about women's studies just how powerful such a program could be to many of the young women she talked with every day: students who wanted to pursue serious study in fields considered "inappropriate" or "too demanding" for women to enter; students wrestling with how to resist pressures to marry coming from family and friends alike. So, upon retiring Mabel willed her gorgeous mahogany desk, replete with brass fittings, to the chair of women's studies. With this gesture she registered her agreement with our attempts to alter the institutional hierarchies that surrounded our little feminist island. Almost thirty years later, that desk remains in the women's studies department, attesting to the warm-spirited and tangible support offered by a woman whose worth was never fully recognized by that same hierarchical structure, which tends to put credentials above human qualities.

My three years as chair of the fledgling program saw much external progress in terms of courses taught, departmental support for releasing current faculty and hiring new faculty to pursue research and teaching that revolved around feminist questions, and financial support for superb feminist scholarship. Sadly, those years also saw an inevitable decline for me personally, as my first year and a half in office was the last phase of my long and destructive alcoholic career. Because my intellectual attention span had been seriously impaired by my drinking, I was forced to teach only works I already knew. Letters of recommendation for students aspiring to law, medical, or graduate school remained buried under piles of increasingly unattended details. And the quality of my personal life deteriorated as I walked in and out of one short-term relationship after another, often with entirely inappropriate women. But women's studies did not suffer in any tangible ways until *after* I stopped drinking; I always gave it my clearest energy, which came between the hazes that followed upon hours devoted to large quantities of bourbon. In fact, no one even suspected that I had a drinking problem, so secretive was I in my habits.

My last year or so as chair, however, was marred—not by active drinking, but by the various levels of withdrawal I experienced as the months without bourbon mounted up. Because a cardinal rule in my childhood upbringing was never to speak about family secrets outside (or inside) the family, I was inordinately slow to seek help from one of the several treatment programs in town. Certainly in those first few months, as I nursed horrific headaches and badly shaking hands, no one in my circle had any idea what I was going through. My sobering-up process, then, was as lonely as nineteen years of alcoholic drinking had been.

Difficult though it may be to imagine, I was less able to function in relation to administrative details than had been the case when I was actively drinking to obliterate the anxiety or pain or loneliness. Even then the irony did not escape me. Try as I did to keep up, the program began to miss crucial deadlines for extra funding and I found myself leaving Mabel's lovely mahogany desk far too early in the afternoon. Each day, I would drive single-mindedly from school to home. Once inside the house, I forbade myself to go out again until the next morning when it was time to go to work. I did this because I was sure that if I set foot outside the front door, I would inevitably find myself in a liquor store purchasing at least one fifth of Jack Daniels Black. Evenings and weekends were very long and very empty, but I refrained from drinking and gradually was able to watch an hour-long television program without becoming so jumpy as to need to find something physical to do. Speaking to no one about this crisis, I stumbled along until three women deeply involved in the women's studies venture asked to meet with me in one of their offices.

It was a cloudy afternoon in late winter, I remember. My hands were still known to shake slightly so that I refrained from using cups and saucers for the quantities of hot tea I drank to replace the liquor. I had almost blown my cover in the weeks right after I stopped drinking: I was at lunch with a colleague in the faculty dining room when I heard the telltale rattle of one piece of china against the other. This turned out to be *my* cup against *my* saucer, a sure sign to anyone paying attention that I was coping with a hangover or withdrawal. I approached this interview with real trepidation, realizing at some cellular level what it would be about. My three colleagues were equally nervous, especially the two who were also old and, I thought, dear friends. What they wanted to tell me was of their displeasure and anger at my low level of work. After reciting their list of grievances, the one I considered an especially close friend said, "If we had anyone else who could step in for the remainder of this year, we'd ask her. But we don't so we have to stick with you. But we want you to know how much we disapprove of how you are running the program."

In the face of such a massive vote of no-confidence, I was speechless. Because I had not told anyone about my struggle with alcoholism, I felt helpless to explain or defend my lapses. Defeated, like Desdemona, by silence and an inability to name myself even to myself, I was unable to remind them of the incredible work I had done for the program. Instead, I went home and locked myself inside my house. That night, as I cried and ate unwanted quantities of food, I probably slid into my secondary addiction of overeating because it seemed at the time less life-threatening than emptying a bottle of Jack Daniels. I understood the principle of sublimation—substituting one behavior for another—from my years as a teenager when I had immersed myself in books, music, and physical exertion to assuage the pain and loneliness I felt because I was unsuccessful at dating boys; even as I tried harder and harder to be appealing to them so that my peers would not treat me as a "freak."

For the rest of that awful year, I worked fiendishly to get women's studies ready to apply for permanent status within the College of Liberal Arts. To this end I spent evenings and weekends writing documents full of just the phrases that would endear us to the various councils and deans who would have to approve our degree-granting major. Those marathon efforts were successful; shortly before I stepped down, the program became a full-fledged department. I also persuaded several departments to advertise for and hire feminist faculty to augment our already strong staff. Several faculty, denied tenure at the department level, were promoted because I organized campaigns and wrote special letters about their excellence. Finally, I prepared the documentation and paved the way for our first national assessment conducted by a committee of feminist scholars led by Florence Howe, a nationally known leader in the field and a cofounder of the increasingly successful Feminist Press.

Immediately after my term as chair, I took a year's leave without pay, partly to see if there was any other way for me to earn a living, and partly to give myself time to begin healing from alcohol abuse by me and from the harsh treatment of me by people I had assumed were friends. If they and I met, by chance rather than design, conversation was stilted and superficial—the weather, national politics, good movies, the weather. Usually I have told myself the rift came because of my sobering up and not being as much "fun" as I had been in our past. But remembering that confrontation again to write of it here has brought home to me, in undeniable ways, the real cause of our friendship's demise. Those two women seem to remain haunted by their behavior, and I remain scared of what they might say or do, even though I have forgiven them for the agonizing session.

Whatever pain I suffered while serving as chair of women's studies was and continues to be more than offset by the sheer thrill associated with the job. Of the many stunning "firsts," two stand out: a course in courtly love across cultures and centuries;

and the first single-authored books and edited collections of articles articulating feminist research principles and results in the humanities and social sciences. The course on courtly love was taught by a series of extraordinary faculty in French literature, history, English, art history, and the classics. As coordinator, I attended all lectures so I could introduce the lecturer and later facilitate student discussions. Lots of coughing and blowing told me students were showing up when they probably should have been home in bed, but excitement ran so high that absences were simply unknown. I still can shut my eyes and see the slides provided by the art history professor: images on Greek and Roman amphora that were echoed in medieval French and later English tapestries of the courtier paying homage to his lady. I was being taught to see connections across time and space, to stop dividing culture linearly, and to question the very notion of disciplinarity—lessons I integrated into all my subsequent teaching and research. The course, with all its cross-fertilization, reinforced my growing sense of a preference for permeable rather than rigid disciplinary boundaries—even if the latter, "hard" taxonomy, continued to be rewarded more generously by the academic system.

My other clear memory revolves around a reception held sometime in the early 1980s to display and honor books and substantial articles written by our faculty. We served standard fare for such campus events in those days: some kind of dark pink punch and plates of uninteresting if overly sugared cookies. Everyone present—faculty, students, and staff—was exhilarated. Much of what was written in the pages of those publications had never before been said; our work was subversive and transgressive. In the early twenty-first century, feminist academics often assume that their projects will receive the same consideration as any others, and, though challenges to feminist scholarship have become more subtle rather than disappearing altogether, this self-confidence is entirely appropriate. But, no matter how glad I am for my younger colleagues' comfort level, I have would not have missed the sheer exuberance and esprit de corps accompanying such events as our punch and cookie gathering.

As universities like Minnesota were forced at last—by anti–Vietnam War protests, a newly revived women's movement, and a national insistence on ethnic studies programs—to grapple with issues of racism, sexism, and the role of faculty and students in governing large educational institutions, I let myself be appointed to several key committees. Two such assignments remain powerfully etched in my memory: chairing an all-university committee charged with drafting a statement on academic freedom and responsibility; and serving on a blue ribbon committee to address the grievances of black students on campus. I was asked to serve on the committee on academic freedom and responsibility by the vice president for academic affairs, a man who seemed genuinely dedicated to making the educational process both rigorous and humane and who sensed my commitment to similar values.

I soon found myself in heady territory, holding private consultations with that vice president about our progress in drawing up some standards for faculty behavior. Early in the process, he told me to call him by his first name, a request followed rather blatantly by a request that I chair the committee. Both moves played dangerously into my need to find "good fathers" somewhere within the university structure, since my immediate and logical mentors in the English department refused to take me seriously. I was too young and naïve in the ways of institutional politics to grasp that he was looking for a patsy to undertake passage of a document that most faculty scorned. He and his cronies were being pressured by a state legislature angry over what it perceived as license on the part of faculty: they had heard far too many stories of faculty who refused to distribute syllabi on the first day of class or who set new assignments during the closing weeks of a term when students were already beginning to prepare for final examinations. The senior administrator's request, then, probably arose from his mounting anxiety. My "yes" to chairing, however, was based squarely in my own idealism: I believed that, as a professional, helping frame and gaining acceptance for such a document was simply the right thing to do. If doctors and lawyers had internally designed ethical statements by which all members agreed to abide, why were faculties exempt from minimal standards of accountability?

Many months of meetings that stretched into the late evenings finally yielded what I had wanted from the outset: a carefully argued, articulate document outlining what we as professors owed our students and employers—owed in exchange for the uncommon privilege of being able to think, say, and research what fired our passions or seemed to us true. As the document moved to the senate floor, it fell to me as the committee's chair and the document's author to make the case to a group of mostly older colleagues long accustomed to enjoying freedom without being asked to give anything in exchange.

When a highly respected and archconservative member of the law school faculty rose to the microphone and introduced a motion to table, I had no choice but to speak from the heart. My throat constricted as I rose to say something very like this:

> "Working at a university is something very few Americans are allowed to do and I, for one, am deeply grateful for the opportunity. Surely I owe the administration something more than showing up at my office or classroom. If I refuse to give that 'something,' I turn a liberty into a license.
>
> "This document asks such paltry things of me—giving students a clear idea of what I intend to do in my classes before I begin doing it; keeping office hours or informing my chair why I cannot do so; being available to assist graduate students even when I have been released from classroom duties; respecting colleagues whose views and approaches to research and teaching differ from my own but are well-meant and sincere; restraining myself from making publicly damaging remarks about internal matters of governance best left to debate within the walls of this campus. If I am unwilling to do this, I wonder if I deserve the extraordinary latitude granted me in the tenure code. I ask you, before you vote to table, to ask yourself what you are grateful for in relationship to your employment at the University of Minnesota."

The motion to table was defeated, and I went home with a sense of pride at having found honest words to express how I felt. The experience forced me to think through fundamental questions about what it means to be a professor at a huge, fairly impersonal university: To whom am I responsible and upon whom do I depend in order to do my work effectively? Surely I am accountable to my students, but how about my legislators, many of whom are also parents, who allocate tax monies needed for public education and struggle to understand our working conditions? How often do I take time to register how important to my cognitive and pedagogical endeavors the following human beings are: staff women who keep the whole educational enterprise going from day to day; the janitorial staff who make my physical environs livable; transit drivers who ensure that I and many more get from one part of campus to another, or even to campus at all? In short, arguing for the passage of this tame declaration of the reciprocity between privileges and responsibilities sharpened my awareness of the highly stratified world in which I worked.

Between staving off the tabling ploy and the document's actual passage, however, stood a series of tortuous meetings during which the actual debate took place. As matters evolved, it became clear that not even all committee members were actively committed to the statement. Two or three of them spoke out as we debated each section, but most remained utterly silent or hinted when they did speak that they no longer agreed with the premise behind the statement. Because the administration worried that the state legislature might act quickly to impose behaviors on the faculty, they demanded that the senate meet weekly until the document had been affirmed or denied. I had to be in attendance at all these long, contentious meetings. A series of white male faculty—there were no faculty of color and only the most meager scattering of white women on that august body—rose to speak about the "mischievous" nature of what I had written. My patience was tested in ways for which I was not prepared: I had to listen quietly while full professors (I was an associate professor at the time) excoriated the committee for capitulating to administrative pressure, for questioning the integrity of people senior in rank and reputation, and for trying to erase individual freedom.

At the end of several hours of wrangling by senators and exhausting restraint on my part, I would drive home to a cold and empty apartment and, because it was the late 1960s and several years before my decision to sober up, drink myself into oblivion. But I kept returning to the podium, slowly but surely taking the document through that reluctant body, accepting any amendment that did not butcher our original intentions. Between meetings, I amended the document, often typing into the morning, manuscript on one side of my typewriter and bourbon bottle and glass on the other. I still remember the false elation and momentary sense of power I felt as I left the meeting hall, having cajoled

through rhetoric and persistence men senior to me in every way
to vote "yes" when they honestly wanted to vote "no." The saga
ended when I delivered what was still an elegant piece of academic prose to the academic vice president, accepted his verbal
thanks, and returned to my department—where most of my senior colleagues continued to vote against my promotion to full professor on grounds which were never made explicit but which
remained ironclad and painfully repetitive.

My other significant service assignment from roughly the same
turbulent period resulted from serious allegations of discrimination by African American students. The president appointed a
blue ribbon committee, charged with investigating the allegations
and presenting him with a program to address wrongdoings,
including "benign neglect"—an apparent inability to escape from
ethnocentric myopia long enough to consider what members of
another culture might need—on the part of his minions. As one of
only two faculty members asked to serve on the committee, I felt
both complimented and vulnerable. Except for one white alumna,
I was also the token female. Other members included a white liberal judge, two white alumni, two prominent members of the
white business community, a respected African American faculty
member at a local liberal arts college, and the white president of
the Federal Reserve Bank for the district including Minneapolis.
Looking over the roster, the federal reserve president, Hugh
Galusha, awakened all my prejudices about bankers with
addresses in the most exclusive Twin Cities suburb. It also produced discomfort and ambivalence because of the presence of
only one person of color on a committee charged to address the
explicit concerns of students of color.

At the first of our many evening meetings, "Mister" Galusha (as
I firmly intended to call him) stormed into the regents' room fifteen
minutes late, wearing tiny silver-rimmed glasses with an obviously
hand-tailored suit and carrying an elegant, soft calfskin briefcase.
His first words, spoken in a flurried but nonetheless privileged
tone, were: "It's impossible to find parking on this campus. Can't
you people at least create space for committee members from
downtown?" My teeth were set instantly on edge. By the end of
that first session, however, I was having to step back from my initial and intense distaste for this man. His theories about why black

students were feeling aggrieved matched my own point for point, while his assertions of how the university might alter its behavior in the future were even more far-reaching than mine. It was Hugh, for instance, who voiced an uneasiness I shared about there being on the committee only one representative from any community of color. Over the months of being sequestered with this group of mostly white, high-powered citizens, I came to admire and like Hugh tremendously. (I relinquished my vow about what I would call him by the second meeting. Nevertheless, I did consider to what extent our ease together, as we slogged through increasing evidence of misguided institutional negligence, might not depend upon our both being radical white Democrats, separated though we were by class, sexuality, and gender. Even then I knew how tense the atmosphere could become for all parties involved when political and racial divides existed within such committees.)

Not only was Hugh a person of great integrity and total commitment to social justice, but he loved literature and language. His passionate love of language prompted him to telephone me in the middle of a day to say "I found a word" and proceed to talk animatedly about its etymology. When I discovered that he was the only other person I knew who owned a hardback copy of James Lipton's *Exaltation of Larks*, I knew I had met some kind of comrade. As the weeks of meetings wore on, we branched out to have extended conversations about Shakespeare; when Hugh learned that I was about to teach a course on the Bard, he asked if he might attend a class or two. Though that prospect raised my anxiety level several notches, I agreed. The visits allowed him to see me in my professional milieu, the place where I was on surest ground, where I trusted my knowledge and insights most. Mutual respect was added to our growing list of positive connections, and a few months after the blue ribbon committee had turned in its rather scathing report, Hugh approached me about editing a series of pamphlets for the Federal Reserve. The purpose was to make the Reserve's objectives and values known and understood by a broader cross-section of the populace in his region, i.e., Minnesota, the Dakotas, Iowa, and Wisconsin. Thrilled at the chance to put my writing to some useful purpose, I soon found myself working with highly competent officers of the bank who gave me information that I was to render accessible to the public. As it turned out, I was the perfect person for the job since I understood almost nothing about how the Federal Reserve Bank functioned within North American culture. I successfully edited four pamphlets, which I recently came across while cleaning out my files; a rush of renewed pride at my adaptability and usefulness washed over me, together with an intense feeling of missing the man who had hired me to write them.

As a human being, Hugh enjoyed challenges, physical as well as intellectual. So, when a local newspaper reporter organized a strenuous mountain-climbing expedition for a group of top-level executives, he signed on. The expedition was scheduled for late in the winter season to avoid bad weather, but the unexpected happened. Caught in a violent snow and windstorm, the party took shelter inside a cave-like space, hoping to wait out the turbulence. Extreme cold followed the snow; the leader had not planned for the unexpected when rationing survival equipment and provisions, and the whole event lasted far longer than anyone could have predicted. Everyone in the party suffered major physical damage and several died. Hugh Galusha was among those who perished. When news reached me, my fury at the organizer for taking a group into harm's way with inadequate knowledge knew no bounds. Eventually I had to put him on my Eighth Step list in AA and make an indirect amends, since he is now dead. Sometimes, when I pass the elegant building that housed the Federal Reserve Bank in those days, I feel the gorge rise inside me momentarily, but mostly I just miss Hugh with fresh sharpness.

Working on that committee became much more emotionally demanding than had been my chairing of the committee on academic freedom and responsibility. I was asked to join the blue ribbon committee by the president, a man about whom I entertained complicated personal feelings. When I agreed to serve, I was looking for something more than proximity to academic power. I wanted a deepening—and deeper—relationship with the president. My knowing him had begun quite by chance: in my third year at the university, I won a college-level award for distinguished teaching and had to attend a banquet in order to receive it. I knew we had a new president but, since I had seldom even seen the previous one, I thought little of it until someone told me he intended to be in the audience for the awards presentation. Probably our dean invited him to help the College of Liberal Arts register in the new administration's consciousness. When a tall, hauntingly attractive man entered the banquet hall a little after we were all seated, I knew he must be our new leader. He heard me say the few words required of the three winners, words about having advanced undergraduates in large introductory lecture courses work as recitation leaders, about the gains to all concerned from letting such students teach.

Two weeks after that event, I was astounded to hear on the other end of my office phone a mature woman's voice saying, "The president would like to have an appointment with you." Making and keeping that appointment was the beginning of a strange friendship between the lanky, white-haired man and me. After our initial meeting, which took place in his office, he asked if we might talk over lunch. Usually such events took place at an elegant old gentleman's club in downtown Minneapolis, but we did not go there because he was embarrassed by the fact that, though it was 1967, female guests were still expected to enter by the side door. While that gender fiasco was the original motive for eating lunch elsewhere, a more tangled one supplanted it as our friendship developed. Within a month of beginning our midday trysts, we settled on a famous seafood restaurant, located in a part of town midway between Minneapolis and St. Paul, whose menu was too expensive for most faculty to afford. I name our meetings "trysts" because they contained from the start an element beyond the academic or collegial. Current scholars reconceiving same-sex relationships in periods prior to the twentieth century speak of a homoerotic dimension, meaning that they included sensual attraction but stopped short of being sexual. If there can be homoerotic relationships, then why not heteroerotic ones, in which a woman and a man feel powerful sensual connections without becoming sexual partners? That is what went on between the gaunt university president and me; we were drawn to each other along powerful axes, though I suspect we both tacitly knew we would never make love.

So we kept meeting for those protracted and elegant lunches. A discreet chauffeur driving a long black sedan would pick me up outside my building at the appointed hour, and we would proceed smoothly and quietly through the ride from school to our luncheon site. We always sat as far back in the semi-darkened space as possible, away from foot traffic, not hiding exactly but definitely not wanting to make conversation with people who might recognize him. The lunches, never spaced longer than three weeks apart, were long and intense. After two stiff whiskey sours for me and two double scotches and soda for him, we each enjoyed a large, cracked Dungeness crab newly flown in from the West Coast, served with warm crusty bread and a small Boston lettuce salad dressed simply with lemon and a pinch of salt.

Conversational topics ranged from books we liked to personal difficulties—mine with my department, his with his home life. At times, we just sat quietly, one of his heavily veined hands with elegant, tapered fingers covering mine in a way that made my heart race. Those lunches were precious to us, offering two obviously lonely people "time out" from their official lives, time to inhabit a fantasy world in which talk was effortless and silence an embrace. Though recently I have puzzled over what my relationship with this man might have meant, at the time I felt no ambivalence or doubt, just gratitude—and a quickened sense of his and my own body, held in magical solution for a couple of hours once a month. The lunches ended only when the president resigned amid vicious criticism about poorly managed fundraising efforts and bungled responses to student protests. My ardent defenses of him stirred memories from my adolescence of a marvelous man who had come in as principal and was fired because of a high school athlete's allegation that my hero had made a pass at him. While I never can know whether the charge was true or not, I know with certainty that my principal was the first male to take me seriously, showing me that art and literature could move or excite someone.

Each of these pivotal men in my life occupied some ambiguous space between longed-for father and fantasy lover. Both held powerful positions within the world of education, a fact not lost on me in relation to my many years as a teacher. What remains lost to me is how to "fit" them into my long, exclusive, and happy life as a lesbian. Were they, finally, "safe" men for me to play out erotic attractions for? Certainly both were married and significantly older than I, though neither of those variables can, by itself, prevent people from falling in love or having sexual relationships. Was I attracted to them because both *talked* to me, whereas my biological father was a private man with everyone and quite taciturn with me, his unexpected second daughter whom he called "Son"? If either man had crossed an invisible but solid boundary between erotic talk and sexual practice, would I have joined him? So far I have no lucid answers to these questions, but asking them seems important even from this vast distance.

In the moment of the 1970s, however, I continued to defend my passionate friend while the university slid into bad times financially and politically. As the anti–Vietnam War protests dragged on, the administration, wanting things to be settled, became increasingly impatient with faculty members tacitly supporting the student dissidents. The president left campus at a crucial moment in this escalating environment; when told by telephone that one of his minions was threatening to call city riot police onto campus, he stayed out of town and let it happen. Many others and I were manhandled and maced during that debacle, but the real damage was to my heart and spirit. The man toward whom I felt such intense attraction and devotion, and with whom I had spent so many intimate hours, betrayed me and, more importantly, himself. (Of course, others may have felt equally betrayed, but I was losing one of the most important friendships of my adult life, so those possible "others" did not matter to me.) When the president finally returned to campus, his shame was monumental, made evident to me in his late-night calls in which he tried over and over to make what he had done acceptable. He never succeeded and, within a matter of months, resigned his high office. Once out of the presidency, he did not call to arrange lunches or even office visits behind tightly closed doors. At first, I wanted him to so he would see that my fidelity could endure public ridicule. Eventually, I felt a kind of numb relief from knowing that the call was not going to come. My fidelity was not withstanding my deeply private disappointment and might not have been strong enough to carry me through a face-to-face meeting. When he died, not long thereafter, I did not attend the funeral. If the bouts of uncontrollable sobbing at the thought of him and of our strange but unique time together was an indication, my love would have been all too apparent to his wife and daughter. Since I wished them well in some vague way, I stayed home, frozen in my desk chair during the time I reckoned the church service would take. Once I envisioned the casket on its way to the cemetery, I had to get outside my apartment. I walked for over an hour, hardly aware of where I was going, my vision blurred by a steady stream of tears I now believe were for me and not for him. With whom was I going to have that electric connection now that all possibility for any rapprochement with him as a private citizen was erased by his death? If memory serves me well, shortly after this traumatic experience I took up with a certain too-young lesbian who told me six months later that she was bored because she was not learning anything "new" from me.

The other major factor contributing to my deeper emotional involvement in the blue ribbon committee's work stemmed from my southern background. Race had never been an abstract concept or distant concern for me. From earliest childhood, I had understood that *white* was an entirely different reality than *black* and that everything social, economic, sexual, political, and educational depended upon which race a person was designated by society. From as early as my junior high school years, I also tended to side with those whose skin color was deemed "opposite" to mine, identifying at some perhaps appropriated (if sincere) level with the oppressed rather than the oppressors—even as I contributed to or benefited from that oppression. I now believe that my identification with the black people of my Alabama childhood sprang from a subconscious belief that neither they nor I could "blend in" with the southern landscape. So I reached out to the more obvious "misfits," taking perverse comfort in (while simultaneously feeling genuine empathy with) their cruel function as scapegoats for all that white people could not face about ourselves. Part of why I fled the South (the rest had to do with escaping family and the intolerable heat and humidity that threatened to mildew my brain) turned around my inability to hold my tongue on issues of race, having lost three close college friends the day I referred to Martin Luther King, Jr. as *Doctor* King. My recognition of King's proper title was an affront to blatant Alabama racism. Once in the North, I discovered to my dismay that racism existed there too but on a far more subtle level. That subtlety made this brand of racism seem to me more insidious than its southern counterpart, a perception echoed by a friend of mine who remarked one day, "You know, Toni, you and I share more reality about racism, even though at home we'd be on opposite sides of the issue, than these Minnesotans who say they aren't racist because they never even *saw* a black person until they got to college in the big city." Though I laughed at the time, I gradually came to understand just how profound her statement was; I watched myself gravitate to the few people of color at the university and felt their ease in talking with me. No matter where they came from geographically, they seemed to trust me, paradoxically, *because* rather than *in spite of* my southern origins.

When in the 1960s African American students began petitioning universities and colleges for more than passive admission into their inner sanctums, I immediately agreed with—and felt I understood—their arguments. The currency of any institution of higher education is its curriculum, the medium through which established theories and new knowledge are conveyed to future generations. Hence, efforts to establish black studies programs seemed both timely and logical. From personal experience I understood that admitting someone to a formerly restricted domain did not assure success or even survival. Consequently, complaints about insufficient or even nonexistent advising programs for black students on campus struck a clear if painful chord. Working to make life more tolerable for such students did not take me away from my own struggles to win recognition from the same academy. As a white woman and lesbian professor, my struggles to survive inside academe were both like and unlike those of black women and men enrolled as students. General marginalization tactics, both personal and institutional, excluded us all in a parallel manner. But we diverged along crucial axes of privilege, e.g., my opportunity to "pass" if willing to conform to cultural norms for white women versus the impossibility for those students (or faculty, should we ever hire any) ever to go "unremarked," no matter what they might or might not do.

Several of us on the blue ribbon committee insisted that we hear testimony from some of the grievants and their staff support personnel. Listening to one example of "benign neglect" after another inflamed my suspicion that the university thought it had fulfilled its "liberal obligation" simply by admitting black students; that no more funds or time or creative thinking was warranted by this minute (hence, to them, economically insignificant) portion of the student body; and that a decision to withdraw by such students reflected individual weakness or deficiency rather than any institutional failure. Witnesses accused the university of failing to recruit black students actively, of insufficient efforts to hire faculty of color, of preferring graduate students from Asia and Africa to undergraduates of color from the United States, and of offering grossly inadequate support to retain those few black students who managed to matriculate. Hugh Galusha joined me in adding to this list the indefensible absence of Native American students at a university located amidst a burgeoning local population representing several indigenous nations.

We spoke truth to power, calling the university "insensitive" and "passive" in its approach to African American students. Though we stopped short of using the "simplest" term—i.e., *racist*—we did direct them to address unexamined institutional racism immediately and vigorously. We handed the administration a list of specific programmatic initiatives that could begin to undo the harm done and make the University of Minnesota slightly more inviting to students of color. We suggested the university open cultural centers that would provide academic tutors, formal advisers, informal "buddies," study lounges, small emergency loans, and a full-time advocate who would speak to individual faculty on behalf of students of color. From the major advising office involved in the students' allegations, we strongly urged a formal apology. And, to their surprise, we stipulated that central administrators meet with us face-to-face; we wanted to ensure that none of them could avoid the affective dimension of our report, which was found in the appendices full of horror stories told to us by one student after another. That evidence had mounted until we could no longer dismiss or trivialize such stories as paranoid fantasies or willful exaggerations. By refusing to displace blame onto individuals already at risk, we wanted to leave those in power with a clear indictment, "even" of places like the university, of inherent racism. We insisted that our state's premier institution of higher education recognize this level of racism and then combat it in every conceivable way.

While our motives were the best and our list of demands altogether appropriate, I have often wondered what it actually meant that this group—comprising ten white males, two white females, and one African American male—presumed to speak to the needs of African American students on campus. Certainly it is important for whites to take on issues of race, especially our own whiteness as a racial category. Yet such action too often verges on paternalism; in this instance, it also muted the original voices raised in protest. We substituted our own because we knew that our speech—coming mostly from white scholars and high-powered citizens, and peppered with bureaucratic rhetoric to blunt the plain speech of social justice—had a better chance of being heard by those with the power and the purse.

Our final meeting caused palpable embarrassment among the several vice presidents who stammered about "good intentions." Most of us were having none of it; we wanted from the university full recognition of the complainants' demands and a clear promise to begin changing the racist (albeit unconsciously so) environment. We got the latter because the administrators could find no other way out of the conundrum into which our findings placed them. But we never heard anything as simple, clean, and human as "I'm sorry we let such a situation exist long enough to provoke these valid complaints." Sensitivity-training workshops were held for staff working directly with African American students; funding and advising channels were streamlined and clarified; additional support programs were put in place to address the needs of this small but growing population; the blue ribbon committee got a lavish thank-you from the president and disbanded. The precipitating situation was bettered, and the cohort of aggrieved students resumed their studies and moved ahead with their educational programs. But that was thirty years ago, and my university still prefers graduate students from Asia or Africa to U.S. undergraduates of color. Almost no Native Americans attend the university, and the percentage of matriculated students of color remains constant, or, in one or two instances, actually smaller than it was ten years ago. Clearly, it is easier for members of a university committee to unlearn their own racist attitudes than it is for the institution as an entity to erase or even ameliorate everyday practices that discriminate against anyone who is not part of the white majority.

Around 1972, the vice president for student affairs resigned under several heavy clouds involving, among other things, more allegations from African American students of his insensitivity to and neglect of their concerns. I could easily imagine how they might feel this way, remembering the ludicrous incident in which he had tried to be "one of the oppressed." The occasion was the day after several black students at Jackson State University had been shot by police, about a week after several white students at Kent State University had succumbed to the same awful fate. The small but vocal association of African American students at Minnesota staged a noontime rally on the steps of Northrup

Auditorium, the largest and most centrally located building on our campus. In addition to their own leaders, a few white faculty and the vice president for student affairs were invited to speak to the assembled crowd. I was honored to be one of the faculty so chosen and had refrained from drinking the night before so that I could write the clearest set of comments possible. My name had probably come to the planners' attention because of my outspoken support in the college assembly meeting for the formation of a black studies program. Most faculty members had sat in grim silence the afternoon a group of male community activists marched to the front of the auditorium where our usually sedate meeting was taking place. Our visitors stood resolutely, unloaded but impressive rifles at their sides, while articulate black students outlined cogent reasons for establishing such an interdisciplinary program. Only one other person besides me risked going to the microphone to urge swift passage of the proposal, and I feel sure one of the students made a note of both our names.

As the crowd gathered for the noon rally in protest of the senseless murders, I stationed myself near one of the massive Doric columns of the auditorium and right beside a black woman whom I knew slightly because my partner, working at a local community college, had helped her gain admission to the university. Anna and I agreed, as fellow southerners who had been taught, among other things, that we were categorically different from one another, that we actually shared more perceptions about race than would ever be possible between someone from the North and someone from the South, regardless of their color configuration. We both understood that the national outrage over Kent State as opposed to the relatively quiet expressions about what had happened at Jackson State only underscored an inherently northern racism, perhaps harder to combat than the flagrant brand practiced in our native states of Mississippi and Alabama.

When the vice president took the microphone, my fellow southerner and I assumed he would utter liberal platitudes and step aside for our fierier rhetoric. Not disappointing us, he did precisely that. But to my embarrassed astonishment, he ended his remarks by raising an uncertain and limp fist and uttering in his extremely white, mid-western voice, "Power to the People." Anna and I could barely contain our laughter. Quickly I altered what I was about to say so as not to give the faintest suggestion that I was appropriating language reserved for those on the inside of the equation. Certainly I had, in the past, been willing to speak for others quite capable of speaking for themselves—incest survivors, recovering lesbian alcoholics, even the black women who had worked for my mother. But witnessing the complete travesty of the vice president's words and gesture, I was able to stay focused on my own reactions to what had happened on two college campuses and, importantly, the racist manner by which the largely white press had covered each incident.

It was not long before that sycophantic man was stepping down from his office and I was being encouraged to assume his position. A telephone call late one evening from the vice president for academic affairs—the same man who had taken me into the academic responsibility trap—assured me that the administration was "ready to hire a woman"; all I needed to do was apply. The temptations were several and powerful: I believed I would be good at the job because I would enlist the advice of actual students who knew firsthand how well or poorly the university was meeting their daily and long-term needs; my feminist soul understood the value to women faculty, staff, and students of having a woman in such a high administrative position; sitting down with the rest of the president's cabinet carried with it a certain, undeniable cachet to someone denied the seminars and promotion commensurate with her knowledge and performance. I agreed to apply and actually began framing statements about my approach to governance and my overall philosophy about providing student services.

Just before I formally entered those sentences onto an application form, I had an epiphany not unlike the one that had pushed me to pour out all the liquor in my house and come out as a lesbian a few years earlier. Miraculously, I was able to see through the illusions of having power or influence to what my life would become if I took that job. What I saw sent me running from the process: such a central position carried with it a drastic reduction in one's teaching load—one reason some people accepted such positions in the first place—depriving me thereby of the one and only safe space connected with my professional life. It also guaranteed the virtual loss of a private life, and, even though mine lacked a great deal just then, I was still able to imagine a reality in which I might want a weekend to drive to Chicago to see paintings at the Art Institute, or an evening at home with someone who found me interesting and fun to be with, or simply time to go for a long walk in the early morning light instead of showing up for a breakfast meeting with people whose values I barely understood and certainly did not share.

As soon as it was appropriate to make phone calls the next morning, I called the vice president who was pressuring me and told him I would not be applying. I only told him that I was unwilling to be taken out of the classroom to such an extent, and how could he argue with that? Between my epiphany and the telephone call, I had come up with an excellent recommendation and a sop to Cerberus: I would agree to serve on the search committee. He accepted my decline, perhaps with a muffled sigh of relief since it meant putting off having to learn to work with a woman as his equal, and seemed pleased enough to have me join the group of faculty charged with finding the next person for the job. My candidate made it to the final round of interviews and, with some careful maneuvering, I convinced one or two hesitant colleagues to make him the offer. Minnesota hired for the first time a person of color to fill a major administrative position. That man was a superb vice president for student affairs for many years, and I saved myself from a self-destructive brink. I have never had the slightest regret.

I learned invaluable lessons from those two committee assignments and from my near-miss experience with becoming a high-level administrator. I learned that too many of my colleagues did not want anyone to dictate to them even the most basic behaviors, that they were like the people about whom John Milton was thinking when he wrote "License they mean when they cry liberty," and that I was fundamentally unlike them. Investigating the university's treatment of African American students brought home to me that I was "whiting" them and their history out of my curriculum as surely as my more philistine colleagues were ignoring linguistic and cultural differences as a way to gloss over major power asymmetries. From my brush with centralized academic power, I learned that Virginia Woolf was right when she encouraged young women newly admitted to Oxford and Cambridge to resist membership in the "clubs" to which they might soon be invited. Rather, she implored them to cling tenaciously to their membership in a cultural confederacy she liked to term the "Outsiders Society." By removing my hat from the vice presidential ring, I escaped a mind- and spirit-crushing position and left myself open to whatever might come next in my personal and professional life.

Coming Full Circle

I would move into the 1990s, then, with clarity and humility. Happy in what was becoming a very long-term relationship with Susan and no longer dependent on alcohol or food to numb my feelings about work, I had to devise a more constructive modus operandi or else leave the academy. Open to possibilities outside my usual field of vision, I agreed to help the woman associate vice president for human resources meet the challenge of applying to a local foundation that funded programs to improve undergraduate teaching. When she asked me to join three other faculty in reading a draft proposal, I said "yes." Revising the original document to emphasize its attention to the intersection of diversity and excellence in teaching, we signed off on the final proposal and sent it to the Bush Foundation.

After preliminary exchanges via telephone, e-mail, and fax, we learned that we had made the first cut and should prepare for an on-campus visit from the foundation's chief officer and a board member flying in from Boston. The foundation's significant caveat was this: the university needed to present to the review team a list of faculty members willing to direct such a program were it to receive funding. Our associate vice president approached me to see if I might stand as one of those individuals and, after discussion with my partner and a few close friends, I decided to go along with this plan and see what it might yield.

The day of the visit, I wore my most feminine clothes—a skirt filled with pastel flowers, a soft pink blouse, and a beaded necklace. One of my male colleagues, upon seeing me in the hall of our building, was so surprised by my attire that he collided with a student because his gaze was fixed on me. Unable to speak truthfully

281

to the moment, however, he tried to disguise his amazement by blathering on about some request we had recently gotten from our chair. I felt an odd sense of relief when he finally broke down and asked me if I was going to a funeral.

Our proposal to the Bush Foundation requested funds to establish a year-long program designed to train assistant professors to teach more effectively and creatively. The program presented a chance I could not afford to resist, even if it meant serious disruption of my own writing agenda: through the years I had sorely missed a community forum in which pedagogy could be explored. As a graduate student, I had enjoyed lively and, often, heated conversations about the relative merits of lectures versus discussion sessions, or the risks and gains of asking students to speak personally about what they had studied. Once a professor, however, such talk vanished from my academic landscape as each of us shut herself or himself inside an insular classroom. Now people were willing to pay me to initiate lively and, often, heated conversations about old and new topics pertaining to classroom teaching and student learning.

At the interview I met Humphrey Doermann, a man I would add soon after to my short but cherished list of men whom I could admire and for whom I could feel genuine affection. I knew already of this fine man and the work he had accomplished while serving for many years as president of the Bush Foundation. Colleagues had described him as smart and hard to fool with empty rhetoric, but no one had prepared me for his impassioned commitment to making education more lasting and friendly for young people. Because I had nothing to lose—my life would not be hindered if I did not get the job as director of this program—I decided to say exactly what I believed in response to questions from him and the pleasant board member from Boston. These two obviously sophisticated men treated both me and my ideas with interest and respect, departing markedly (and amusingly) from the wide-eyed surprise of my blundering male colleague prior to the interview/funeral.

Humphrey and I liked each other right away, an affinity that only grew stronger with time. He exuded a quiet enthusiasm for post-secondary teaching, matched by a crisp intellect that saw right through academic boondoggles. My honest assessment of the place of teaching at a large research university must have passed muster: we received the grant under the condition that a colleague and I would run the program for its initial three-year phase.

Choosing to remain at a huge research university has often caused me discomfort because my clear commitment to teaching runs afoul of my institution's focus on publishing one's research, becoming nationally and internationally known in one's field, and protecting oneself behind a closed office door except when it is absolutely necessary to be available to students. And, many times before this formal conversation with Humphrey, I had admitted to myself how ambivalent I feel about schools like the University of Minnesota, how sometimes I have felt like a displaced person. Perhaps my sense of displacement stems from the particular college I inhabit. On our campus, the collegiate unit in which teaching is prominent and rewarded is General College or GC, as it is called. The student body in GC reflects the changing face of our culture and society, composed largely of African American and Latina/o students of usual undergraduate ages, poor women and many single mothers of all racial backgrounds, and older women who draw primarily from their experience as housewives. These students want to hold better-paying and more challenging jobs than taking orders at Arby's or McDonald's, or caring for other women's children while the mothers work at jobs entirely different from taking orders at Arby's or McDonald's. Classes are small; all students have ready access to computers and the Internet; and faculty are hired because they are innovative and rigorous teachers whose research often arises directly out of their classroom experience. And yet, teaching of this caliber does not receive the university-wide respect or support it deserves because the institutional reward system is keyed to activities falling under phrases like "original research," "international ranking," and "federal grants." Furthermore, in the prevailing academic taxonomy, teaching is a distinctly "feminine" aspect of academe, never to be confused with the more "masculine" facets such as research, publication, and reputation. But those faculty members working in GC actually deliver on one of the putative and high-minded goals of any public university—the imparting of knowledge to the area's daughters and sons—while ignoring some of the difficult realities of modern academic life.

It is not that I do not want people to create new knowledge through primary research or to rethink older approaches by applying new perspectives to old texts. I enjoy doing both when the impulse arises from curiosity or irritation at what I consider serious misreadings of authors and works. But at major research universities, such activity is privileged over all other intellectual or pedagogical interests, forcing everyone to research incessantly and to write innumerable articles and books, the value or usefulness of which can become debatable. Thankfully, in Humphrey Doermann we found someone in a powerful position at a major funding agency who genuinely believed that even institutions like the University of Minnesota were obliged to *teach*, and superbly. Serendipity renewed my commitment to sharing with other educators what I had learned through extensive reading of educational research—an oxymoron for many of my colleagues—and from decades of direct classroom experience.

The Bush Faculty Development Program for Excellence and Diversity in Teaching began in earnest in the fall of 1991. The program served fifty professors each year during its initial phase, and thirty each subsequent year. My co-director was a friend, a professor in American studies and American Indian studies who cares as much if not more than I about making knowledge accessible to a diverse student body. Carol and I were an ideal team, running this highly successful program for three years without a single major disagreement over content or process. This extraordinary working relationship can be attributed to the virtual absence of competitive genes in either of our make-ups—and to our massive respect and affection for each other.

The program drew each cadre of assistant professors from across the university spectrum, and we made a crucial decision early in the process to group them along multidisciplinary lines. No small group ever included two people from the same or even closely related departments because we wanted to create spaces comfortable enough to allow people to admit difficulty, even failure, without fear of retribution in a "home" department. Each small group comprised five faculty members and a resource teacher, a leader who would facilitate discussions and present information not about field-specific matters but about teaching in general.

To this end, I worked to acquaint all participants with certain principal aspects of excellent teaching by staging six programs attended by everyone enrolled in a given year. Session topics included active and collaborative learning, since extensive research indicates the multiple rewards of both to students; various elements of diversity, both in student populations and in curricula, emphasizing how such diversity impacts student learning; the incorporation of technology into the classroom, asking always whether such innovations could truly enhance learning or whether they were simply "gadgets" to capture student attention; modalities to break up and so enliven the traditional lecture format, acknowledging the need for such courses even as we stressed the potential inefficiency and stagnation accruing to them; student learning styles and faculty teaching styles, with much discussion about ways faculty can expose students to a variety of both; and the role of faculty in learning venues other than the traditional classroom, e.g., tutorials, graduate education, independent study, various forms of clinical experience, and community-service learning.

Of course, I thoroughly enjoyed being paid to talk about what thirty years in the classroom had taught me about pedagogy. But I also took delight in meeting scores of dedicated and immensely interesting young women and men who restored my faith in the future of higher education. Former participants and I greet one another with glee whenever we meet, and I have heard from many of them as their careers progress and flourish. Almost every person who has participated in our program has been awarded tenure and promotion, often expressing in her or his dossier that working in the program had improved the person's overall rating and evaluation by department colleagues.

Our argument to department chairs and deans was simple: release these new faculty from some aspect of their work early in their tenure at Minnesota and avoid a series of mistakes and difficulties resulting from little or no preparation for classroom teaching. We guaranteed that with this approach, junior faculty would feel less harassed by their teaching agendas and so would like the work more; and that these young academics would actually save precious time en route to promotion by amassing an array of pedagogical strategies they could rely upon in virtually any classroom setting.

Early in the course of directing this exciting program, I learned what I had always suspected to be true, namely that people coming out of Ph.D. programs, even at the most prestigious institutions, might be brilliant in their subject areas but often had only the vaguest inklings of how to convey that brilliance to nineteen-year-olds. An application to the pilot program from a young engineering scholar said it all. When asked why he wanted to participate, he responded, "I graduated at the top of my class at MIT and feel entirely ready to launch my research agenda. But I have never been in charge of a classroom and have absolutely no idea how to proceed in the fall." My initial reaction was to curse the academic paradox that creates depositories of knowledge (aka researchers) who cannot transmit that knowledge to students (aka teachers). Instead, I felt elated to realize that by admitting this frightened young man to our program, we were giving him an excellent chance to learn how to proceed or even to excel in his upcoming classroom environment. For nine months, I watched as he eagerly soaked up all that was offered. He wrote us during his second year of teaching to say that his student evaluations had improved markedly and that his confidence in his ability to help others learn the engineering that so excited his intellectual imagination had increased in ways he had never dreamed possible.

As the number of young faculty successfully completing the program grew, I allowed myself to feel grateful and useful. Grateful to the woman administrator who had offered me the chance to meet and work with so many sterling individuals who would, without even knowing it, enliven my faith in my profession. Useful because I could see inexperienced teachers come to regard my years of trial and error, together with my openness to educational research, as an invaluable resource. One of my fondest memories from my eight-year stint directing this program turns around an exchange I had with a participant whose home field was some, to me, esoteric facet of biology. Each year I sent all participants a series of "tip sheets," documents that elaborated simple pedagogical strategies deployed by me or colleagues with whom I had talked about teaching. A favorite of mine was this: when beginning study of a new play or novel, I often asked students to come to class ready to speak as one of the work's characters. This device forces students to examine the motives and reactions of at least one figure in the work even as it also grants them permission to "be" someone other than themselves for a few moments. To works distant in time and language, it also lends focus and relevance. As students frame a statement or hurl an accusation, they do so in words befitting arguments they might actually have with parents, enemies, or sexual partners.

A few weeks after I sent out my description of this classroom activity, I received a note from the faculty member in biology, telling me he had put the strategy into practice in his own class.

Struck by the playful and serious value of my assignment, he had become determined to adapt it to his own purposes, distant as they might seem from a discussion of a Shakespearean play or a novel by Virginia Woolf. He decided to use my scheme to help beginning students understand the makeup of molecular compounds, asking each student to come to class as one of the molecules found in the equation they were working on. He then insisted that they speak in the voice of the molecule, saying what it did for the compound and how it interacted with other molecules and even how it felt to be that molecule. The results were not only hilarious but pedagogically exciting: on tests, students displayed a deeper understanding not only of the particular molecular particle they may have taken on as a momentary persona but of the entire compound of which their particular molecule was a part. My young colleague was astounded and delighted to see that a pedagogical strategy that works in one learning environment may work equally well in a very different context. Elated and moved by the bravery and openness of that young man and others like him entering the profession, I knew that I could retire feeling calm and excited about the future.

In 1999, when I left the program's directorship, I initiated a phased retirement schedule. During an annual eye examination, my ophthalmologist discovered that the pressure on my eyeballs was beyond the normal range. She cautioned me about my potential risk for glaucoma and asked me to return in only three months for a follow-up test. Driving home from that appointment, I had flashed back to childhood when my mother had spoken in dire tones about glaucoma, afraid of it for herself because of having seen it ruin her relatives' and friends' ability to read or do fine needlework or, eventually, to drive their automobiles. I felt scared enough to tell my partner right away, though I might have forgotten similar medical news about some other part of my body. It was only a caution, and I have a habit of ignoring minor pain because it does not seem worth the energy needed to worry about it. But eyes are precious to me, not just because I love to read, but because observing the visual world around me constitutes a major source of pleasure in my life. I would be devastated if I were unable to see tiny wildflowers in early spring or spot a filthy penny in the gutter or watch the sun go from gray to pink to blood orange to mauve to gray as it rises.

My partner and I consulted both our medical encyclopedia and an alternative manual about healing herbs and dietary remedies. Though each had a distinctive and predictable outline of treatment for glaucoma, they shared one comment that became significant: physical or emotional stress may exacerbate ocular pressure—in other words, pressure of one kind may cause pressure of another. As weeks began to separate me from the office visit and its intense light, shone into my eyes in order to examine the optic nerve, my concern did not abate. I kept imagining the ghoulish machine that needed to touch my eyeball in order to gauge pressure on it and became convinced that radical changes in my life were called for. I let myself sink deep inside, a strangely sedate, reflective move for me, since I usually prefer to "meditate" while painting a wall or jogging in my neighborhood. Lists of places I have never been and sights I have only dreamt of seeing began forming in my mind: animals in Kenya or Tanzania; the Grand Canyon and Mesa Verde, beloved by Willa Cather as a safe repository for her erotic feelings for women's bodies; original El Greco paintings, full of strange Spanish storm clouds and elongated ascetics; icebergs along the Alaska coastline; ancient temples in Kyoto. But then I found myself fending off other, more practical concerns: working until our house is paid for; staying put in women's and GLBT studies to be sure lesbians are not erased entirely by new research on queer theory and transgender identity; waiting to retire until my two new colleagues have tenure and my last three Ph.D. candidates have degrees.

After this uncustomary period of sedate reflection, I came to realize that I was incapable of merely cutting down at the university. After all, I have long viewed with contempt and scorn those colleagues who teach classes and schedule bare-bones office hours at times guaranteed to discourage students from appearing, e.g., 7:30 A.M. or 4:30 P.M., only to flee back to their research at the first possible moment. Furthermore, as one of the most senior members of my department and college, I was no longer given easy committee assignments; service now entailed lengthy involvement in complex projects. Simultaneously and inevitably, my advising had become heavily focused on graduate students, each one of whom needed both a long-term commitment and the best of my intellectual acumen as a reader and critic of her or his work.

I decided that the only way I could limit my effort was to limit the terms of employment—to go to half time, voluntarily taking a significant pay cut. In this way I could continue performing whatever I did with the same degree of passionate engagement that I had come to expect of myself and still have more time at home to relax, be with Susan, and perhaps even to write. My preference was to remain the director of the faculty development program. The directorship position had been defined as half-time; as one result, my department was given money to hire a graduate student to teach courses equaling half my yearly teaching load. Naturally, the cost of hiring that student was considerably less that half my salary as a full professor. When presented with the opportunity to retain my services but actually pay half my salary, the administration balked. Irritated that their commitment to improved teaching still did not rise to a significant monetary investment, I was also sad to give up something so rewarding. Eventually, I spoke with the well-meaning woman who had hired me, telling her of my dilemma. Though she was personally sorry to see me go, she saw nothing to be gained from trying to change her superiors' minds. I resigned the position in June 1999.

Since handing over the program to an excellent successor, I have continued to pay an annual visit to the group. For example, my former co-director, Carol, and I have conducted workshops on multicultural pedagogy. Whereas resistance to this subject used to come from faculty in the physical sciences and engineering fields, even they now realize that the students facing them day after day are not all white, middle-class, young adult males. This has allowed us to move the discourse toward more sophisticated levels, e.g., which pedagogical strategies may contain hidden dangers or sources of discomfort for students with cultural backgrounds different from the usual or predictable. While I have enjoyed my afternoons with each new "crop," I realize that this small service to a program about which I care deeply will not be overly missed.

Nevertheless, my strong interest in multicultural pedagogy prompts me to consider writing articles about what I think and know, so as to reach a broader audience. The first such essay would be a cautionary tale for white faculty in the humanities not to expropriate literature by writers of color in a well-meant effort to form (premature) alliances. I would insist that the material realities enveloping characters not marked as "white" are substantially and crucially different from those surrounding their putatively white counterparts. Letting our students erase such differences may allow them to "identify" with fictional characters that might otherwise remain too "strange" for the usual white, middle-class, heterosexual undergraduate; but in doing so we fail to challenge the very social structures and perspectives that splinter human experience into "normal" and "other" classifications. It also romanticizes and subverts what most serious writers of color whom I read want to accomplish, and so is a dangerous—and counterproductive—pedagogy. If I can articulate some of my ideas for a broader audience, I may discover some like-minded colleagues outside Minnesota. I certainly will satisfy my own conviction about both the literary excellence and the political urgency of this writing.

My last two years in the academy have been spent, then, teaching two English literature courses during one semester, and holding office hours to talk with students as I complete service on a few all-university committees during the other semester. My penultimate year (1999–2000), I offered a seminar in the feminist essay as distinct from the feminist scholarly article, and a course in GLBT literature for undergraduates. The English department had instituted the GLBT course and wanted me as its first instructor. At first I hesitated: I knew next to nothing about bisexual literature; was not in the habit of reading gay writers beyond E. M. Forster, Paul Monette, and Walt Whitman; and was familiar only with Leslie Feinberg's *Stone Butch Blues* as a powerful transgender narrative. But, happy to see my department make such writing more visible, I agreed to offer the course. With the help of a generous colleague at one of the private liberal arts colleges near Minneapolis, I amassed a presentable offering by gay writers, both white and African American. (My particular resource was not able to provide me with stories by gay members of other communities of color.) About half the readings were by lesbians across time and ethnicities. In the syllabus, I acknowledged my ignorance of bisexual material and my admittedly "token" inclusion of Feinberg as the only transgendered author. Since I would never teach the course again, I agreed to let it grow to whatever size student demand dictated. Enrollment leveled off at about forty, just large enough to be demanding and just small enough to keep me from having a teaching assistant.

The seminar was another story entirely. Perhaps because I had been teaching so little for the past eight years, perhaps because the department had admitted fewer students without curtailing the number of seminars, and perhaps because my curricular tastes no longer corresponded with the general direction of graduate study, my seminar enrolled only four students, all white women. This shocked me, since I historically had turned away students pleading to take whatever course I was about to offer. But my recovery program tells me to "stick with the winners," so I focused on the ones who showed up rather than dwelling as I would have in the past on those in absentia. The students challenged themselves to complete vast amounts of reading each week, to contribute far more than if the seminar had been fully subscribed, and to write in a voice that combined the personal with the scholarly. By the end of the term, each had produced a creditable essay quite different from a scholarly article they might author.

When asked to declare my choices for my final two courses, I surprised myself: rather than opting for southern lesbian writers or radical feminist poetry, I chose to teach an honors section of Shakespeare and a senior seminar in which we read numerous elegies, beginning with Milton's "Lycidas," together with several novels with distinctly elegiac themes. Behind this decision may lie my sense that feminist subject matter and pedagogy have made their way into virtually all progressive classrooms; or perhaps it reflects my desire to end as I had begun—teaching Renaissance literature and a genre that has always moved me. In any case, I returned to my roots without apologies and let myself revel in language as familiar to me as my own fingers and toes. The Shakespearean plays I selected—*Antony and Cleopatra, Coriolanus, Troilus and Cressida, Measure for Measure, Cymbeline,* and *The Winter's Tale*— are among my absolute favorites. As for the elegy course, I taught standard nineteenth-century poems (written by one white male on the occasion of the death of another white male), and novels (by Morrison, Frazier, and Kingsolver) having pronounced elegiac themes. New to my presentation of the standard fare was an emphasis on the homoerotic elements and same-sex love to be found in the works of Milton, Tennyson, Whitman, and Monette.

As a footnote to this circular path, I have recently sorted through all the books in my office and sold or donated most of them. The exceptions—ones that have been transferred to our basement for safekeeping and potential future use—are all from the sixteenth and seventeenth centuries. Even if I never open them again, I cannot discard them; they feel like ancient friends who deserve to be kept and at least visited periodically while I am doing the weekly laundry.

On the first day of the fall 2000 semester, a stunning Minnesota day, I announced to my thirty undergraduates registered to study Shakespeare with me that I was retiring, that they were one of my last two classes, and that the onus on them was to provide me with nothing but positive memories. Though this was said in a semi-joking manner, those young people (plus the one returning older woman) took me at my word and worked their hearts and brains out for fourteen weeks, leaving me alternately thrilled and moved to tears as I exited from yet another incredibly impassioned session. They read extra material in books and on the Internet; they met in their small groups outside class to be even better prepared for certain days; they struggled with my main written assignment to construct a two-column reading notebook with emotive responses on the left buttressed by text-based analyses on the right. More than anything, I wanted them to experience firsthand the intimate and unavoidable connections between their brains and the rest of their bodies.

Perhaps the tone-setting event occurred at the end of our second week together. I had begun class with *Antony and Cleopatra* since it was the one play on my list that I thought many might have read or at least seen on film. I wanted to help them, as overachieving honors seniors, to brush off their creative faculties early in the course, so I assigned an out-of-class exercise in which half the students would present the world of Rome and the other half the world of Egypt. My instructions made it clear that I did not want talking heads or a series of factual handouts. Instead, I urged them to "become" those worlds, to present atmosphere, to take us to the settings in which the play's two colossal figures lived and from which they might try to break free through their sexual liaison.

On the day they were to present, I found the classroom in complete disarray. The teacher's desk had been pushed against the blackboard wall while the student desks lined the other three sides. Students were scurrying in and out of nearby bathrooms, trailing white bed sheets and other "props," giggling like happy children turned out to play. To my delight, both groups had caught the spirit of the assignment, bringing pita bread, hummus, and exotic juices for Egypt to serve; Roman meal bread, grapes, and an unopened bottle of red wine (alcohol cannot be served on campus) for Rome to offer. Both groups had conducted extensive research into their respective culture's religion, music (a boom box gave us rhythms for belly dancing from Egypt and martial cadences for Rome), dress, political structures and practices, and visual arts, providing elaborate and often decorative handouts for reading at our leisure.

I have two indelible memories of this occasion. In one, a young man and woman sashay into the room arm in arm. He is carrying a purse, wearing high-heeled shoes and a white brassiere over his black blazer; she sports thick boots and a leather vest, with an army surplus helmet on her head. Together they spoke as Cleopatra does when she tells her serving women about the night she and Antony cross-dressed in order to make love, not as their public selves but as some other manifestation of who they "are": "That time—O times!— / I laughed him out of patience; and that night / I laughed him into patience; and next morn, / Ere the ninth hour, I drunk him to his bed; / Then put my tires and mantles on him, whilst / I wore his sword Philippan" (2.5.18–23).

In the other never-to-be-forgotten scene, three male students carry Cleopatra horizontally into the room, placing her delicately onto our now luxuriously covered desk, from which she begins speaking to her audience in languid tones about the charms and allurements of her country. Because students had needed one another to bring off the assignment and because the assignment had allowed them to "play," the level of trust and connection skyrocketed on that second Thursday. From then on, I never had to worry about participation or cooperation, just about how to get them to stop jabbering before class began or once they were working in small groups during class. Several times I questioned the wisdom of my decision to stop teaching, since my pedagogical antennae seemed in excellent shape for my curricular swan song. But the pull of open days in which to do only things I chose, together with the ability to offer an evening class at any time I might want to, kept me to my June retirement date.

As the last day of classes approached, which would be the last day of all such classes for me, I kept thinking about how to end. On the final Thursday of the term, Susan picked me up in the late afternoon as she had every Tuesday and Thursday since Labor Day and asked her usual question: "How did it go today?" I burst into tears because both classes that day had given so unstintingly as we analyzed Shakespeare's *Winter's Tale* and Morrison's *Paradise*. When I could speak I blurted out, "They were so splendid and I want to tell them so on Tuesday but I know if I try I'll just cry and that's not fair to them since they can't do any of the things they might feel like doing because I'm their teacher." By the time we were pulling into our garage, Susan had suggested the perfect solution—write a letter and give each student a signed copy. The letter would allow me to say what I wanted to without burdening them with my inevitable tears to which they could extend no usual responses because of their status as students and mine as teacher.

I spent much of that weekend composing the letter, choosing a piece of clip art that suggested the Renaissance, printing the letters on dark ecru paper, and signing each by hand. As I went off to class Tuesday morning, I felt I had things under control—right up until I reached the door and heard Adam, the tallest class member, say, "You can't go in there yet." All traces of control slid from my grasp as I realized that the students were enacting plans of their own for how to end our course and my teaching career. When finally allowed to enter, I was met with applause from the class as I made my way to the left-handed desk reserved for me. (During the semester, I had made various students move their own desks as I dragged out one of the two provided for the likes of me by a world still oblivious to its southpaw writers.) What happened next stunned me in its brilliance: seven students "staged" the final scene of *The Winter's Tale*, a scene in which a statue of Hermione, who was horribly maligned by her husband early in the play and who has been supposed dead for the past sixteen years, gradually comes to life as that repentant husband allows himself to fall increasingly under the magic of art and illusion. The scene, in my opinion, is one of the most moving in all of Shakespeare, but also one of the hardest to bring off in our cynical and overstimulated age. But those seven young people, only three of whom had any experience acting, made us all cry in that drab classroom with no real props or costumes, perhaps reclaiming some of the same clean lines found in original productions, where all emphasis had fallen on the words and expressions of actors, without the mixed addition of theatrical devices. My own passionate response to this play may have had a small part in their ability to reclaim the power of the scene across time. But I suspect that what enabled them most was their own surrender to the magic of the scene—and their deep wish to give me something entirely memorable as a special thank-you for my unstinting efforts throughout the semester.

When they finished, the room burst into loud and long applause, and I felt the full triumph of my brand of pedagogy: no longer were students recognizing the teacher as some fount of knowledge, wonderful as their echoing applause had been in my first years. Rather they and, importantly, I the teacher were applauding other students and themselves. I had succeeded in shifting the focus from the act of teaching to the act of learning, a process involving the removal of me from the center of all equations and the installation of students as crucial elements in the acquisition of information, intellectual skills, and, most excitingly, a voice. I felt proud and justified in the face of years of scorn from many colleagues who remain convinced that I am not teaching students appropriately or rigorously enough. I believe that if the English department conducted a survey of the students in that Shakespeare class—and the scores of students I have taught in other similarly structured courses over the years—with peers who experienced a more traditional lecture format as undergraduates, my students would retain more interest in literature and have a firmer grasp of how to read and critique it.

Coda

As I move what remains of my academic life from 310A Lind Hall to our three-story home in south Minneapolis, I am quite sure that I am choosing *the important over the urgent:* specific relationships with Susan and friends over continued contact with prearranged groups of people; gardening over grading; reading what interests or challenges me over what I need to have "ready" for class on Monday; writing what will be of use to me first, and then to women and men trying to figure out how to live. Writing this new series of memoiristic essays also has shown me that, as for southern writer Dorothy Allison, there are two or three things I know for sure:

- I know that my life as an academic has given me incredible rewards. No other workplace could have afforded me the flexibility or variety of assignments or introduced me to as many fascinating people. I feel blessed to be among the minority of workers in late capitalistic America who can honestly say s/he enjoyed doing what s/he did for pay, certainly most of the time. Simultaneously, this life has caused me excruciating pain on more than one occasion, and exposed me to a level of verbal attack and violence no one should have to endure just for the money to live. I have experienced the very paradoxes that drew me initially into studying Renaissance literature. While teaching at the University of Minnesota, I have also encountered, wrestled with, and even come to be comfortable amidst some of these insoluble conundrums. I have grasped my white privilege in an oppressively racialized society even as I have been able to articulate more fully the levels of gender and sexual oppression to which I have been subjected. I have come to understand the

profound paradox of loving to work and be of use to students
and those colleagues who value what I know and believe, and
fiercely desiring open time away from that work and those people. Though most of my time as a professor has been gratifying,
rewarding, even thrilling, thirty-seven years is enough.

My point of view no longer coincides with most of my younger
colleagues, a fact made painfully clear to me over the last ten
years as I have tried with limited success to befriend new faculty
in my department. The profession of literary studies has under-
gone a sea-change that leaves me on an isthmus inhabited by
older colleagues, a few students, and younger faculty who try to
resist the over-professionalization of our field. I can fulfill my
wish to talk about literature by offering community classes like
the ones my partner and I have been teaching for some twenty
years, and by an occasional session at the local American
Association of University Women (AAUW), or monthly meetings of a women's book group that I have facilitated for almost
thirty years. I can keep up with where literary studies is headed
by conversing with former Ph.D. candidates presently building
their own careers at colleges and universities across the country.
And, fortunately, the teenaged daughter of a good friend has
agreed to take me to where the next groups of boundary-defying
young people congregate.

• I know that working with the young has kept me from stagnating
  or becoming afraid of the world outside academe. When students
  were protesting an immoral war, I was at the barricades with
  them; when they insisted that curricula reflect their own multiple
  lives, I took such eminently sensible proposals to the proper
  authorities in order to get them instituted; when students
  appeared in my classes in black clothes and fingernails, followed
  a few years later by variously colored hair and body piercings, I
  went below that camouflage to find what pain or anger it masked,
  and to listen carefully to what they wanted to say about the books
  we were reading and the issues that commanded their attention.
  This openness has not always been easy. I still cringe when bright
  young scholars use ugly or vague words when I know they could
  muster more precise and effective diction. I worry when I am told
  that we are living in a post-feminist or post-lesbian moment, when
  the world seems to me dangerously close to taking back some of

the hard-won gains for all women, people of color, lesbians, gays, and transgendered people.

• I know that I stop teaching the beauty and power of language feeling exactly the same urgency about that beauty and power that I did when I began doing so almost forty years ago. A major facet of my work at the university has been to help students see the tremendous value of story and of well-chosen words in a world too often manipulated and abused by lies, silences, and false speech. They have not always wanted to hear me because I refuse to alter my own rather elaborate speech to suit their minimalist ears. To do so would be disrespectful, or so it seems to me, in perhaps the most serious way possible for a teacher of literature. I look forward, however, to unlocking my own word hoard more often, wrestling with the ideas that currently float or march through my consciousness every day, hoping to catch more of them than has been possible while practicing my profession.

• I know that writing about my own struggles in an attempt to find clarity and meaning, both in my work life and in my personal life, has been of incalculable value. As I have come to grasp the enormous potential for memoir as a genre, capable of situating me between the worlds of pure fact and sheer make-believe, I have been able to connect the various aspects of my existence in new and healing ways. People who read the results tell me that it is useful to them as they sort through the chaotic remnants of their own pasts and as they shape a present in which they can express more of what they feel. Whenever I hear this, I flash to these lines in Marge Piercy's moving poem "To Be of Use":

> I love people who harness themselves, an ox to a heavy cart,
> who pull like water buffalo, with massive patience,
> who strain in the mud and the muck to move things forward,
> who do what has to be done, again and again.

Memoir has come of age during my lifetime; today women and men are writing their way out of confusion and invisibility by recounting what remains memorable from their pasts as witness to their survival and, more importantly, as evidence of their capacity to overcome difficulties with grace and fortitude. I am proud to count myself among this assembly of ordinary citizens refusing efforts to silence us from within or from without.

So I come to the end of a long and rewarding career during which I have met a rather large number of amazing people and formed a few lasting friendships. I have also grown from being a person who drank too much to be able to think straight or write clearly or make intimacy work for her into someone whose eyes are uncommonly bright, whose hand is uncommonly steady, and who wakes each morning in the same house with the woman she found almost twenty-five years ago and began to hope she might get to know better.

I have also been allowed to "handle" some of the most remarkable writing in existence. This last fact continues to awe me: How many people can say that they have earned a comfortable living by reading, digesting, analyzing, and conveying magnificent prose and poetry written by women and men from backgrounds as varied as they are numerous? How many of us enjoy performing at least one of the central acts of her or his profession? How many U.S. citizens, trying to decipher false messages sent by politicians backed by millionaires, can look back and picture themselves blocking traffic on a major street in their hometowns, or bending the rules of some insensitive institution in order to rescue a talented but misguided young person, or weeping over the last scene of a Shakespearean play s/he had taught scores of times before? I got to do it all, and in one of this country's loveliest cities, where my life-partner happened to be residing at just the moment we both were ready to do the continuing and hard work required of any meaningful long-term relationship. No matter what trouble or pain has come my way as a result of my irrational decision back in the winter of 1964, I cannot possibly regret making it. Although I am about to sever all official ties with the university that has been my professional home for so long, I know in my heart that I am not fleeing where I have been—but racing toward whatever destination might be next.

DISCOVER THE BEST WOMEN WRITING
Memoir and Autobiography from the Feminist Press

Across Boundaries: The Journey of a South African Woman Leader by Mamphela Ramphele. $14.95 paper, $19.95 cloth.

Always from Somewhere Else: A Memoir of My Chilean Jewish Father by Marjorie Agosín. $18.95 cloth.

Among the White Moon Faces: An Asian-American Memoir of Homelands by Shirley Geok-lin Lim. $12.95 paper, $22.95 cloth.

Black and White Sat Down Together: The Reminiscences of an NAACP Founder by Mary White Ovington. $10.95 paper, $19.95 cloth.

Cast Me Out If You Will: Stories and Memoir by Lalithambika Antherjanam. $11.95 paper.

A Cross and a Star: Memoirs of a Jewish Girl in Chile by Marjorie Agosín. $13.95 paper.

A Day at a Time: The Diary Literature of American Women Writers from 1764 to the Present, edited by Margo Culley. $16.95 paper.

Fault Lines by Meena Alexander. $12.95 paper.

Harem Years: The Memoirs of an Egyptian Feminist, 1879–1924 by Huda Shaarawi. $12.95 paper.

Juggling: A Memoir of Work, Family, and Feminism by Jane S. Gould. $17.95 paper.

A Lifetime of Labor: The Autobiography of Alice H. Cook by Alice Cook. $15.95 paper, $29.95 cloth.

Lion Woman's Legacy: An Armenian-American Memoir by Arlene Voski Avakian. $14.95 paper.

The Little Locksmith by Katharine Butler Hathaway. $14.95 paper.

The Maimie Papers: Letters from an Ex-Prostitute by Maimie Pinzer. $19.95 paper.

Memories: My Life as an International Leader in Health, Suffrage, and Peace by Aletta H. Jacobs. $18.95 paper.

The Seasons: Death and Transfiguration by Jo Sinclair. $12.95 paper.

Songs My Mother Taught Me: Stories, Plays, and Memoir by Wakako Yamauchi. $14.95 paper.

Streets: A Memoir of the Lower East Side by Bella Spewack. $10.95 paper, $19.95 cloth.

These Modern Women: Autobiographical Essays from the Twenties, edited by Elaine Showalter. $8.95 paper.

To receive a free catalog of the Feminist Press's 200 titles, call or write the Feminist Press at the City University of New York, 365 Fifth Avenue, New York, NY 10016; phone: (212) 817-7920; fax: (212) 817-1593; website: www.feministpress.org. Feminist Press books are available at bookstores or can be ordered directly. Send check or money order (in U.S. dollars drawn on a U.S. bank) payable to the Feminist Press. Please add $4.00 shipping and handling for the first book and $1.00 for each additional book. VISA, Mastercard, and American Express are accepted for telephone orders. Prices subject to change.